SURREALIST LOVER RESISTANT

Robert Desnos

SURREALIST LOVER RESISTANT

COLLECTED POEMS

Translated and introduced by

Timothy Adès

2017

Published by Arc Publications,
Nanholme Mill, Shaw Wood Road
Todmorden OL14 6DA, UK
www.arcpublications.co.uk

978 1906570 69 9 (pbk)
978 1906570 95 8 (hbk)
978 1908376 77 1 (ebk)

Cover design by Tony Ward
Printed by Lightning Source

This volume would not have seen the light of day
but for the generosity of a large number of people who made a
financial contribution towards the cost of its production through
the Kickstarter programme. The publishers are deeply grateful
to all those who have made publication possible. A list of
sponsors appears at the end of this volume.

Arc Classics:
New Translations of Great Poets of the Past
Series Editor: Jean Boase-Beier

ACKNOWLEDGEMENTS

The translator gratefully acknowledges Mme Marie-Claire Dumas and Éditions Gallimard, for excerpts from her commentary on 'Against the Grain' and 'The Bath With Andromeda', in *Œuvres* (1999, pp. 1156-7); Éditions Gallimard, for 'Crépuscule d'Été' and 'L'Étoile du Matin', both in *Destinée Arbitraire,* and all other poems in *Œuvres,* 1999.

Thanks are due to the editors of the following publications, in which some of these translations have appeared: *Acumen 50* ('That Lovely Woman'); *A Dada Reader* (Tate: from Rrose Sélavy: 'Elegant Canticle of Salomé Salomon'); *Agenda 45* ('Beautiful After-Midnight', 'The Voice of Robert Desnos'); *Agenda 46/3* ('The Legacy'); *Agenda 50/1-2* ('Robert the Devil' – poem by Louis Aragon); *Centres of Cataclysm* (Bloodaxe Books / MPT: 'Tomorrow', 'Springtime'); *Comparative Criticism 25* ('Contrée'); *Essential Poems and Writings of Robert Desnos* (Black Widow Press: 3 poems from 'Contrée' – 'The River', 'The Summer Night', 'The Voice'); *In Other Words* (3 poems from 'Contrée' – 'The Countryside', 'The Harvest', 'The Equinox'); *Journal of the Centre for Research into Surrealism* ('Rrose Sélavy', 'Ballad of Fantomas'); *Long Poem Magazine 5* ('The Ode to Coco'); *Magma 36* (part of 'Flint and Fire'); *Modern Poetry in Translation* ('I've dreamed so much', 'No, Love is not dead', 'Never Another', 'Blind', 'Beautiful After-Midnight', 'The Poem to Florence', 'Bagatelles', 'Ballad of the Wine-glass', 'Ballad of the Butcher', 'Seasons', 'Tomorrow', 'Springtime'); *Outposts* ('The Countryside'); *PN Review 200* ('The Dream in a Cellar', 'Morning Star', 'Woman Be Serious', 'At Dawn', 'Cease from Crying Calixto', 'Tale of Fol-Fan-Fifer'); *Poetry Review* ('The Friday of the Crime'), *Salzburg Poetry Review 22, 2012* ('Handkerchieves at the Nadir', 'Cold Throats'); *The High Window* ('Phantom', 'Andromeda Saved'); *Translation and Literature* ('Siren-Anemone', 'Birth of the Monster' [from 'Andromeda'], 'The Escaper').

CONTENTS

TIME OF CONFLICT
WITHOUT YVONNE, WITHOUT ANDRÉ BRETON 1929-30

LOVER – YOUKI FOUJITA
POEMS 1930-32

RESISTANT

POEMS PUBLISHED IN 1943

1942-43

Contrée / Against the Grain

Le Bain Avec Andromède / Bathing With Andromeda

INTRODUCTION

Robert Desnos (both the s's are sounded) is, to this translator, the most exciting French poet of the last century. Already in his early twenties he found his way to the nascent Surrealist Movement in Paris, when it was just a little club. Surrealism set him free from the normal constraints of reason, relevance, coherence. At the same time he was immensely gifted in the traditional, probably timeless, poetic skills of rhyme and metre, alliteration and wordplay.

Desnos was born in Paris on 4 July 1900, the son of a licensed poultry and game dealer at the Halles Market. In his youth he was secretary to Louis de Gonzague Frick, the poet and critic who was close to Apollinaire. He became a journalist as a young man, and remained one for most of his life. Among the Surrealists in 1922-4 he composed, while asleep or hypnotised, two hundred elaborate and witty super-spoonerisms which he credited to the inspiration of Rrose Sélavy, the fascinating altera ego invented by Marcel Duchamp (see my translator's note on p. 49 for further discussion). For this, the Surrealists' leader, André Breton, proclaimed him the 'prophet' of the movement. Desnos wrote a Surrealist novel, *Liberty or Love*. Like most of the Surrealists, he fell out with Breton; he soon attached himself to Georges Bataille, writing in the magazine *Documents*.

Some of his great love-poems were inspired by the night-club singer Yvonne George (see my translator's note on p. 89). These are poignant poems of love rejected, and being in free verse, are easier to translate than much of his other poetry, two reasons for their appearance in several English anthologies. In the years 1929 and 1930 Desnos was in conflict in both his literary and his private life: he had left Breton's little club to take Surrealism out into the world, and Yvonne was dying of drink and drugs. He worked through this difficult period (see my translator's note on p. 113) with a series of big poems, in the historic alexandrine metre or in mixed metres, ending with an epic, *The Night of Loveless Nights*. He discovered the true

love of his life in Lucie Badoud (Youki Foujita), who inspired many poems, mostly rhymed and metrical: the longest of that phase is *Siramour.* He moved on into radio with listeners sending in their dreams for him to interpret on air: he had a huge following. *The Ballad of Fantomas* was broadcast as a 'superproduction'.

Desnos wrote a hundred poems for children – *Flowersongs* and *Storysongs* are much-loved classics in France, 'The Ant' being a favourite since it was sung by Juliette Gréco – but these are not included in this volume. He also wrote lyrics for songs, commercials and the cinema.

The gathering storm in Europe culminated in war and the occupation of France by German troops. Desnos, already a member of the Popular Front, responded by becoming an active Resistant (see my translator's note on p. 365) and being inspired to write the great sequences *Against the Grain, Bathing With Andromeda* (see Marie-Claire Dumas' introductory note on pp. 476-7), and *Calixto,* full of meaning yet able to pass the censor (sadly, he never saw them in print). Other poems like 'This Heart Which Hated War' struck directly at the oppressor, heralding the return of freedom.

In 1944, Desnos was arrested and deported. After a year of suffering and slavery, he died of typhus at the Terezin death-camp on 8 June 1945. He is the only writer honoured with two quotations at the Monument to the Martyrs of the Deportation, close to the cathedral of Notre-Dame in his home city of Paris.

Timothy Adès

ROBERT DESNOS TIMELINE

1900 Born in Paris, son of a licensed dealer in poultry and game at Les Halles.
1902 Family moves to 11 rue St-Martin, and in 1913 to 9 rue de Rivoli.
1914 Studying English at Herne Bay, Kent.
1918 First poems published: encouraged by Louis de Gonzague Frick. Not called up to the military.
1919 Secretary to Jean de Bonnefon, man of letters: often in National Library.
1920-21 Military service in France and Morocco.
1921 Introduced to André Breton by Benjamin Péret.
1922-4 Linked to *Littérature* magazine. Automatic writing. Sessions of hypnotic sleep: super-spoonerisms of *Rrose Sélavy*: great success.
1923-6 Literary critic, film critic, editor of *Paris-Soir, Le Soir, Paris-Matinal*; meets Artaud, Leiris, Hemingway, Gertrude Stein…
1924 Acclaimed by André Breton and others in *Surrealist Manifesto.* Smitten by nightclub singer Yvonne George.
1926 Moves into André Masson's old studio, 43 rue Blomet with artist Georges Malkine: a place ideal for relaxing with friends.
1926-7 Novel *Liberty or Love!* and poems, inspired by Yvonne (unmoved).
1928 Cuba with Alejo Carpentier; film with Man Ray; walking tour of Burgundy with artist Foujita and his wife Youki (Lucie Badoud). Linked to Georges Bataille's *Documents* magazine.
1929 Denounced by Breton in *Second Surrealist Manifesto.*
1930 Angry response. Desnos in *Third Surrealist Manifesto* says Surrealism is now in the public domain. Yvonne dies of drink and drugs. Big poem, *The Night of Loveless Nights.*
1930-2 Penury.
1931 Foujita entrusts Youki to Desnos, and returns to Japan.

1932 Into radio: advertising slogans, jingles. *Ballad of Fantomas,* music by Weill. Children's poems for Hyacinthe and Tristan Deharme.

1933 A bigger *Fantomas* broadcast with Artaud and Carpentier.

1934 With Youki at 19 rue Mazarine. Antifascist, joins Common Front.

1935 In Spain, meets poets Neruda and Lorca.

1936 Broadcasts Walt Whitman's poem *Salut au Monde,* with music.

1937-8 Chorales for Lorca, the Spanish Republicans, the Museum of Man.

1938 Interprets radio listeners' dreams: huge following.

1939 War: Sergeant. Forced retreat, 250km; captured, released, demobilised.

1940 Journalist, access to enemy despatches, passes these to Resistance. Active Resistant. Sued by pro-fascist Céline over a hostile review.

1942 Slaps another pro-fascist who later denounces him.

1943 Novel against drugs, *Le Vin est Tiré.* Poems, pseudonymous.

1944 Arrested. *Against the Grain* and *Bathing with Andromeda* published; *Calixto* not till 1962. *Storysongs for Good Children* published. Deported to Auschwitz, transferred to Buchenwald, then Flossenbürg. Slave labourer at Flöha: cleaner in an aircraft factory. Brutalised. Still writing letters to Youki.

1945 Murderous forced march to Terezin: arrives 9 May, the war in Europe having ended. Dies of typhus at Terezin on 8 June.

1915-1922

AQUARELLE...

Les soldats ont brûlé la ferme et le château,
Abattu le donjon, la ruine romaine,
Qui, triomphant du temps, de la foudre et de l'eau,
D'un long passé restaient une preuve certaine.
Leurs débris maintenant détournent le ruisseau...
Monuments de tristesse et de guerre et de haine.
Les soldats ont brûlé la ferme et le château,
Abattu le donjon, la ruine romaine...

L'oiseau ne chante plus à l'ombre du rameau,
Le cerf ne vient plus boire à la fraîche fontaine,
Le lièvre a déserté le sinueux réseau
Des taillis épineux dont il fit son domaine...
Les soldats ont brûlé la ferme et le château,
Abattu le donjon, la ruine romaine...

1915

CASQUÉS DU HEAUME

Casqués du heaume et cuirassés,
S'en sont partis les gens de guerre.
Les chemins creux sont défoncés
Où nous cachions nos amours printanières.

Car l'homme doit aimer son frère
Comme l'oisel aime l'oisel!
Et partir avec lui la terre
Comme ils se partissent le ciel.

WATERCOLOUR...

The soldiers burnt the castle and the farm,
The tower and the Roman ruins are lost.
They triumphed over thunder, rain and time,
Stood as the sure proof of a lengthy past.
Today what's left of them obstructs the stream...
Landmarks of war and hatred and distress.
The soldiers burnt the castle and the farm,
The tower and the Roman ruins are lost.

Birds sing no longer in the leafy gloom,
Nor does the fresh spring quench the roebuck's thirst,
The hares have left the brush that was their home,
A thorny thicket, sinuous, compressed...
The soldiers burnt the castle and the farm,
The tower and the Roman ruins are lost...

1915

IN HELMET

In helmet and in breastplate
They went to fight the wars.
The sunken lanes are smashed to bits
That hid our spring amours.

For man must love his brother
As two birds of a feather
Share earth with one another
The way they share the weather.

Casqués du heaume et cuirassés
S'en sont partis les gens de guerre.
Les chemins creux sont défoncés
Où nous cachions nos amours printanières.

Mais peu s'en soucie la nature,
Les fleurettes poussent aux prés,
L'oisel jargonne en la ramure,
Le cerf en rut court les forêts.

Et nous aussi devons aimer,
Viens-t-en ès champs et feuillage
Nous livrant aux jeux printaniers,
Oublier la guerre sauvage.

Casqués du heaume et cuirassés,
S'en sont partis les gens de guerre.
Les chemins creux sont défoncés
Où nous cachions nos amours printanières.

de **PROSPECTUS, 1919**

DÉDICACE

À Louis Aragon

Et j'ai dit qu'il fallait rire
et j'ai dit qu'il fallait chanter;
Laurent Tailhade, Apollinaire,
Je suis venu par les allées...

In helmet and in breastplate
They went to fight the wars.
The sunken lanes are smashed to bits
That hid our spring amours.

It's all the same to nature,
Buds blossom in the meadow,
Woods run with rutting roe-deer,
Birds chirp in leafy shadow.

And we must do our loving,
Find fields and trees once more,
Find spring and fun of living,
Forget the savage war.

In helmet and in breastplate
They went to fight the wars.
The sunken lanes are smashed to bits
That hid our spring amours.

from **PROSPECTUS, 1919**

DEDICATION

To Louis Aragon

I said that we needed some laughter,
I said that we needed some song:
Two poets are in the hereafter,
Straight alleys I just came along.

Je suis venu jusqu'à la rade:
un cargo-boat y accostait,
on déchargeait des marmelades
de cœurs meurtris et de fruits blets.

Mais quand j'ai voulu savoir l'heure,
mais quand j'ai cherché mon cœur
dans la poche de mon gilet,
j'ai vu qu'un archer vainqueur
vers le soleil vous emportait!

ICI ON PEUT APPORTER
À René Crevel

Je suis passé dans une rue étrange
où des enfants blonds compissaient leurs langes.

À la porte d'un restaurant
un écriteau était collé:

ICI ON PEUT APPORTER SON MANGER

À la porte d'un hôtel meublé
un écriteau était collé:

ICI ON PEUT APPORTER SON AMOUR

I came and I saw in the roadstead
A tanker at anchor, a boat,
And jellies and jams were unloaded,
What a mess, broken hearts, rotten fruit.

I was checking the time on my gnomon,
I felt for my heart in my pocket,
I saw a victorious bowman
Take you up to the sun, like a rocket!

BRING YOUR OWN

To René Crevel

I went along a strange road where
blond children weed in their baby-wear.

On the door of an eating-house
was fixed a sign:

YOU MAY BRING YOUR OWN FOOD HERE

On the door of a lodging-house
was fixed a sign:

YOU MAY BRING YOUR OWN LOVE HERE

MON TOMBEAU

À Eugène et Lucienne de Kermadec

Mon tombeau mon joli tombeau,
il sera peint au ripolin
avec des agrès de bateau
et des tatouages de marin.

Sur mon tombeau un phonographe
chantera soir et matin
la complainte du guerrier cafre
navré d'un coup d'œil libertin.

Sur mon tombeau un phonographe
récitera cette épitaphe

LIBERTÉ ÉGALITÉ FRATERNITÉ

CUISINE BOURGEOISE

À Pierre Scordel

Sur les tempes le père a deux virgules
Il sait jouer du clairon
Vous pourrez lire son nom
sur les murs des cellules
des casernes d'Afrique.

Pour exciter les mâles
après dîner dans les rues transversales
La mère
rattache sa jarretière

La fille est bonne à tout faire
à tout faire chez un vieux monsieur

MY TOMB

To Eugène and Lucienne de Kermadec

My tomb O so pretty
they'll paint it de luxe
with nautical fittings
and sailors' tattoos

On my tomb a phonograph
night and day shall sound romance
singing of a savage brave
smitten by a wanton glance

On my tomb a phonograph
shall recite this epitaph

LIBERTY EQUALITY FRATERNITY

HIGH-CLASS CUISINE

To Pierre Scordel

On his brows the father has two commas
He's a certified bugler
You can read his name
on the cell walls
of the Africa barracks

To excite the males
after dinner in the between-streets
the mother
adjusts her garter

The daughter's made for all work
for all work at some old gent's

Et maquillé le fils dans les bars clandestins
à l'entour de la Madeleine
du soir au petit matin
erre comme une âme en peine.

Il déjeune tous les jours dans cette famille
Il y boit tous les jours la même camomille
Il y mange tous les jours de la
CUISINE BOURGEOISE

IL EST INTERDIT DE CRACHER

À Georges Gautré

Il est interdit de cracher par terre
et le plafond est de forme circulaire.

Une poule a pondu
sur les fauteuils de cuir et d'or
mais nul coq du futur
n'en sortira jamais Poussin.

Les œufs à la coque nul ne les a brisés
Vienne un bandit de l'Orénoque
en Peau-Rouge déguisé.

Bouche ouverte à l'instar d'un ténor
Jean Richepin lit un discours
sur la rosière de Nanterre,

IL EST INTERDIT DE CRACHER PAR TERRE

And the son mascara'd in sleazy bars
somewhere near the Madeleine
from sundown into the small hours
goes wandering like a soul in pain

Daily at breakfast in the family he
daily drinks that camomile tea
daily eats
HIGH-CLASS CUISINE

NO SPITTING

To Georges Gautré

No spitting on the ground
and the ceiling's round.

A chicken laid an egg [or so I'm told]
on the well-stuffed chairs of leather and gold
but never shall any cockerel
hatch as a Poussin from that chick-shell.

Eggs boiled in their shells
that no-one broke, though
Come an Orinoco
buccaneer in his native gear.

Mouth like a tenor, what a gaper
Jean Richepin reads a learned paper
on Nanterre's May-Queen, rosed and crowned,

NO SPITTING ON THE GROUND.

AUX PETITS OIGNONS

Je sais un champion de billard
qui porte perruque et lorgnon
qui à Londres, dans le brouillard,
avec la femme d'un mercier
FAIT L'AMOUR AUX PETITS OIGNONS
sans l'aimer ni la remercier.

Dans ce fromage il a laissé
Quatre molaires et son faux nez.
Passez-moi le sel de Ninive
Servez, servez-moi des olives,

Pour évoquer dans mon assiette
La Canebière et la Joliette.

COCKTAIL COULEUR TANGO

Dans un cocktail couleur tango
je buvais les yeux de ma belle:
l'un est vert l'autre mirabelle,
je buvais les yeux de Margot.

Margot mon rêve, au pas d'un tango,
a piétiné l'image frêle,
ses yeux aux couleurs rebelles
troublés par mon chalumeau.

Le divin cocktail de ses larmes,
par un beau soir à Monaco.
Ô fées Méditerranéennes
Je l'ai bu au son d'un tango.

ALL THE TRIMMINGS

I know a billiard star, he's big,
He wears a pince-nez and a wig,
In London fog the dirty dog
Pleasures the lady of a banker,
MAKING LOVE WITH ALL THE TRIMMINGS.
Doesn't love her, doesn't thank her.

He left in this bed of roses
Four back teeth and two false noses.
Pass the salt of Nineveh, please
Serve me olives from olive-trees,

Recreate, on my plate,
Marseilles harbour, bay of Nice.

TANGO-COLOURED COCKTAIL

The tint of my cocktail is tango,
I was drinking the eyes of my belle.
One is green, one is gold-mirabelle!
I was drinking the eyes of Margot.

My vision was dancing the tango,
She kicked the frail dream to a frazzle,
The rebel-hued eyes of Margot
Were troubled by my little nozzle.

That cocktail divine of her tears
At sundown in Monte Carlo
(O Mediterranean fairies!)
I drank to the sound of a tango.

NEUVE JEUNESSE

Nous irons au cinéma
Rendre nos devoirs à Charlot
Mais n'irons-nous pas sur l'eau
Visiter YOKOHAMA?

Le nègre des Batignolles
où est-il? et son banjo?
La putain qui m'appelait coco
et qui posait les vierges folles?

Les cerises en sac de papier
que je croquais dans mon dodo
Polichinelle et le Pompier
qui chantaient ho ho ho ho?

Toutes les fleurs de Colombo,
tous les whyskies de Singapour
et les remparts de Saint-Malo
et les débris de mes amours

La mer a noyé tout cela

Je ne suis plus qu'un petit garçon
qui mange du chocolat
et qui joue au ballon

PROSPECTUS

Tous les vieillards dans la maison
Ont détraqué leurs pendules,
Il fait nuit en toute saison
Dans la maison des trop crédules.

EARLIEST YOUTH

Off to see the flicks to-day:
Charlie's there to be adored.
We can simply step aboard,
Dock at Yokohama Bay.

Minstrel of the music-halls,
Where's he now with his banjo?
With her crazy virginals,
Tart who called me Romeo?

Cherries in the Land of Nod
From a paper bag, tra-la?
Mr Punch and PC Plod
Gaily singing ha-ha-ha?

All Colombo's pretty flowers,
Chota pegs in Singapore
And St Malo's walls and towers
And my loves intact no more.

Now the deep has drowned all that

I'm a little lad, that's all,
Eating up my chocolate,
Playing with my great big ball.

PROSPECTUS

All the old men living here
Broke their clocks, can't make them go,
It is night all round the year
At the Credulous Château.

Ils ont renversé les potiches
La concierge a rompu le cordon,
Tous les vieillards de la maison
Ont des chevelures postiches.

Montent les cris de la rue;
Voici frissonner leurs bedaines,
Voici sonner sonner le glas
Et passer le cri de leur haine
Raccommodeur
FAÏENCE ET PORCELAINE

L'ODE À COCO

Coco! perroquet vert de concierge podagre,
Sur un ventre juché, ses fielleux monologues
Excitant aux abois la colère du dogue,
Fait surgir un galop de zèbres et d'onagres.

Cauchemar, son bec noir plongera dans un crâne
Et deux grains de soleil sous l'écorce paupière
Saigneront dans la nuit sur un édredon blanc.

L'amour d'une bigote a perverti ton cœur;
Jadis gonflant ton col ainsi qu'un tourtereau,
Coco! tu modulais au ciel de l'équateur
De sonores clameurs qui charmaient les perruches.
Vint le marin sifflant la polka périmée,
Vint la bigote obscène et son bonnet à ruches,
Puis le perchoir de bois dans la cage dorée:
Les refrains tropicaux désertèrent ta gorge.

They've upset the chinaware,
La concierge has bust the bell,
All old men that here do dwell
Fix false pieces in their hair.

Street-cries coming up the stairs;
See their paunches palpitate,
Hear the death-knell toll again
Hear them cry their cry of hate
Repairs
FAIENCE AND PORCELAIN

THE ODE TO COCO

Coco! Green parrot of concierge with gout,
Perched on a paunch, its bilious monologues
Arouse the barks of large and angry dogs,
Make zebras and wild asses dash about.

Nightmare, its black beak plunging in a skull:
Two grains of sunshine under eyeball's peel
Will bleed at night on a red eiderdown.

A bigot-woman's love has turned your soul.
Once like a turtle-dove you puffed your neck,
Coco! and noised to equatorial sky
Your tuneful cries that charmed the parrot-hens.
Came sailorman whistling a clapped-out polka,
Came nasty bigot-woman's frilly bonnet,
The wooden perch inside the gilded cage:
The tropic songs fell silent in your throat.

Rastaquouère paré de criardes couleurs
Ô général d'empire, ô métèque épatant
Tu simules pour moi grotesque voyageur,
Un aigle de lutrin perché sur un sextant.

Mais le cacatoès observait le persil
Le bifteck trop saignant, la pot-bouille et la nuit,
Tandis qu'un chien troublait mon sommeil et la messe
Qui, par rauques abois, prétendait le funeste
Effrayer le soleil, la lune et les étoiles.

Coco! cri avorté d'un coq paralytique,
Les poules en ont ri, volatiles tribades,
Des canards ont chanté qui se sont cru des cygnes,
Qui donc n'a pas voulu les noyer dans la rade?

Qu'importe qu'un drapeau figé dans son sommeil
Serve de parapluie aux camelots braillards
Dont les cors font souffrir les horribles orteils:
Au vent du cauchemar claquent mes étendards.

Coco! femme de Loth pétrifiée par Sodome,
De louches cuisiniers sont venus, se cachant,
Effriter ta statue pour épicer l'arôme
Des ragoûts et du vin des vieillards impuissants.

Coco! fruit défendu des arbres de l'Afrique,
Les chimpanzés moqueurs en ont brisé des crânes
Et ces crânes polis d'anciens explorateurs
Illusionnent encor les insanes guenons.

Coco! Petit garçon savoure ce breuvage,
La mer a des parfums de cocktails et d'absinthe,
Et les citrons pressés ont roulé sur les vagues;
Avant peu les alcools délayant les mirages
Te feront piétiner par les pieds durs des bœufs.

Exotic nabob of the gaudy hues,
General of empire, showy immigrant,
Weird traveller, to me you represent
A lectern-eagle on a sextant roost.

The cockatoo surveyed the half-done steak,
The parsley and the hotpot and the dark:
A dog disturbed my slumber and the mass
With false alarms of doom, a raucous bark
To terrify the sun and moon and stars.

Coco! a spastic rooster's strangled cry,
The chickens laughed at it, the flighty dykes:
Ducks, thinking they were swans, emitted quacks.
We longed to drown them in the estuary.

What if he dreams a flag he often sees
Is used to keep the rain off bully-boys,
Whose bunions agonise their beastly toes?
My flags flap loudly on the nightmare breeze.

Coco! Lot's wife that Sodom turned to stone,
Louche cooks come creeping up, to whittle down
Your effigy for impotent old men,
To spice the odours of their stews and wine.

Coco! Forbidden fruit of Afric trees,
Death's-heads stove in by jeering chimpanzees,
And still some bygone expedition gulls
Demented monkeys with its polished skulls.

Coco! Small boy, sample this heady brew,
Cocktails and absinthe give the sea their smells,
And lemonades go rolling on the waves:
Mirages are delayed by alcohols:
You will be trampled by hard hooves of bulls.

La roulette est la lune et l'enjeu ton espoir,
Mais des grecs ont triché au poker des planètes,
Les sages du passé, terrés comme des loirs,
Ont vomi leur mépris aux pieds des proxénètes.

Les maelstroms gueulards charrieront des baleines
Et de blancs goélands noyés par les moussons.
La montagne fondra sous le vent des saisons,
Les ossements des morts exhausseront la plaine.

Le feu des Armadas incendiera la mer,
Les lourds canons de bronze entr'ouvriront les flots
Quand, seuls sur l'océan, quatre bouchons de liège
Défieront le tonnerre effroi des matelots.

Coco! la putain pâle aux fards décomposés
A reniflé ce soir tes étranges parfums.
Elle verra la vie brutale sans nausée
À travers la couleur orangée du matin.

Elle marchera sur d'humides macadams
Où des phallophories de lumières s'agitent;
Sur les cours d'eau berceurs du nord de l'Amérique
Voguera sa pirogue agile, mais sans rame.

Les minarets blanchis d'un Alger idéal
Vers elle inclineront leur col de carafon
Pour verser dans son cœur mordu par les démons
L'ivresse des pensées captée dans les bocaux.

Sur ses talons Louis Quinze elle ira, décrochant
Les yeux révulsés des orbites des passants!

Ô le beau collier, ma mie
Que ces yeux en ribambelle,

The moon's roulette-wheel puts your hopes at stake.
Greeks fixed the planets' poker-game, it's fake:
Ancient great minds, like dormice in their burrows,
Spewed hatred at the feet of flesh-procurers.

Maelstroms with jaws shall sweep away the whales
And the white seagulls that monsoons have drowned.
Mountains shall founder in the winter gales,
And dead men's bones heap up the rolling ground.

The sea shall catch alight, Armadas burn,
Heavy bronze cannon prise apart the flood;
Tossed on the ocean wave, four corks alone
Defy the thunder that the sailors dread.

Coco! The pallid tart whose rouges fade
Sniffed, just this evening, your exotic balm.
She'll peer through daybreak's over-oranged shade,
And watch life's brutishness without a qualm.

She'll walk wet roads macadamised with tar
Where phallophorias of torches waggle;
Currents caressing North America
Shall waft her neat pirogue without a paddle.

White towers of an ideal Algiers
Shall bend to her their necks like jars,
Pour in her heart that demons nipped
Wild thoughts inside a phial trapped.

On claw-like heels of Louis Quinze she'll go, raised high:
She'll disconnect, rip out the eyes of passers-by.

O beautiful necklace my darling
These eyes with their fairy train

Ô le beau collier ma mie
Que ces têtes sans cervelle.

Nous jouerons au bilboquet
Sur des phallus de carton-pâte,
Danse Judas avec Pilate
Et Cendrillon avec Riquet.

Elle vivra, vivra marchant
En guignant de l'œil les boutiques
Où sur des tas d'or, souriant aux pratiques,
D'un peu plus chaque jour engraissent les marchands.

Elle vivra marchant,
Jusqu'à l'hospice ouvrant sa porte funéraire
Jusqu'au berceau dernier, pirogue trop légère,
Sur l'ultime Achéron de ses regrets naissants.

Ou bien, dans un couvent de nonnes prostituées,
Abbesse au noir pouvoir vendra-t-elle la chair
Meurtri par les baisers de ses sœurs impubères?

Lanterne en fer forgé au seuil des lupanars,
Courtisanes coiffées du seigneurial hennin,
Tout le passé s'endort au grabat des putains
Comme un banquier paillard rongé par la vérole.

Saint Louis, jadis, sérieux comme un chien dans les quilles
Régissait la rue chaude aimée des Toulousains,
Le clapier Saint-Merry, proche la même église,
Mêlait ses chants d'amour aux nocturnes tocsins.

La reine Marie Stuart obtint par grand'prière
Que d'un vocable orgiaque on fit Tire-Boudin,
J'aime beaucoup ces rues Tiron, Troussenonnains,

O beautiful necklace my darling
These heads without any brain

Our game of cup-and-ball had
Two papier-mâché phalli
Let Judas dance with Pilate
Riquet with Cinderella.

She shall live, shall walk and live,
Eyeing up the golden pile,
Smart boutiques where traders thrive,
Please their clients, daily smile.

She shall live, shall live and walk,
Walk till hospice lych-gates yawn,
Closing cradle, frail pirogue,
Nascent regrets' last Acheron.

Or in a convent where the nuns are hookers,
Abbess of dark power, will she sell the flesh
Purple with her pubescent sisters' kisses?

Wrought-iron lantern at bordello-doors,
Courtesans coiffed with hennin of milord,
The past is lulled asleep on beds of whores,
Like a lewd banker whom the pox has gnawed.

St Louis, pensive as a dog on quills:
They loved that steamy street he once controlled,
Toulouse men did. Meanwhile St Merri's bells
Mixed love-songs with the warning-notes they tolled.

Queen Mary Stuart pleaded to obtain,
Out of an orgiast's word, Rue Tire-Boudin.
I love them, Rue Tiron, Rue Troussenonnains,

Où trafiquait à l'enseigne des jarretières
Les filles aux doigts blancs, aux langues meurtrières.

Holà! l'estaminet s'ouvre sur l'horizon,
Les buveurs ont vomi du vin rouge hier soir
Et ce matin, livide et crachant ses poumons,
Syphilitique est morte la putain sans gloire.

Que le vent gonfle donc la voile des galères
Car les flots ont échoué sur les grèves antiques
Des cadavres meurtris dédaignés des requins,
Les crabes ont mangé tous les cerveaux lyriques,
Une pieuvre s'acharne après un luth d'argent
Et crève un sac soyeux où sonnaient les sequins!

Tabac pour la concierge et coco pour la grue!
Je ne priserai pas la poudre consolante
Puisqu'un puissant opium s'exhale de mes nuits,
Que mes mains abusées ont déchiré parfois
La chair sanglante et chaude et vierge mais dolente!

Quels bouquets, chers pavots, dans les flacons limpides,
Quels décombres thébains et, Byzance orgueilleuse,
Les rêves accroupis sur le bord d'un Bosphore
Où nagent les amours cadencées et nombreuses

J'ai des champs de pavots sournois et pernicieux
Qui, plus que toi Coco! me bleuiront les yeux.
Sur Gomorrhe et Sodome aux ornières profondes,
J'ai répandu le sel fertilisant des ondes.

J'ai voulu ravager mes campagnes intimes,
Des forêts ont jailli pour recouvrir mes ruines.
Trois vies superposées ne pourraient pas suffire
À labeur journalier en saccager l'empire.

'Nun Tucking Street', where at the Sign of the Garter
White-fingered girls turned tricks, with tongues of slaughter.

Hey there! The bar is open, far away,
The wine they vomited last night was red.
Spewing her lungs and ghastly pale today,
The inglorious syphilitic tart is dead.

Let galleon-sails inflate with wind,
For waves have beached on antique strand
Bruised corpses that the shark disdains,
The crabs ate all the lyric brains,
A squid craves twelve-stringed silver tunes,
Bursts a silk bag of loud doubloons!

Fags for the concierge, co-co for the crane.
I shall not sniff the powders that console:
Strong is the opiate my nights exhale,
Hot is the flesh my ravaged hands have torn,
Sanguine and virginal and yet in pain.

Dear poppies, what bouquets in limpid glass,
What Theban ruins, what Byzantine pride,
Dreams crouching by a crowded Bosporus,
Awash with loves all bobbing on the tide.

Coco! my poppy-fields, much more than you,
Perverse and sly, shall make my eyes go blue.
Sodom, Gomorrah! On your rutted plain
I strewed rich salt from the abundant main.

I thought to lay my inner landscapes waste.
Forests sprang up, hid my remains away.
Not three successive lives could have sufficed
To sack that empire, toiling day by day.

Le poison de mon rêve est voluptueux et sûr
Et les fantasmes lourds de la drogue perfide
Ne produiront jamais dans un esprit lucide
L'horreur de trop d'amour et de trop d'horizon
Que pour moi voyageur font naître les chansons.

Écrit en 1919, publié en 1930.

Voluptuous and sure is my dream's poison.
The treacherous drug's heavy phantasmagoria
Cannot engender in a lucid spirit
The dread of too much love, too much horizon.
Songs conjure, on my journey, all that terror.

Written in 1919, published in 1930.

SURREALIST

WORDS PLAY, WORDS MAKE LOVE
1922-1926

RROSE SÉLAVY

Translator's Note

This is one of Surrealism's essential texts. The group around André Breton started sessions of hypnosis or self-hypnosis on 25 September 1922. It was René Crevel's idea, and at first he was voluble, but Desnos had earlier practised automatic writing, transcribing some of his dreams, and he soon became the one who spoke, drew or wrote under hypnosis. On the 28th they got him to write a poem.

Marcel Duchamp had invented Rrose Sélavy (Éros, c'est la vie; arrosez la vie..., as a fascinating female altera ego, and pronounced the first few crude examples of her intricate, spooneristic, poetic tongue-twisters. On 7 October, Francis Picabia asked Desnos for more of these, and Desnos said at once 'Dans un temple en stuc de pommes...' Soon the puns were flowing, especially if Breton was present. A hundred and seventy-four sentences appeared in *Littérature* no. 7, Dec 1922. 'Words have finished playing', wrote Breton: 'words are making love'; and in 1924: 'Surrealism is the order of the day and Desnos is its prophet.' And later: 'Anyone who never saw his pencil, unhesitating and prodigiously fast, commit these amazing poetic equations to paper, and who could not rule out premeditation as I could, might well appreciate their technical perfection and wonderful skill, but cannot imagine how much it all meant at the time, and the positively oracular importance it took on.' (*Nadja*, 1928). But the novelty and the effect had worn off: Desnos became aggressive, the audience nervous. The sessions ended after some alarming incidents early in 1923. Breton said he, Éluard and Desnos would write no more: Desnos dissented.

'I wasn't afraid to mystify,' Desnos said later. 'The mystifier may unwittingly do important things.'

These translations have been done very freely in the hope of catching the poetry, originality and mystery of the original.

1 Dans un temple en stuc de pomme le pasteur distillait le suc des psaumes.
2 Rrose Sélavy demande si les Fleurs du Mal ont modifié les mœurs du phalle: qu'en pense Omphale?
3 Voyageurs, portez des plumes de paon aux filles de Pampelune.
4 La solution d'un sage est-elle la pollution d'un page?
5 Je vous aime, ô beaux hommes vêtus d'opossum.
6 QUESTION AUX ASTRONOMES: Rrose Sélavy inscrira-t-elle longtemps au cadran des astres le cadastre des ans?
7 Ô mon crâne étoile de nacre qui s'étiole.
8 Au pays de Rrose Sélavy on aime les fous et les loups sans foi ni loi.
9 Suivrez-vous Rrose Sélavy au pays des nombres décimaux où il n'y a décombres ni maux?
10 Rrose Sélavy se demande si la mort des saisons fait tomber un sort sur les maisons.
11 Passez-moi mon arc berbère, dit le monarque barbare.
12 Les planètes tonnantes dans le ciel effrayent les cailles amoureuses des plantes étonnantes aux feuilles d'écaille cultivées par Rrose Sélavy.
13 Rrose Sélavy connaît bien le marchand du sel.
14 ÉPITAPHE: Ne tourmentez plus Rrose Sélavy car mon génie est énigme. Caron ne le déchiffre pas.
15 Perdue sur la mer sans fin Rrose Sélavy mangera-t-elle du fer après avoir mangé ses mains?
16 Aragon recueille *in extremis* l'âme d'Aramis sur un lit d'estragon.
17 André Breton ne s'habille pas en mage pour combattre l'image de l'hydre du tonnerre qui brame sur un mode amer.
18 Francis Picabia l'ami des castors
Fut trop franc d'être un jour picador
À Cassis en ses habits d'or.
19 Rrose Sélavy voudrait bien savoir si l'amour, cette colle à mouches, rend plus dures les molles couches.

RROSE SÉLAVY

1 In an apple-plaster temple the pastor distilled the sap of psalms.
2 Rrose Sélavy asks if Baudelaire's 'The Wicked Blooms' hath unblockéd wombs: hopefully, Omphalé, you've a view.
3 Travellers, pamper the Pamplona fillies with peafowl feathers.
4 Is the solution of a sage the pollution of a page? [un page, a page-boy.]
5 I love sir's bosom that wears opossum.
6 QUESTION FOR ASTRONOMERS: Will Rrose Sélavy for decades enter the annual cadastre in the astral quadrant?
7 Oh, my knackered noddle, star-struck nacreous nodule.
8 Where Rrose Sélavy lives, they love wolves and fools who are heaven's and all men's outlaws.
9 Will you harass Rrose Sélavy as far as the decimal numbers nothing dismal encumbers?
10 Rrose Sélavy wonders if the demise of seasons decides the destiny of demesnes.
11 Pass me my Barbary quiver, says the barbaric vizier.
12 Thunderous planets above scare the quails, lovers of Rrose Sélavy's wondrous plants whose leaves are scales.
13 Marcel Duchamp, marchand du sel: Rrose Sélavy knows the salt-seller well.
14 EPITAPH: Torment Rrose Sélavy no more, for enigma's my genius. Nor can Caron con it.
15 Adrift on endless waters, will Rrose Sélavy eat first her hands, then her fetters?
16 Aragon harvests in extremis the spirit of Aramis on a bed of tarragon.
17 André Breton doesn't come dressed as a mage to combat an image of the thunder-hydra, bitter and barking.
18 Francis Picabia, too frank for
A confidant of beavers, or,
Red-caped and draped in toison d'or,
A prancing Cassis picador.
19 Rrose Sélavy wonders if love is the fly-paper that prepares soft sofas for foreplay.

20 Pourquoi votre incarnat est-il devenu si terne, petite fille, dans cet internat où votre œil se cerna?
21 Au virage de la course au rivage, voici le secours de Rrose Sélavy.
22 Rrose Sélavy peut revêtir la bure du bagne, elle a une monture qui franchit les montagnes.
23 Rrose Sélavy décerne la palme sans l'éclat du martyre à Lakmé bergère en Beauce figée dans le calme plat du métal appelé beauté.
24 Croyez-vous que Rrose Sélavy connaisse ces jeux de fous qui mettent le feu aux joues?
25 Rrose Sélavy c'est peut-être aussi ce jeune apache qui de la paume de sa main colle un pain à sa môme.
26 Est-ce que la caresse des putains excuse la paresse des culs teints?
27 Le temps est un aigle dans un temple.
28 Qu'arrivera-t-il si Rrose Sélavy, un soir de Noël, s'en va vers le piège de la neige et du pôle?
29 Ah! meurs, amour!
30 Quel hasard me fera découvrir entre mille l'ami plus fugitif que le lézard?
31 Un prêtre de Savoie déclare que le déchet des calices est marqué du cachet des délices: met-il de la malice dans ce match entre le ciel et lui?
32 Voici le cratère où le Missouri prend sa source et la cour de Sara son mystère.
33 Nomades qui partez vers le nord, ne vous arrêtez pas au port pour vendre vos pommades.
34 Dans le sommeil de Rrose Sélavy il ya un nain sorti d'un puits qui vient manger son pain la nuit.
35 Si le silence est d'or, Rrose Sélavy abaisse ses cils et s'endort.
36 Debout sur la carène le poète cherche une rime et croyez-vous que Rrose Sélavy soit la reine du crime?
37 Au temps où les caravelles accostaient La Havane, les caravanes traversaient-elles Laval?

20 What set your complexion withering, little girl, boarding where your eye came by another ring?
21 The riverside diversion of a racecourse, there's Rrose Sélavy's resource.
22 Rrose Sélavy may don prison's drab garb, yet her mount ranges on mountain-ranges.
23 Rrose Sélavy passes the palm that lacks the glamour of martyrs to Lakmé the lamb-herd of Chartres on the Beauce's flat metal calm, by name beauty.
24 Do you think Rrose Sélavy knows those ticklish jokes that make for tingling cheeks?
25 Rrose Sélavy is perhaps the apprentice apache who flanned his brat with the flat of his hand.
26 Does the canoodling of shoddy wenches condone the idling of shady haunches?
27 Time is an agile eagle in a temple.
28 What if Rrose Sélavy, on a night of Yule, steers for the snare of the snow-white pole?
29 Ah, lover! All over!
30 Why's it my luck to pick from the pack, at hazard, a friend more fickle than the lizard?
31 A curate in a chalet sees the cachet of delicacy in the lees of his chalice: does he meet his celestial match with malice?
32 This crater affords the Missouri its source and Sarah's court its mystery.
33 Nomads en route for the North, do not pause at the port to trade your pomades.
34 Rrose Sélavy sleeps well as a small fellow out of a well wolfs her loaf at twelve.
35 If silence is golden, Rrose Sélavy lowers her eyelids for close-down.
36 Craning on the careen, the poet seeks a rhyme: do you see Rrose Sélavy as the queen of crime?
37 When caravels were making fast at La Havana, were caravans snaking past Laval?

38 QUESTION D'ORIENT: À Sainte-Sophie sur un siège de liège s'assied la folie.
39 Rrose Sélavy propose que la pourriture des passions devienne la nourriture des nations.
40 Quelle est donc cette marée sans cause dont l'onde amère inonde l'âme acérée de Rrose?
41 Benjamin Péret ne prend jamais qu'un bain par an.
42 P. Éluard: le poète élu des draps.
43 ÉPITAPHE POUR APOLLINAIRE: Pleurez de nénies, géants et génies au seuil du néant.
44 Amoureux voyageur sur la carte du tendre, pourquoi nourrir vos nuits d'une tarte de cendre?
45 MARTYRE DE SAINT SÉBASTIEN: Mieux que ses seins ses bas se tiennent.
46 Rrose Sélavy a visité l'archipel où la reine Irène-sur-les-Flots de sa rame de frêne gouverne ses îlots.
47 From Everest mountain I am falling down at your feet for ever, Mrs Everling.
48 André Breton serait-il déjà condamné à la tâche de tondre en enfer des chats d'ambre et de jade?
49 Rrose Sélavy vous engage à ne pas prendre les verrues des seins pour les vertus des saintes.
50 Rrose Sélavy n'est pas persuadée que la culture du moi puisse amener la moiteur du cul.
51 Rrose Sélavy s'étonne que de la contagion des reliques soit née la religion catholique.
52 Possédé d'un amour sans frein, le prêtre savoyard jette aux rocs son froc pour soulager ses reins.
53 DEVISE DE RROSE SÉLAVY:
Plus que poli pour être honnête
Plus que poète pour être honni.
54 Oubliez les paraboles absurdes pour écouter de Rrose Sélavy les sourdes paroles.
55 ÉPIPHANIE: Dans la nuit fade les rêves accostent à la rade pour décharger des fèves.

38 EASTERN QUESTION: At Santa Sophia a kirkstall of cork's a seat of insanity.
39 Rrose Sélavy proposes that the perishing compost of passions become the nourishing repast of nations.
40 What is this unfounded tide whose sour flow floods Rrose's steely soul?
41 Benjamin Péret's regimen is perfect: his early bath is his yearly bath.
42 Paul Éluard, poet, the élite of the sheets.
43 Epitaph for Apollinaire: Weep dirges, giants and geniuses, on the void's edges.
44 Amorous voyager on the tender chart, why nourish your nights on a cinder tart?
45 THE MARTYRDOM OF ST SEBASTIAN: The garters suit him but his bust's wrong.
46 Rrose Sélavy has seen the archipelago where sea-queen Irene with an ash-sprig rules her isles.
47 From Everest mountain I am falling down to your feet for ever, Mrs Everling. *[Desnos composed this one in English.]*
48 Would André Breton be already damned to tonsure in hell cats of jade and amber?
49 Rrose Sélavy calls on you not to mistake the verrucas of the breast for the virtues of the blest.
50 Rrose Sélavy wouldn't bet egotism gets you a wet bottom.
51 Rrose Sélavy can't believe the religion of catholics arose from the contagion of relics.
52 Seized with reckless love, the Alpine parson spreads his frocks to the rocks to ease his loins.
53 RROSE SÉLAVY'S MOTTO:
Beyond the polite to be decent
Beyond the poet to be dishonoured.
54 Forego the absurd parabolas, go for Rrose Sélavy's misheard parables.
55 EPIPHANY: In the small hours, dreams moor at the mole to unload beans.

56 Au paradis des diamants les carats sont des amants et la spirale est en cristal.
57 Les pommes de Rome ont pour les pages la saveur de la rage qu'y imprimèrent les dents des Mores.
58 Lancez les fusées, les races à faces rusées sont usées!
59 Rrose Sélavy proclame que le miel de sa cervelle est la merveille qui aigrit le fiel du ciel.
60 Aux agapes de Rrose Sélavy on mange du pâté de pape dans une sauce couleur d'agate.
61 Apprenez que la geste célèbre de Rrose Sélavy est inscrite dans l'algèbre céleste.
62 Habitants de Sodome, au feu du ciel préférez le fiel de la queue.
63 Tenez bien la rampe rois et lois qui descendez à la cave sans lampe.
64 Morts férus de morale, votre tribu attend-elle toujours un tribunal?
65 Rrose Sélavy affirme que la couleur des nègres est due au tropique du cancer.
66 Beaux corps sur les billards, vous serez peaux sur les corbillards!
67 Du palais des morts les malaises s'en vont par toutes les portes.
68 Rocambole de son cor provoque le carnage puis carambole du haut d'un roc et s'échappe à la nage.
69 De cirrhose du foie meurt la foi du désir de Rrose.
70 Amants tuberculeux, ayez des avantages phtisiques.
71 Rrose Sélavy au seuil des cieux porte deuil des dieux.
72 Les orages ont pu passer sur Rrose Sélavy, c'est sans rage qu'elle atteint l'âge des oranges.
73 Ce que Baron aime c'est le bâillon sur l'arme!
74 Les idées de Morise s'irisent d'un charme démodé.
75 Simone dans le silence provoque le heurt des lances des démones.
76 Les yeux des folles sont sans fard. Elles naviguent dans des yoles, sur le feu, pendant des yards, pendant des yards.

56 In the paradise of diamonds the carats are amorous, the spiral is crystal.
57 Roman persimmons taste to pages as if gnawed in rages by jaws of Moors.
58 Let rockets be fired, the crooked-faced races are tired!
59 Rrose Sélavy declares her skull's nectar is the elixir that bitters the sky's bile.
60 At Rrose Sélavy's 'agapê' or love-feast, papal paste is tasted in an agate-glazed sauce.
61 Learn that Rrose Sélavy's celebrated gesture is etched in celestial algebra.
62 People of Sodom, fear the fire of heaven, prefer the fever of the rear.
63 Keep to the ramp, rulers and rules braving the cellar with no lamp.
64 Is your tribe forever at a tribunal, dear downhearted departed?
65 Rrose Sélavy can trace black ancestors back to the Tropic of Cancer.
66 Classy torsos on tables of nurses, you will be carcases in hearses!
67 Maladies issue from every orifice of cadavers' palaces.
68 Rocambole blows his cornet to start carnage and swims clear, cartwheeling off a lofty crag.
69 Rrose's desire of love for ever dies of cirrhosis of the liver.
70 Lovers with tuberculosis, use your phthisical advantages.
71 In the Elysian fields, Rrose Sélavy wears deceaseful weeds.
72 Savage gales range over Rrose Sélavy, who reaches without outrage the age of oranges.
73 Jacques Baron's fun, bayonet-jerks on gun!
74 Morise's ideas are iridescent with obsolescent promise.
75 Simone's silences launch the crunch of demonesses' lances.
76 Mad broads with eyes undaubed sail through yards and yards of fire in yawls.

77 Le mépris des chansons ouvre la prison des méchants.
78 Le plaisir des morts c'est de moisir à plat.
79 Aimez, ô gens, Janine, la fleur d'hémérocalle est si câline.
80 Sur quel pôle la banquise brise-t-elle le bateau des poètes en mille miettes?
81 Rrose Sélavy sait bien que le démon du remords ne peut mordre le monde.
82 Rrose Sélavy nous révèle que le râle du monde est la ruse des rois mâles emportés par la ronde de la muse des mois.
83 DICTIONNAIRE LA RROSE: Latinité – les cinq nations latines. La Trinité – l'émanation des latrines.
84 Nul ne connaîtrait la magie des boules sans la bougie des mâles.
85 Dans un lac d'eau minérale Rrose Sélavy a noyé la câline morale.
86 Rrose Sélavy glisse le cœur de Jésus dans le jeu des Crésus.
87 CONSEIL AUX CATHOLIQUES: Attendez sagement le jour de la foi où la mort vous fera jouir de la faux.
88 Au fond d'une mine Rrose Sélavy prépare la fin du monde.
89 La jolie sœur disait: «Mon droit d'aînesse pour ton doigt, Ernest.»
90 Cravan se hâte sur la rive et sa cravate joue dans le vent.
91 Dans le ton rogue de Vaché il y avait des paroles qui se brisaient comme les vagues sur les rochers.
92 Faites l'aumône aux riches puis sculptez dans la roche le simulacre de Simone.
93 QUESTION: Cancer mystique chanteras-tu longtemps ton cantique au mystère?
94 RÉPONSE: Ignores-tu que ta misère se pare comme une reine de la traîne de ce mystère?
95 La mort dans les flots est-elle le dernier mot des forts?
96 L'acte des sexes est l'axe des sectes.
97 La suaire et les ténèbres du globe sont plus suaves que la gloire.
98 Frontières qui serpentez sur les cimes vous n'entourez pas les cimetières abrités par nos fronts.

77 Evil opinions of singsongs prise open villains' prisons.
78 The sport of the departed is to spread and be rotted.
79 Janine, we do all love her, the day-lily's such a wheedler.
80 On what pole does the ice-pack splinter the poets' smack?
81 Rrose Sélavy knows the goblin of gloom cannot gobble the globe.
82 Rrose Sélavy tells us the world's rattle is the ruse of male rulers embattled in the whirl of the monthly muse.
83 LA RROSE DICTIONARY: Latinity: the five Latin nations. The Trinity: latrine emanations.
84 To command all the magic of boules, imagine the candle of the males. [Boules: the lobbing game.]
85 Rrose Sélavy submerged the moral wheedler in a mere of mineral water.
86 Into the sport of every Croesus Rrose Sélavy slips the very heart of Jesus.
87 ADVICE TO CATHOLICS: Sagely await the day of faith when death shall have you enjoy the scythe.
88 Rrose Sélavy's going down a mine, making ready for Armageddon.
89 Ernest, says his pretty sister, by your third right digit, buy my birthright.
90 Cravan wends on the wave and his cravat waves in the wind.
91 In Vaché's roguish drawls, words crashed like waves on rocky shores.
92 Give some alms to the rich and etch in the rocks the effigy of Simone.
93 QUESTION: Mystical cancer, how long will your song be a mystery canticle?
94 ANSWER: Aren't you aware your misery preens like a queen on this mystery's train?
95 Is a watery death a wreath for the doughty?
96 The act of the sexes is the axis of the sects.
97 Sweeter than glory are the shrouds and shadows of the globe.
98 Our brows harbour cemeteries that a maze of boundaries on summits omits.

99 Les caresses de demain nous révèleront-elles le carmin des déesses?
100 Le parfum des déesses berce la paresse des défunts.
101 La milice des déesses se préoccupe peu des délices de la messe.
102 À son trapèze Rrose Sélavy apaise la détresse des déesses.
103 Les vestales de la Poésie vous prennent-elles pour des vessies, ô! Pétales.
104 Images de l'amour, poissons, vos baisers sans poison me feront-ils baisser les yeux?
105 Dans le pays de Rrose Sélavy les mâles font la guerre sur la mer. Les femelles ont la gale.
106 À tout miché, pesez Ricord.
107 Mots êtes-vous des mythes et pareils aux myrtes des morts?
108 L'argot de Rrose Sélavy, n'est-ce pas l'art de transformer en cigognes les cygnes?
109 Les lois de nos désirs sont des dés sans loisir.
110 Héritiers impatients, conduisez vos ascendants à la chambre des tonnerres.
111 Je vis où tu vis, voyou dont le visage est le charme des voyages.
112 Phalange des anges, aux angélus préférez les phallus.
113 Connaissez-vous la jolie faune de la folie? – Elle est jaune.
114 Votre sang charrie-t-il des grelots au gré de vos sanglots?
115 La piété dans le dogme consiste-t-elle à prendre les dogues en pitié?
116 Le char de la chair ira-t-il loin sur ce chemin si long?
117 Qu'en pensent les cocus? Recette culinaire: plutôt que Madeleine l'apotrophage, femmes! imitez la vierge cornivore.
118 Corbeaux qui déchiquetez le flanc des beaux corps, quand éteindrez-vous les flambeaux?
119 Prométhée moi l'amour.

99 Will the morning of caresses reveal to us the carmine of goddesses?
100 The eyeliners of goddesses lull the idleness of goners.
101 The militias of goddesses disregard the delights of missals.
102 On her trapeze see Rrose Sélavy appease the distresses of our divine mistresses.
103 Do poesy's Vestals take you for vesicles, Petals?
104 Love's images, fishes, will your poisonless kisses make me lower my eyes?
105 In the land of Rrose Sélavy, males scour the shores in warships, females pick and scratch at sores.
106 [*À tout péché, miséricorde:* for every sin, there is mercy.]For all malefactors, atonement; for all male punters, an ointment. [*Ricord: famous doctor.*]
107 Words, are you myths which match the myrtles of death?
108 Can Rrose Sélavy's artful talk turn a swan into a stork?
109 The laws of our desires are leisureless dice.
110 Impatient heirs, usher your forebears into the chamber of thunders.
111 I live where you live, urchin whose mug is the magic of journeys.
112 Phalanx of angels, prefer the phallus to the angelus.
113 Do you know the jolly lovely faun of folly? She is yellow.
114 Does your bloodstream carry cowbells at your blubbing's beck and call?
115 Does piety in dogma consist in pitying dogs?
116 For the fleshly calèche it's a long lane, will the carnal car go far?
117 What are cuckolds thinking? Hints for women cooking: Don't mimic the apostrophagic madeleine, copy the cornivorous virgin.
118 You crows rifling fine torsos' haunches, when will you stifle your torches?
119 Prometheuth! Promitheth, promitheth!

120 Ô ris cocher des flots! Auric, hochet des flots au ricochet des flots.

121 L'espèce des folles aime les fioles et les pièces fausses.

122 DEFINITIONS DE LA POÉSIE POUR: *Louis Aragon:* À la margelle des âmes écoutez les gammes jouer à la marelle.

123 *Benjamin Péret:* Le ventre de chair est un centre de vair.

124 *Tristan Tzara:* Quel plus grand outrage à la terre qu'un ouvrage de vers / verre? Qu'en dis-tu, ver de terre?

125 *Max Ernst:* La boule rouge bouge et roule.

126 *Max Morise:* À figue dolente, digue affolante.

127 *Georges Auric:* La portée des muses n'est-ce pas la mort duvetée derrière la porte des musées?

128 *Philippe Soupault:* Les oies et les zébus sont les rois de ce rébus.

129 *Roger Vitrac:* Il ne faut pas prendre le halo de la lune à l'eau pour le chant «alla» des poètes comme la lune.

130 *Georges Limbour:* Pour les Normands le Nord ment.

131 *Francis Picabia:* Les chiffres de bronze ne sont-ils que des bonzes de chiffes: j'ai tué l'autre prêtre, êtes-vous prête, Rrose Sélavy?

132 *Marcel Duchamp:* Sur le chemin, il y avait un bœuf bleu près d'un banc blanc. Expliquez-moi la raison des gants blancs maintenant?

133 *G. de Chirico:* Vingt fois sur le métier remettez votre outrage.

134 Quand donc appellerez-vous Prétéritions, Paul Éluard, les répétitions?

135 Ô laps des sens, gage des années aux pensées sans langage.

136 Fleuves! portez au Mont-de-Piété les miettes de pont.

137 Les joues des fées se brûlent aux feux de joies.

138 Le mystère est l'hystérie des mortes sous les orties.

139 Dans le silence des cimes, Rrose Sélavy regarde en riant la science qui lime.

140 Nos peines sont des peignes de givre dans des cheveux ivres.

120 O laugh, the waves, coachmen are chortling! Olaf, the waves, catch many rattling! All of the waves crash ricochetting!
121 The species of fair fools loves phials and false pieces.
122 DEFINITIONS OF POETRY FOR: *Louis Aragon:* Hear the scales play hopscotch at the edge of souls.
123 *Benjamin Péret:* Belly of flesh, flurry of brush.
124 *Tristan Tzara*: What harms earth worse than a glass-work or a verse-work? What say you, earthworm?
125 *Max Ernst:* Max points! The red ball rolled and bowled.
126 *Max Morise:* For a disappointed fig, dig a fascinating dyke.
127 *Georges Auric:* Isn't this the import of the muses: behind the museums' portals, the bed-rolls of mortals?
128 *Philippe Soupault:* Geese and zebus are neguses in this rebus.
129 *Roger Vitrac:* Don't take the moon's halo hung to light the lagoon for the poets' hallo sung too like the moon.
130 *Georges Limbour:* The Normans' destiny is the North's mendacity.
131 *Francis Picabia:* Numbers in bronze make a ragamuffin bonze: I rubbed out the second reverend, are you ready, Rrose Sélavy?
132 *Marcel Duchamp:* On the road was a blue bull by a blanched bench. Tell me now, what reasons for white mittens?
133 *G. de Chirico:* Remit your outrage twenty times on your métier.
134 Paul Éluard, when will you call repetitions Preteritions?
135 O lapse of senses, wager years on wordless pensées.
136 Rivers! Come and bring the pawnbrokers the poor broken bridge-crumbs.
137 Fairies' faces burn as a bonfire blazes.
138 Mysterious are the hysterias of foundered mortals under nettles.
139 In the silence of highland snows, Rrose Sélavy smiles at the science of filing nails.
140 Our misfortunes are hair-combs of hoar-frost in fuddled tresses.

141 Femmes! faux chevaux sous vos cheveux de feu.
142 Dites les transes de la confusion et non pas les contusions de la France.
143 De quelle plaine les reines de platine monteront-elles dans nos rétines?
144 La peur, c'est une hanche pure sous un granit ingrat.
145 Les menteurs et les rhéteurs perdent leurs manches dans le vent rêche quand les regarde Man Ray.
146 Si vous avez des peines de cœur, amoureux, n'ayez plus peur de la Seine.
147 À cœur payant un rien vaut cible.
148 Plus fait violeur que doux sens.
149 Jeux des mots jets mous.
150 Aimable souvent est sable mouvants.
151 Robert Delaunay: de l'eau naît, gare à hameçon.
152 Ma peur se reflète sur le verre comme un vapeur sur la mer.
153 DÉFINITION DE L'ART PAR RROSE SÉLAVY: La vache tuberculeuse traite sans pitié jusqu'à perdre par mois la moitié d'un pis.
154 Sans pâlir, Desnos a fait mourir sur son pal bien des désirs.
155 Monte à l'échelle, Drieu la Rochelle, pour étonner Dieu.
156 Est-ce que Rrose Sélavy découvrira en Amérique le fleuve d'alcool où boivent les lamas cholériques?
157 Aller jeter ses prières à l'église, autant jeter ses pierres à l'éclipse.
158 Dans le crâne de l'abbesse se livre le combat du crabe et de l'ânesse.
159 Rrose Sélavy a découvert que la particule des nobles n'est pas la partie noble du cul.
160 C'est dans l'art que les pions se taillent leur part du lion.
161 Pourquoi le problème de la vie est-il la proie des vis blêmes?
162 Rrose Sélavy fonde une banque antarctique sur la banquise antiartistique.
163 Rrose Sélavy met du fard au destin puis de son dard assure ses festins.

141 Fair ladies! False horses in your fiery tresses.
142 Say the trances of confusion, not the contusions of France.
143 From what plain will the platinum Reginas rise to our retinas?
144 Fear is a pure femur under ingrate granite.
145 Man Ray's gaze unsleeves the mayhem-ranters, romancers orating in the harsh breeze.
146 Lover, if you suffer pain, never fear the river Seine.
147 (*À cœur paisible, rien ne vaut tant:* To a heart at peace, nothing is worth the same.) To a heart that pays, nothing is worth its aim.
148 (*Plus fait douceur que violence:* Gentleness does more than violence.) Vile force does more than gentle sense.
149 Wordplay, wet spray.
150 Soft, sunlit, bland, oft built on sand.
151 Robert Delaunay: Rowboat Water-born! Beware the barb.
152 My fear in the mirror appears as a marine vapour.
153 DEFINITION OF ART BY RROSE SÉLAVY: The merciless cow with tuberculosis loses in one month half an udder.
154 Desnos does not pale as he deals with desires on his pole.
155 Scale the ladder, Drieu la Rochelle, to shock the Lord.
156 Will Rrose Sélavy discover the alcohol river quaffed by choleric llamas in America?
157 Praying in pews with bibles is like spraying the eclipse with pebbles.
158 In an abbess's cranium, a crab grapples an ass.
159 Rrose Sélavy has learnt that nobility's noble title is no buttock's notable tackle.
160 Poor pawns in art pare as their share the lion's part.
161 Why are life's ifs and buts the problem prey of pale bolts and nuts?
162 On the anti-artistic ice-pack, Rrose Sélavy starts an Antarctic savings bank.
163 Rrose Sélavy tarts up the fates and her dart starts the feasts.

164 L'heure du stupre prévaut sur la stupeur des pauvres hères.
165 Les pensées des hommes aiment les pensums.
166 Le dogme fatal du Christ ce n'est après tout que le cristal des fats.
167 Assassin des luths as-tu tué le salut des saints?
168 Les yeux caves de Max Ernst estiment les cavernes où s'amusent les statues et où s'inscrivent les maximes de sa muse: Ernestine.
169 La dilection des femmes est-elle le dilemme de la fiction et des nombres?
170 Les enfants des hommes sont une somme de fantômes et de sang un peu.
171 Juchés sur des éléphants les fantômes femelles inscrivent au ciel l'oméga mystérieux égal des équations planétaires.
172 L'orgueil de Rrose Sélavy sait s'évader du cercle qui peut se clore comme un cercueil.
173 Le gras légat sorti du cloître a vraiment l'éclat d'un goitre.
174 Les fats ignorent la vertu des glas quand les glaces refusent de refléter leur face.
175 Au gala des astres s'inscrit en astragales ce nom: Gala.
176 La lame qui tranche l'affliction des âmes dévoile-t-elle aux amis la fiction de l'affection?
177 À l'ironie des pages blanches oppose, sans rage agonie, le silence pire que le rire.
178 Les orages qui masquent Orion à nos visages n'en suppriment pourtant pas la vision.
179 Qu'il est fragile ce mur! flots mulots agiles qui cherchez votre lot dans la nuit.
180 Gastronomes! les rêves des astronomes vous noieront-ils sur les grèves?
181 DÉFINITIONS DE LA POÉSIE POUR: *Paul Éluard:* Affres de l'amour dans quelle nuit ai-je savouré votre fruit âpre?
182 *André Breton:* Le plus beau titre des hommes, c'est de jeter à la hotte (hopp!) les pitres coiffés de mitres.

164 The period of debauches pips the stupor of poor wretches.
165 Mankind's thoughts take kindly to a schoolkid's impots.
166 What's the fatal dogma of Christ, after all, but the crystal of fops and fags?
167 Assassin of psalteries, have you slaughtered the salvation of saints?
168 Max Ernst's cavernous eyes assess the caves of statues' amusement, carved with his Muse's maxims: Ernestine.
169 Is a predilection for the female the dilemma of fiction and the numeral?
170 The human brood is a phantom squad with a squirt of blood.
171 Female phantoms perched on elephants scriven on heavens the mysterious omega that fits planetary equations.
172 The self-regard of Rrose Sélavy forges clear as the circle closes like a shroud.
17 The gross legate from the cloister has all the éclat of a goitre.
174 Swells don't respect tolling knells when looking-glasses won't reflect their longing glances.
175 At the astral gala this name is written in astragals: Gala.
176 Does the knife in severing the souls' affliction unveil to pals affection's fiction?
177 Without rage in agony, place against blank pages' irony the silence worse than mirth.
178 The hurricanes that occlude Orion don't obtrude on our vision.
179 This wall is so fragile! Waves, field-mice so agile, seeking your fate by night.
180 Gastronomers! Will astronomers' dreaming snores drown you on marine sea-shores?
181 DEFINITION OF POETRY FOR: *Paul Éluard:* Love's throes, in what late hours did I browse your sloes?
182 *André Breton:* And no better matter than to drop the mitred nutters (whoops!) into a hopper.

183 *Robert Desnos:* Corps d'amour, quel jour me pendrai-je à la corde d'amour?
184 *Jacques Baron:* Les corps des femmes comme des camées le corps des forts comme des camées de femmes.
185 *Simone Breton:* Daniel de Foe inventez un simoun fou pour Simone.
186 123 appelle immédiatement le chiffre 1234 pour les esprits épris de lucidité. Esaü est mort, manque d'eau.
187 C'est encore infiniment plus commode que de regarder la poitrine, encornée de seins clairvoyants en cornée, des étoiles non encore nées.
188 Pleurs ébahis, pelures des abbayes, vous trompez les abeilles.
189 Où est la Parysi's est la paralysie.
190 Rails d'émail, vous passez comme des rois sur nos émois.
191 Que secrète la glande secrète du périnée de l'aigle des Andes ou des Pyrénées?
192 Les miracles de Rrose Sélavy sont des aveux mauves comme les éclairs.
193 Télémaque, tel est camée.
194 Qu'importe au repos de nos oiseaux sur les roseaux le loir, aux yeux comme de l'or, qui dort?
195 Quand Man Ray is coming away...: on pourra voir un Far West war festin.
196 Dans les stalles de glace râle Tristan Tzara.
197 Amour aux mains hostiles, quel malin déroba les hosties?
198 Les malheurs des concitoyens n'influent pas sur la chaleur des cons mitoyens?
199 Amour! homard dans les fjords froids.

183 *Robert Desnos:* Love's limbs, how soon shall I limber love's noose?
184 *Jacques Baron:* Female torsos just like cameos tough male torsos like female cameos.
185 *Simone Breton:* Daniel Defoe, devise a daffy simoon for Simone.
186 123 calls up at once the number 1234 for spirits smitten with lucidity. Esau died for lack of water.
187 It's far handier than to look at the chest, horned with breasts clairvoyant in cornea, of stars not yet born here.
188 Bemused apple-peels of abbeys, your boo-hoos bamboozle bees.
189 Where La Parysi's is, there is paralysis.
190 Enamelled rails, you sail like untrammelled royals above our travails.
191 What is secreted by the Andean or Pyrenean eagle's secret perineal gland?
192 Rrose Sélavy's miracles are vows mauve as éclairs.
193 O Telemachus, tell me cameos.
194 To our birds at rest on reeds, what good is the dormant dormouse whose eyes are as gold?
195 When Man Ray is coming away, we'll see a Far West war-fest.
196 In a sub-zero cattle-stall, Tristan Tzara rattles his last.
197 Love in the fingers of foes, what rogue rifled the wafers?
198 Does the public fate of a community affect the pubic heat of common property?
199 Love! Lobster in frozen fjords.

21 heures le 26-11-22

En attendant
en nattant l'attente
Sous quelle tente?
mes tantes
ont-elles engendré
les neveux silencieux
que nul ne veut sous les cieux
appeler ses cousins
en nattant les cheveux du silence
six lances
percent mes pensées en attendant

Les moules des mers
aux moules des mères
empruntent leur forme d'œil,
Homme – houle d'aimer.

Ail de ton œil,
je t'aime à cause de cela.

Nos tâches tachent
tour à tour
les tours
d'alentours.

Plutôt se pendre aux pins,
s'éprendre des yeux peints,
que de gagner son pain
où les fleuves vont s'épandre.

9 pm, 26-11-22

WAITING
plaiting the waiting
attendant on it
Into what tent
my aunts went
to engender those noiseless nephews
that none of us under the heavens
wants to call our cousins?
Plaiting the braids of silence
six lances pierce my pensées? my pansies
waiting

A MARINER'S mussels
acquire ocular form from
a mother's moulds,
man – tumorous amorous.

GARLICQUOR-Eyes,
I love you for that.

OUR TOIL spoils
turn turn about
the towers
all round about.

GO HANG in pain from a pine to die,
dangle and pine for a painted eye,
better than earning our bread
where running waters spread.

MORDS le mors de la mort Maure silencieux.
cils! aux cieux
dérobez nos yeux.

Non, nous n'avons pas de nom.

PLUS QUE la nuit nue
la femme vient hanter
nos rêves, pareils à Antée
antes des désirs renaissants.

Nos pères! C'est parce que vous n'aviez pas les yeux pers.

Changez vos cœurs au pair avec les dollars
Change ton cœur, opère sans douleur.

MES CHANTS sont si peu méchants
Ils ne vont pas jusqu'à Longchamp
Ils meurent avant d'atteindre les champs
où les bœufs s'en vont léchant
des astres
désastres

L'AN est si lent.
Abandonnons nos ancres dans l'encre,

mes amis.

TANT d'or.
Passez les patries à l'épreuve du tan
et du temps
et encore du taon.

BITE the bitter bit, it's mortal, Moor of silence.
eyelids! filch our eyes
from the skies.

No, we've no name, none.

MORE THAN nude night, woman haunts
our dreams, as giant Antaeus
haunted by yearnings reborn.

Our paren'ts! Seeing your eyes aren't seagreen.

Change your hearts at par rate with our dollars,
Change of heart, operate without dolours.

MY DITTIES are not a bit naughty nor dirty
Non-runners non-starters at Ascot
they perish far short of the pastures
where ox-tongues are tickling
galactic
disasters

THE YEAR D-R-ags, wordless. My D-R friends,
let's D-R-own our anchors in the D-R-ink.

POTS of gold.
Put patriotism to the test of tan
of time
and of ticks.

L'ART est le dieu lare
des mangeurs de lard
et les phares dévoilent le fard
des courtisans du Far-West qui s'effarent.

LES CHATS hauts sur les châteaux
d'espoir
Croquent des poires d'angoisse
la nuit
l'ennui
l'âme nuit.

Et puis il y a le puits
qui s'enfonce dans la terre
où s'atterrent
les faibles
que brise la brise.

Poète venu de Lorient
que dis-tu de l'orient?
l'or riant

LES MÛRES sont mûres le long des murs
et des bouches bouchent nos yeux.

Les porcs débarquent dans les ports
d'Amérique
et de nos pores
s'enfuient les désirs.

ART: dear little god
    of eaters of lard
    while headlights of cars
    unmask the mascaras
    of scared wild west tarts.

CATS up on castles,
    high hopers,
sup pear suppers of agonies
    night
    nuisance
    heart-hurt

Then, well, the well,
deep thrust down where
    the weak touch down,
    the breeze-bruised
    suffer zephyrs.

Poet of Lorient,
    what of the orient?
    laughter of gold

BLACKBERRIES burgeon on bulwarks,
our eyes are gagged by gabs.

Porkers pour into ports
of America
out of our pores
ooze desires.

Vos BOUCHES mentent,
vos mensonges sentent la menthe,
Amantes!

Cristaux où meurt le Christ
reflétez la froide beauté
de Kristiana.
nos traditions?
notre addition!

LES PONTS s'effondrent tous
au cri du paon qui pond
et les pans des ponts
transforment les rivières.

aux lacs des lacs
meurent les paons
enlisés dans la gomme laque

P'OASIS

Nous sommes les pensées arborescentes qui
fleurissent sur les chemins des jardins cérébraux.
– Sœur Anne, ma Sainte Anne, ne vois-tu rien
venir… vers Sainte-Anne?
– Je vois les pensées odorer les mots.
– Nous sommes les mots arborescents qui
fleurissent sur les chemins des jardins cérébraux.

YOUR LIPS lie,
your lies stink of mint,
minxes!

Crystals where Christ dies,
Reflect the cold beauty
of Kristiania.
We've the patrimony?
We've to pay the money!

THE BRIDGES all go under
at the peahen's pang,
the bridges' panels
transform the channels.

in snares of meres
in gumlac shellac
the peahens flounder
and founder

POESY'S P'OASIS

We are the poet-tree pansies, the *pensées* that flower on the paths
in gardens of the brain.
– Sister Anne, my St Anne, do you see nothing coming
towards St Anne's?
– I see *pensées* giving their scent to words.
– We are the poet-tree words that flower on the paths of gardens
of the brain,

pensées = thoughts, also pansies

De nous naissent les pensées.
– Nous sommes les pensées arborescentes qui
fleurissent sur les chemins des jardins cérébraux.
Les mots sont nos esclaves.
– Nous sommes
– Nous sommes
– Nous sommes les lettres arborescentes qui
fleurissent sur les chemins des jardins cérébraux.
Nous n'avons pas d'esclaves.
– Sœur Anne, ma sœur Anne, que vois-tu venir vers
Sainte-Anne?
– Je vois les Pan C
– Je vois les crânes KC
– Je vois les mains DCD
– Je les M
– Je vois les pensées B C et les femmes M E
et les poumons qui en ont AC de l'R L O
poumons noyés des ponts NMI.
Mais la minute précédente est déjà trop AG.
– Nous sommes les arborescences qui fleurissent sur
les déserts des jardins cérébraux.

DIALOGUE

– Rien ne m'intéresse.
– Rie, en aimant, Thérèse.

we give birth to *pensées*.
– We are the poet-tree *pensées* that flower on the paths of gardens
of the brain.
Words are our slaves.
– We are
– We are
– We are the poet-tree letters that flower on the paths of gardens
of the brain.
We have no slaves.
– Sister Anne, sister Anne, what do U C coming…
towards St Anne's?
I C Pan CCCCC
I C skulls after N N G O R E S assault
I C hands that passed A O A
I love 'M
I C L O *pensée* and A D R D R L A D
I C lungs that have had more than N F F A R N C
lungs drowned on N M E bridges
But the P R E V S minute is already 2 O E R E
– We are the poet-trees that flower in the deserts of gardens of the
brain.

DIALOGUE

'Lo, I've nothing to interest my little soul.'
'Laugh, now think to win, Terry, smile at hell's hole.'

de **LANGAGE CUIT**

ÉLÉGANT CANTIQUE DE SALOMÉ SALOMON

Mon mal meurt mais mes mains miment
Nœuds, nerfs non anneaux. Nul nord
Même amour mol? mames, mord
Nus nénés nonne ni Nine.
Où est Ninive sur la mammemonde?

Ma mer, m'amis, me murmure:
«nos nils noient nos nuits nées neiges»
Meurt momie! môme: âme au mur.
Néant nié nom ni nerf n'ai-je!

Aime haine
Et n'aime
haine aime
aimai ne

MN
NM
NM
MN

Literal Version

My pain dies but my hands mime
Knots nerves not rings. No north
Even/same love soft breasts? bites
Naked breast nun nor Ninus.

ELEGANT CANTICLE OF SALOMÉ SALOMON

My members' mess maimed, my mitts may mime
Nerves knots not nicknacks. Nor, north, gnaw
My mellow marrow's amorous mammaries?
No naked knocker nun nor Ninny no.

Where's Nineveh on the Mamma Mundi?
My mates, my mer-mam murmurs me:
"One's Niles annihilate one's natally niveal nights."
Murdered mummy, my messmate, immure my Om:
Nothingness, name, nor nerve, nay, naught have I none!

N M EE	Enemies
& E M NN	Endearments
& D M NN	And the immense
N M EE	Anomies

M N	Love hate
N M	& Love not
N M	Hate love
M N	I loved not

Literal Version

Where's Nineveh on the Mamma Mundi?
My sea [mother], my dears, murmurs to me:
'Our Niles drown our nights born snow.'
Die, tomb-stuff! Youngster soul to the wall:
Nothingness negated name nor nerve have I not!

UN JOUR QU'IL FAISAIT NUIT

Il s'envola au fond de la rivière.
Les pierres en bois d'ébène, les fils de fer en or et la croix sans branche.
Tout rien.
Je la hais d'amour comme tout un chacun.
Le mort respirait de grandes bouffées de vide.
Le compas traçait des carrés
et des triangles à cinq côtés.
Après cela il descendit au grenier.
Les étoiles de midi resplendissaient.
Le chasseur revenait carnassière pleine de poissons
Sur la rive au milieu de la Seine.
Un ver de terre marque le centre du cercle sur la circonférence.
En silence mes yeux prononcèrent un bruyant discours.
Alors nous avancions dans une allée déserte où se pressait la foule.
Quand la marche nous eut bien reposé
nous eûmes le courage de nous asseoir
puis au réveil nos yeux se fermèrent
et l'aube versa sur nous les réservoirs de la nuit.
La pluie nous sécha.

LA COLOMBE DE L'ARCHE

Maudit!
soit le père de l'épouse
du forgeron qui forgea le fer de la cognée
avec laquelle le bûcheron abattit le chêne
dans lequel on sculpta le lit
où fut engendré l'arrière-grand-père
de l'homme qui conduisit la voiture
dans laquelle ta mère
rencontra ton père.

ONE DAY WHEN IT WAS NIGHT

He flew off to the bottom of the river.
Stones of ebony wood, steel wires of gold, a cross with no cross-piece.
All nothing.
I hate her with a love like all one each.
The dead man breathed great gulps of emptiness.
The compass traced squares and triangles with five sides.
After that he went down into the loft.
The midday stars were shining.
The hunter returned, his game-bag full of fish
On the bank in the middle of the Seine.
An earthworm marks the centre of the circle
on the circumference.
In silence my eyes uttered a noisy speech.
Then we moved up a deserted avenue where people were thronging.
When marching had given us a good rest
we had the courage to sit down
then as we woke our eyes closed
and dawn poured on us the reservoirs of night.
The rain dried us.

DOVE OF THE ARK

Cursed!
be the father of the wife
of the blacksmith who forged the iron of the axe
with which the woodsman felled the oak
from which was carved the bed
in which was begotten the great-grandfather
of the man who drove the vehicle
in which your mother
met your father.

LES GORGES FROIDES

À la poste d'hier tu télégraphieras
que nous sommes bien morts avec les hirondelles.
Facteur triste facteur un cercueil sous ton bras
va-t'en porter ma lettre aux fleurs à tire d'elle.

La boussole est en os mon cœur tu t'y fieras.
Quelque tibia marque le pôle et les marelles
pour amputés ont un sinistre aspect d'opéras.
Que pour mon épitaphe un dieu taille ses grêles!

C'est ce soir que je meurs, ma chère Tombe-Issoire,
Ton regard le plus beau ne fut qu'un accessoire
de la machinerie étrange du bonjour.

Adieu! Je vous aimai sans scrupule et sans ruse,
ma Folie-Méricourt, ma silencieuse intruse.
Boussole à flèche torse annonce le retour.

À tire d'aile – quick as a bird. This is à tire d'elle!
Tombe-Issoire, Folie-Méricourt – two streets in Paris.

COLD THROATS

Post Office of the past. Soon telegraphing
you'll say that we have perished with the swallows.
Sad postman, wrap your arm around a coffin,
bird-speed her urgently with flowers as follows:

The compass is of bones my heart you'll trust it.
Some tibia marks the pole. The amputees'
hopscotch looks operatic, broken-masted.
Some god, carve hailstones for my tombstone, please!

Tonight I die, my dear Tomb-Issory,
Your glad eye was a mere accessory
of the arcane contraption of good morning,

Farewell! I was your true straightforward lover,
my Folly-Merrycourt, mute interloper.
Bent-needled compass indicates returning.

LOVER

YVONNE GEORGE

HOPELESS LOVE 1926-7

Translator's Note

Desnos adored the night-club singer, Yvonne George. She had many other admirers, and ignored him, dying in 1930 of drink and drugs: 'Ténèbres' (Shadows), the title of the second group, suggests the approach of death. These unrhymed and very touching poems have appeared in English translation quite often, unlike most of Desnos.

At Yvonne's final gala night, organised by Jean Cocteau, Desnos met Youki, the French wife of the Japanese artist Tsuguhara Foujita. In August 1930 the trio went on a walking tour of Burgundy. In 1931 Foujita left Youki who by now was living with Desnos, and returned to Japan. Desnos wrote love-poems that testify to 'the only joys I have known'. In the end she became his wife. It was with the idea of protecting her that he let himself be arrested by the Gestapo.

À LA MYSTERIEUSE

Ô DOULEURS DE L'AMOUR!

Ô douleurs de l'amour!
Comme vous m'êtes nécessaires et comme vous m'êtes chères.
Mes yeux qui se ferment sur des larmes imaginaires, mes mains qui se tendent sans cesse vers le vide.
J'ai rêvé cette nuit de paysages insensés et d'aventures dangereuses aussi bien du point de vue de la mort que du point de vue de la vie qui sont aussi le point de vue de l'amour.
Au réveil vous étiez présentes, ô douleurs de l'amour, ô muses du désert, ô muses exigeantes.
Mon rire, et ma joie se cristallisent autour de vous. C'est votre fard, c'est votre poudre, c'est votre rouge, c'est votre sac de peau de serpent, c'est vos bas de soie… c'est aussi ce petit pli entre l'oreille et la nuque, à la naissance du cou, c'est votre pantalon de soie et votre fine chemise et votre manteau de fourrure, votre ventre rond c'est mon rire et mes joies vos pieds et tous vos bijoux.
En vérité, comme vous êtes bien vêtue et bien parée.

Ô douleurs de l'amour, anges exigeants, voilà que je vous imagine à l'image même de mon amour, que je vous confonds avec lui…
Ô douleurs de l'amour, vous que je crée et habille, vous vous confondez avec mon amour dont je ne connais que les vêtements et aussi les yeux, la voix, le visage, les mains, les cheveux, les dents, les yeux…

J'AI TANT RÊVÉ DE TOI

J'ai tant rêvé de toi que tu perds ta réalité.
Est-il encore temps d'atteindre ce corps vivant et de baiser sur

YOU PANGS OF LOVE!

You pangs of love!
How much I need you and cherish you!
My eyes closing on imaginary tears, my hands for ever stretching to the void.
I dreamed last night of unhinged landscapes and dangerous adventures, as much from death's viewpoint as from life's, and they are both the viewpoint of love.
When I woke you were there, you pangs of love, you desert muses, you importunate muses.
My laughter and joy crystallise around you. It's your make-up, your powder, your rouge, your snakeskin bag, your silk stocking... it's also that little fold between ear and nape, where the neck is born. It's your silk trousers and your fine chemise and your fur coat, your round belly it's my laughter and joys your feet and all your jewels.
How very well-dressed you are, how elegant.

You pangs of love, importunate angels, that's how I imagine you in the very image of my love, can't tell you apart...
You pangs of love, I create and clothe you, can't tell you apart from my love and I know only her clothes and also her eyes, her voice, her face, her hands, her hair, her teeth, her eyes...

I'VE DREAMED OF YOU SO MUCH

I've dreamed of you so much that you lose your reality.
Is there still time to reach that living body and to kiss on those lips the birth of the voice I love?

cette bouche la naissance de la voix qui m'est chère?

J'ai tant rêvé de toi que mes bras habitués en étreignant ton ombre à se croiser sur ma poitrine ne se plieraient pas au contour de ton corps, peut-être.

Et que, devant l'apparence réelle de ce qui me hante et me gouverne depuis des jours et des années, je deviendrais une ombre sans doute.

Ô balances sentimentales.

J'ai tant rêvé de toi qu'il n'est plus temps sans doute que je m'éveille. Je dors debout, le corps exposé à toutes les apparences de la vie et de l'amour et toi, la seule qui compte aujourd'hui pour moi, je pourrais moins toucher ton front et tes lèvres que les premières lèvres et le premier front venu.

J'ai tant rêvé de toi, tant marché, parlé, couché avec ton fantôme qu'il ne me reste plus peut-être, et pourtant, qu'à être fantôme parmi les fantômes et plus ombre cent fois que l'ombre qui se promène et se promènera allégrement sur le cadran solaire de ta vie.

I've dreamed of you so much that my arms, which always
find my own breast even as they clutch at your shadow,
may never close on the contours of your body.
So much that, confronted by one who has haunted and
controlled me for days and for years, I would certainly
become a shadow myself.
O the seesaw of emotions.
I've dreamed of you so much that it's probably too late to
wake up. I'm asleep on my feet, my body exposed to all the
sensations of life and love, and you, the only woman these
days who counts for me, I couldn't touch your mouth or
your brow as well as I could the next one that comes along.
I've dreamed of you so much, walked, talked, slept with your
phantom so much that all that's left to me, perhaps, is
to be a phantom among phantoms and a hundred times
more shadowy than that shadow walking in joy, now and
in time to come, across the sun-dial of your life.

Translator's Note

The last sentence, slightly altered, is inscribed on the walls of the Monument to the Martyrs of Deportation, close to Notre-Dame in Paris. It had come back from Terezin, translated into Czech. In a slightly altered French guise, it was taken to be a new poem, his last, addressed not to a loved one but to Liberty, or to France.

The entire poem 'Ce Cœur Qui Haïssait La Guerre' (see p. 497) is also inscribed there. Robert Desnos is the only writer to be honoured at the Monument with two quotations.

NON L'AMOUR N'EST PAS MORT

Non l'amour n'est pas mort en ce cœur et ces yeux et cette bouche qui proclamait ses funérailles commencées.
Écoutez, j'en ai assez du pittoresque et des couleurs et du charme.
J'aime l'amour, sa tendresse et sa cruauté.
Mon amour n'a qu'un seul nom, qu'une seule forme.
Tout passe. Des bouches se collent à cette bouche.
Mon amour n'a qu'un nom, qu'une forme.
Et si quelque jour tu t'en souviens
Ô toi, forme et nom de mon amour,
Un jour sur la mer entre l'Amérique et l'Europe,
À l'heure où le rayon final du soleil se réverbère sur la surface ondulée des vagues, ou bien une nuit d'orage sous un arbre dans la campagne ou dans une rapide automobile, Un matin de printemps boulevard Malesherbes,
Un jour de pluie,
À l'aube avant de te coucher,
Dis-toi, je l'ordonne à ton fantôme familier, que je fus seul à t'aimer davantage et qu'il est dommage que tu ne l'aies pas connu.
Dis-toi qu'il ne faut pas regretter les choses: Ronsard avant moi et Baudelaire ont chanté le regret des vieilles et des mortes qui méprisèrent le plus pur amour.
Toi quand tu seras morte
Tu seras belle et toujours désirable.
Je serai mort déjà, enclos tout entier en ton corps immortel, en ton image étonnante présente à jamais parmi les merveilles perpétuelles de la vie et de l'éternité, mais si je vis
Ta voix et son accent, ton regard et ses rayons,
L'odeur de toi et celle de tes cheveux et beaucoup d'autres choses encore vivront en moi,
En moi qui ne suis ni Ronsard ni Baudelaire,
Moi qui suis Robert Desnos et qui pour t'avoir connue et aimée,
Les vaux bien;
Moi qui suis Robert Desnos, pour t'aimer
Et qui ne veux pas attacher d'autre réputation à ma mémoire sur la terre méprisable.

NO, LOVE IS NOT DEAD

No, love is not dead in this heart and these eyes and this
mouth that declared its funeral had begun.
Listen, I've had enough of the picturesque, of colours and charm.
I love love, its tenderness and cruelty.
My love has only one name, only one form.
All passes. Mouths press themselves to that mouth.
My love has only one name, one form.
And if one day you remember it,
You, form and name of my love,
One day at sea between America and Europe,
At the hour when the sun's last ray rebounds from the
water's wavy surface, or on a stormy night under a tree in
the country or in a fast motor-car,
On a spring morning in the Boulevard de Malesherbes,
On a rainy day,
At dawn before going to bed,
Tell yourself (I command your familiar phantom) that only I
loved you more, and it's a pity you didn't know.
Tell yourself one must have no regrets: Ronsard before me
and Baudelaire sang the regrets of old women and dead
women who spurned the purest love.
You when you are dead
Will be beautiful, still desirable.
I shall be dead already, all closed up in your immortal body,
in your astounding image present for ever among the
perpetual wonders of life and eternity, but if I live
Your voice and its rhythm, your gaze and its radiance,
The scent of you, the scent of your hair, and much more
besides will live on in me,
In myself who am neither Ronsard nor Baudelaire,
Myself, Robert Desnos, who by having known and loved you
Am their equal;
Myself, Robert Desnos, by loving you
And I wish to add no other report to my memory on this
pitiful earth.

COMME UNE MAIN À L'INSTANT DE LA MORT

Comme une main à l'instant de la mort et du naufrage se dresse comme les rayons du soleil couchant, ainsi de toutes parts jaillissent tes regards.
Il n'est plus temps, il n'est plus temps peut-être de me voir,
Mais la feuille qui tombe et la roue qui tourne, te diront que rien n'est perpétuel sur terre,
Sauf l'amour,
Et je veux m'en persuader.
Des bateaux de sauvetage peints de rougeâtres couleurs,
Des orages qui s'enfuient,
Une valse surannée qu'emportent le temps et le vent durant les longs espaces du ciel.
Paysages.
Moi je n'en veux pas d'autres que l'étreinte à laquelle j'aspire,
Et meure le chant du coq.
Comme une main, à l'instant de la mort, se crispe, mon cœur se serre.
Je n'ai jamais pleuré depuis que je te connais.
J'aime trop mon amour pour pleurer.
Tu pleureras sur mon tombeau,
Ou moi sur le tien.
Il ne sera pas trop tard.
Je mentirai. Je dirai que tu fus ma maîtresse.
Et puis vraiment c'est tellement inutile,
Toi et moi, nous mourrons bientôt.

À LA FAVEUR DE LA NUIT

Se glisser dans ton ombre à la faveur de la nuit.
Suivre tes pas, ton ombre à la fenêtre,
Cette ombre à la fenêtre c'est toi, ce n'est pas une autre c'est toi.
N'ouvre pas cette fenêtre derrière les rideaux de laquelle tu bouges.

JUST AS A HAND AT THE MOMENT OF DEATH

Just as a hand at the moment of death and shipwreck rises up
like the rays of the setting sun, so your glances go flashing
from all directions.
It may be too late to see me now,
But the falling leaf and the turning wheel will tell you nothing
lasts for ever on earth
Except love,
And I want to be convinced of that.
Lifeboats painted in reddish colours,
Storms hurrying away,
A clapped-out waltz carried off by weather and wind in the sky's
long spaces.
Landscapes.
I want the embrace that I long for, and no other,
Perish the cockcrow.
Just as a hand clenches at the moment of death, my heart closes up.
I've never wept since I've known you.
I love my love too much to weep.
You'll weep on my grave,
Or I'll weep on yours.
It won't be too late.
I shall lie. I'll say you were my mistress.
And it's really so futile,
You and I will soon be dead.

UNDER COVER OF NIGHT

To slip into your shadow under cover of night.
To follow your footsteps, your shadow at the window,
That shadow at the window is you, not someone else, it's you.
Don't open that window where you are behind the curtains, moving.

Ferme les yeux.
Je voudrais les fermer avec mes lèvres.
Mais la fenêtre s'ouvre et le vent, le vent qui balance bizarrement
la flamme et le drapeau entoure ma fuite de son manteau.
La fenêtre s'ouvre: ce n'est pas toi.
Je le savais bien.

TÉNÈBRES 1927

LA VOIX DE ROBERT DESNOS

Si semblable à la fleur et au courant d'air
au cours d'eau aux ombres passagères
au sourire entrevu ce fameux soir à minuit
si semblable à tout au bonheur et à la tristesse
c'est le minuit passé dressant son torse nu au-dessus
des beffrois et des peupliers
j'appelle à moi ceux-là perdus dans les campagnes
les vieux cadavres les jeunes chênes coupés
les lambeaux d'étoffe pourrissant sur la terre et le linge
séchant aux alentours des fermes
j'appelle à moi les tornades et les ouragans
les tempêtes les typhons les cyclones
les raz de marée
les tremblements de terre
j'appelle à moi la fumée des volcans et celle des cigarettes
les ronds de fumée des cigares de luxe
j'appelle à moi les amours et les amoureux
j'appelle à moi les vivants et les morts

Close your eyes.
I'd like to close them with my lips.
But the window is opening and the breeze, the breeze weirdly
juggling flame and flag, wraps my retreat in its cloak.
The window is opening: it isn't you.
I knew that.

SHADOWS 1927

THE VOICE OF ROBERT DESNOS

So like the flower and the breeze
the stream the passing shadows
the smile glimpsed that great night at midnight
so like everything joy sorrow
it's last night's midnight rearing its naked torso above the
belfries and poplars
I summon those who are lost in the countryside
old corpses young felled oaks
rags of cloth rotting on the ground and laundry drying
around farms
I summon tornadoes and hurricanes
tempests typhoons cyclones
tidal waves
earthquakes
I summon smoke of volcanoes and cigarettes
smoke-rings of luxury cigars
I summon loves and lovers
I summon the quick and the dead

j'appelle les fossoyeurs j'appelle les assassins
j'appelle les bourreaux j'appelle les pilotes les maçons
et les architectes
les assassins
j'appelle la chair
j'appelle celle que j'aime
j'appelle celle que j'aime
j'appelle celle que j'aime
le minuit triomphant déploie ses ailes de satin et se pose
sur mon lit
les beffrois et les peupliers se plient à mon désir
ceux-là s'écroulent ceux-là s'affaissent
les perdus dans la campagne se retrouvent en me trouvant
les vieux cadavres ressuscitent à ma voix
les jeunes chênes coupés se couvrent de verdure
les lambeaux d'étoffe pourrissant dans la terre et sur la terre claquent
à ma voix comme l'étendard de la révolte le linge séchant aux
alentours des fermes habille d'adorables femmes que je n'adore
pas qui viennent à moi obéissent à ma voix et m'adorent
les tornades tournent dans ma bouche
les ouragans rougissent s'il est possible mes lèvres
les tempêtes grondent à mes pieds
les typhons s'il est possible me dépeignent
je reçois les baisers d'ivresse des cyclones
les raz de marée viennent mourir à mes pieds
les tremblements de terre ne m'ébranlent pas mais font tout
crouler à mon ordre
la fumée des volcans me vêt de ses vapeurs
et celle des cigarettes me parfume
et les ronds de fumée des cigares me couronnent
les amours et l'amour si longtemps poursuivis se réfugient en moi
les amoureux écoutent ma voix
les vivants et les morts se soumettent et me saluent les premiers
froidement les seconds familièrement

I summon grave-diggers I summon assassins
I summon executioners I summon pilots masons and
architects
assassins
I summon the flesh
I summon the one I love
I summon the one I love
I summon the one I love
midnight triumphant spreads its satin wings and sits
on my bed
belfries and poplars bend to my desire
they crumble they subside
those lost in the countryside find me and are found again
old corpses revive at my voice
young felled oaks cover themselves with greenery
rags of cloth rot in the ground and on the ground clap at
my voice like the banner of revolt laundry drying around
farms is worn by adorable women I don't adore who come
to me obey my voice and adore me
tornadoes spin in my mouth
hurricanes redden if possible my lips
tempests roar at my feet
typhoons if possible mess my hair
I receive the drunken kisses of cyclones
tidal waves come to die at my feet
earthquakes leave me unshaken but make all things tremble
at my command
volcano smoke dresses me in its vapours
and cigarette smoke makes me fragrant
and cigar smoke-rings wreathe my head
loves and love so long pursued take refuge in me
lovers listen to my voice
the quick and the dead submit and greet me the first cold the
second familiar

les fossoyeurs abandonnent les tombes à peine creusées et déclarent que moi seul puis commander leurs nocturnes travaux
les assassins me saluent
les bourreaux invoquent la révolution
invoquent ma voix
invoquent mon nom
les pilotes se guident sur mes yeux
les maçons ont le vertige en m'écoutant
les architectes partent pour le désert
les assassins me bénissent
la chair palpite à mon appel
celle que j'aime ne m'écoute pas
celle que j'aime ne m'entend pas
celle que j'aime ne me répond pas.

INFINITIF

Y mourir ô belle flammèche y mouri**R**
Voir les nuages fondre comme la neige et l'éch**O**
Origines du soleil et du blanc pauvres comme Jo**B**
Ne pas mourir encore et voir durer l'ombr**E**
Naître avec le feu et ne pas mouri**R**
Etreindre et embrasser amour fugace le ciel ma**T**

Gagner les hauteurs abandonner le bor**D**
Et qui sait découvrir ce que j'aim**E**
Omettre de transmettre mon nom aux année**S**
Rire aux heures orageuses dormir au pied d'un pi**N**
Grâce aux étoiles semblables à un numér**O**
Et mourir ce que j'aime au bord des flamme**S**.

grave-diggers abandon scarcely-dug graves and declare that
only I can command their nocturnal toil
assassins greet me
executioners invoke the revolution
invoke my voice
invoke my name
pilots steer by my eyes
masons listen to me and get vertigo
architects head off to the desert
assassins bless me
the flesh throbs at my call
the one I love doesn't heed me
the one I love doesn't hear me
the one I love doesn't answer me

INFINITIVE

[Double acrostic: Yvonne George, Robert Desnos]

You are my lovely spark. To perish o**R**
View clouds that melt away like snow and ech**O**
Origins of sun-whiteness poor as Jo**B**
Not yet to die to see the shade surviv**E**
Not die but come to birth with blazing fervou**R**
Embrace and quench dull sky love prone to fli**T**

Gaining the heights abandoning the stran**D**
Efficient to discover what I lov**E**
Omit my name's transmission to the year**S**
Rejoice at storm-times sleep where pines look dow**N**
Grateful to stars that make a domin**O**
Expiring which I love beside the flame**S**.

LE VENDREDI DU CRIME

Un incroyable désir s'empare des femmes endormies
Une pierre précieuse s'endort dans l'écrin bleu de roi
Et voilà que sur le chemin s'agitent les cailloux fatigués
Plus jamais les pas des émues par la nuit
Passez cascades
Les murailles se construisent au son du luth d'Orphée
Et s'écroulent au son des trompettes de Jéricho
Sa voix perce les murailles
Et mon regard les supprime sans ruines
Ainsi passent les cascades avec la lamentation des étoiles
Plus de cailloux sur le sentier
Plus de femmes endormies
Plus de femmes dans l'obscurité
Ainsi passez cascades.

CHANT DU CIEL

La fleur des Alpes disait au coquillage: «tu luis»
Le coquillage disait à la mer: «tu résonnes»
La mer disait au bateau: «tu trembles»
Le bateau disait au feu: «tu brilles»
Le feu me disait: «je brille moins que ses yeux»
Le bateau me disait: «je tremble moins que ton cœur quand elle paraît»
La mer me disait: «je résonne moins que son nom en ton amour»
Le coquillage me disait: «je luis moins que le phosphore du désir dans ton rêve creux»
La fleur des Alpes me disait: «elle est belle»
Je disais: «elle est belle, elle est belle, elle est émouvante».

THE FRIDAY OF THE CRIME

An incredible desire comes over sleeping women
A precious stone falls asleep in the royal blue jewel-box
And see there in the lane the tired pebbles in motion
Never again the footsteps of women thrilling to the night
Pass on, waterfalls
The walls spring up to the sound of Orpheus' lute
and collapse to the sound of Jericho's trumpets
That voice pierces the walls
and my gaze crushes them leaving no ruins
So the waterfalls pass on, with the wailing of stars
No more pebbles on the path
No more sleeping women
No more women in the dark
So pass on, waterfalls.

SKY SONG

Said the daffodil to the shell: 'you glitter'
Said the shell to the sea: 'you echo'
Said the sea to the boat: 'you shudder'
Said the boat to the fire: 'you shine'
The fire said to me: 'I shine less than her eyes'
The boat said to me: 'I shudder less than your heart in her
presence'
The sea said to me: 'I echo less than her name in your loving'
The shell said to me: 'I glitter less than the phosphorus of
desire in your hollow dream'
The daffodil said to me: 'She is beautiful'
I said: 'She is beautiful, she is beautiful, she is thrilling'.

JAMAIS D'AUTRE QUE TOI

Jamais d'autre que toi en dépit des étoiles et des solitudes
En dépit des mutilations d'arbre à la tombée de la nuit
Jamais d'autre que toi ne poursuivra son chemin qui est le mien
Plus tu t'éloignes et plus ton ombre s'agrandit
Jamais d'autre que toi ne saluera la mer à l'aube quand fatigué d'errer moi sorti des forêts ténébreuses et des buissons d'orties je marcherai vers l'écume
Jamais d'autre que toi ne posera sa main sur mon front
et mes yeux
Jamais d'autre que toi et je nie le mensonge et l'infidélité
Ce navire à l'ancre tu peux couper sa corde
Jamais d'autre que toi
L'aigle prisonnier dans une cage ronge lentement les barreaux de cuivre vert-de-grisés
Quelle évasion!
C'est le dimanche marqué par le chant des rossignols dans les bois d'un vert tendre l'ennui des petites filles en présence d'une cage où s'agite un serin, tandis que dans la rue solitaire le soleil lentement déplace sa ligne mince sur le trottoir chaud
Nous passerons d'autres lignes
Jamais jamais d'autre que toi
Et moi seul seul seul comme le lierre fané des jardins de banlieue seul comme le verre
Et toi jamais d'autre que toi.

DE LA ROSE DE MARBRE À LA ROSE DE FER

LA ROSE DE MARBRE immense et blanche était seule sur la place déserte où les ombres se prolongeaient à l'infini. Et la rose de marbre seule sous le soleil et les étoiles était reine de la solitude. Et sans parfum la rose de marbre sur sa tige rigide au

NEVER ANOTHER BUT YOU

Never another but you for all the stars and solitudes
All the trees hacked at nightfall
Never another but you shall trace her path which is mine
The more you recede the bigger your shadow
Never another but you shall greet the sea at dawn when I emerge leg-weary from the dark forests and nettle-patches and make for the foam
Never another but you shall put her hand on my brow and my eyes
Never another but you. I deny falseness and infidelity
This anchored ship you can cut its rope
Never another but you
The eagle shut in a cage slowly gnaws the copper bars green with verdigris
What an escape!
It's Sunday marked by nightingale-song in fresh green woods the boredom of little girls at a fretting canary's cage, while slowly in the lonely street the sun moves its thin line across the hot pavement
We shall pass other lines
Never never another but you
And me alone alone alone like withered ivy in suburban gardens alone as glass
And you never another but you.

FROM THE MARBLE ROSE TO THE IRON ROSE

THE MARBLE ROSE huge and white was alone on the deserted square where the shadows stretched to infinity. And the marble rose alone under the sun and stars was queen of solitude. With no scent the marble rose on her rigid stalk

sommet du piédestal de granit ruisselait de tous les flots du ciel. La lune s'arrêtait pensive en son cœur glacial et les déesses des jardins les déesses de marbre à ses pétales venaient éprouver leurs seins froids.

LA ROSE DE VERRE résonnait à tous les bruits du littoral. Il n'était pas un sanglot de vague brisée qui ne la fît vibrer. Autour de sa tige fragile et de son cœur transparent des arcs-en-ciel tournaient avec les astres. La pluie glissait en boules délicates sur ses feuilles que parfois le vent faisait gémir à l'effroi des ruisseaux et des vers luisants.

LA ROSE DE CHARBON était un phénix nègre que la poudre transformait en rose de feu. Mais sans cesse issue des corridors ténébreux de la mine où les mineurs la recueillaient avec respect pour la transporter au jour dans sa gangue d'anthracite la rose de charbon veillait aux portes du désert.

LA ROSE DE PAPIER BUVARD saignait parfois au crépuscule quand le soir à son pied venait s'agenouiller. La rose de buvard gardienne de tous les secrets et mauvaise conseillère saignait un sang plus épais que l'écume de mer et qui n'était pas le sien.

LA ROSE DE NUAGES apparaissait sur les villes maudites à l'heure des éruptions de volcans à l'heure des incendies à l'heure des émeutes et au-dessus de Paris quand la commune y mêla les veines irisées du pétrole et l'odeur de la poudre elle fut belle au 21 janvier belle au mois d'octobre dans le vent froid des steppes belle en 1905 à l'heure des miracles à l'heure de l'amour.

LA ROSE DE BOIS présidait aux gibets. Elle fleurissait au plus haut de la guillotine puis dormait dans la mousse à l'ombre immense des champignons.

on top of the granite pedestal streamed with all the waters of the sky. The moon stopped pensive in her glacial heart and the goddesses of gardens the goddesses of marble came to try their cold breasts on her petals.

THE GLASS ROSE rang with all the noises of the coast. Not a sob of a breaking wave but made her thrill. Round her frail stem and her transparent heart rainbows turned with the stars. The rain slid in delicate globules down her leaves from which the wind now and then drew a groan to frighten the streams and the fireflies.

THE COAL ROSE was a black phoenix that powder turned into a fire rose. But ever emerging from the mine's gloomy corridors where the miners picked her respectfully to convey her to daylight in her vein of anthracite, the coal rose kept watch at the desert gates.

THE BLOTTING-PAPER ROSE sometimes bled at dusk when the evening came to kneel at her feet. The blotting-paper rose a keeper of all secrets and a bad adviser bled a blood thicker than sea-spray and it was not her own.

THE CLOUD ROSE appeared over doomed cities at the hour of volcanic eruptions of conflagrations of riots and over Paris when the Commune fed into them the conduits iridescent with petrol and the smell of powder it was lovely on January 21 lovely in October in the cold wind from the steppes lovely in 1905 at the hour of miracles at the hour of love.

THE WOODEN ROSE presided over gibbets. She flourished at the top of the guillotine then slept in the moss in the vast shade of mushrooms.

LA ROSE DE FER avait été battue durant des siècles par des forgerons d'éclairs. Chacune de ses feuilles était grande comme un ciel inconnu. Au moindre choc elle rendait le bruit du tonnerre. Mais qu'elle était douce aux amoureuses désespérées la rose de fer.

La rose de marbre la rose de verre la rose de charbon la rose de papier buvard la rose de nuages la rose de bois la rose de fer refleuriront toujours mais aujourd'hui elles sont effeuillées sur ton tapis.

Qui es-tu? toi qui écrases sous tes pieds nus les débris fugitifs de la rose de marbre de la rose de verre de la rose de charbon de la rose de papier buvard de la rose de nuages de la rose de bois de la rose de fer.

THE IRON ROSE had been hammered for centuries by lightning-smiths. Each of her leaves was big as an unknown sky. At the slightest impact she emitted the noise of thunder. But how gentle she was to lovelorn women, the iron rose.

The marble rose the glass rose the coal rose the blotting-paper rose the cloud rose the wooden rose the iron rose will always flower again but today their petals lie shed on your carpet.

Who are you? you who crush under your naked feet the short-lived remains of the marble rose the glass rose the coal rose the blotting-paper rose the cloud rose the wooden rose the iron rose.

THE TIME OF CONFLICT – WITHOUT YVONNE, WITHOUT ANDRÉ BRETON

TRANSLATOR'S NOTE

The following is a summary of a note by Marie-Claire Dumas, editor of the *Complete Works of Robert Desnos* (*Œuvres*, Éditions Gallimard, 1999).

In 1929 the Surrealist movement went into a crisis of cohesion and of politics. Breton and Aragon published a dossier "concerning certain intellectuals with revolutionary tendencies." Desnos was spared, but he abandoned Breton's *La Révolution Surréaliste* and wrote instead for Bataille's magazine *Documents*, which was broad enough to accommodate his interest in popular culture – slang, cheap novels, advertisements.

He was tired of the infighting. Yvonne was a hopeless case; he was smitten with Youki Foujita. He wrote a group of poems, conventional in form, a passionate response to personal events. 'Blind' is dated 16 August, just as the Foujitas left for Japan. 'The Poem to Florence', 16 November, is for a woman friend killed in a car. Placing it at the end of *Body and Goods,* Desnos signalled a break from the surreal:

"The gates have been bolted on Wonderland."

But the break was equivocal, as the insistent theme of blindness may suggest. In 'Blind' the blind woman, her sight restored, wishes her lover blinded. In 'Flint and Fire' the poet appears as deluded ("And I was blind and thought that it was night"); yet "What night was worth the closing of our eyes?" The 'Poem to Florence' begins: "Like a blind man with border-posts to pass", recalling perhaps the blindness of fate. Love is blind: so is death. Of the poems of 1929, 'Siren-Anemone' is the most evocative, seeking to reconcile the siren [or mermaid], Youki's image, with that of Yvonne the anemone, or star-flower.

"Day breaks the siren scrambles on the rocks
Triumphant blooms the sky's anemone"

The two images are closely linked: Youki had a mermaid tattoo; Yvonne in French rhymes with anemone. These are sincere poems, whose 'old-fashioned' poetic methods are adapted to Desnos' own voice and inspiration: poems clearly outside the surrealist norms.

In December, Breton's *Second Manifesto of Surrealism* inflicted a thunderous expulsion. Desnos was banished for backsliding, practising journalism, and inexcusably failing to grasp the purposes of poetry as they now stood. Desnos' reply, offensive and sarcastic, culminated in his own *Third Manifesto of Surrealism* (1 March 1930). Breton had said "It is essential to exclude the public." Desnos flatly contradicted him: "I proclaim that Surrealism has now fallen into the public domain."

SIRÈNE-ANÉMONE

Qui donc pourrait me voir
Moi la flamme étrangère
L'anémone du soir
Fleurit sous mes fougères

Ô fougères mes mains
Hors l'armure brisée
Sur le bord des chemins
En ordre sont dressées

Et la nuit s'exagère
Au brasier de la rouille
Tandis que les fougères
Vont aux écrins de houille

L'anémone des cieux
Fleurit sur mes parterres
Fleurit encore aux yeux
À l'ombre des paupières

Anémone des nuits
Qui plonge ses racines
Dans l'eau creuse des puits
Aux ténèbres des mines

Poseraient-ils leurs pieds
Sur le chemin sonore
Où se niche l'acier
Aux ailes de phosphore

Verraient-ils les mineurs
Constellés d'anthracite
Paraître l'astre en fleur
Dans un ciel en faillite

SIREN-ANEMONE

Who'd see me? I burn
A bright foreign flame
Anemones bloom
By night in my fern

O ferns my two hands
Broke out of their case
In line each one stands
Both lining the ways

Night puts on the style
At braziers of rust
The ferns all the while
Fill up the coal-chest

Anemone of skies
She blooms in my beds
She blooms in the eyes
In the shade of their lids

Anemone of nights
She plunges her roots
In wells' hollow depths
And mines' shady clefts

Would they dare to tread
The loud road that rings
Where steel makes its bed
On phosphorus wings

Would they see, the miners
In anthracite cluster
The blossoming lustre
On bankrupted heaven

En cet astre qui luit
S'incarne la sirène
L'anémone des nuits
Fleurit sur son domaine

Alors que s'ébranlaient avec des cris d'orage
Les puissances Vertige au verger des éclairs
La sirène dardée à la proue d'un sillage
Vers la lune chanta la romance de fer

Sa nage déchirait l'hermine des marées
Et la comète errant rouge sur un ciel noir
Paraissait par mirage aux étoiles ancrées
L'anémone fleurie aux jardins des miroirs

Et parallèlement la double chevelure
Rayait de feu le ciel et d'écume les eaux
Fougères surgissez hors de la déchirure
Par où l'acier saigna sur le fil des roseaux

Nulle armure jamais ne valut votre angoisse
Fougères pourrissant parmi nos souvenirs
Mais vous charbonnerez longtemps sous nos cuirasses
Avant la flamme où se cabrant pour mieux hennir

Le cheval vieux cheval de retour et de rêve
Vers les champs clos emportera nos ossements
Avant l'onde roulant notre cœur sur la grève
Où la sirène dort sous un soleil clément

L'anémone fleurit partout sous les carènes
Déchirées aux récifs dans l'herbe des forêts
Dans le tain des miroirs sur les parquets d'ébène
Et surtout dans nos cœurs palpitant sans arrêt

In this starry shiner's
Incarnate the siren
Nocturnal anemone
Blooms in her garden

The powers lurched the storm-winds cried aloud
Dizziness on the lightning-rod The siren
Flashed at the bowsprit of a furrow ploughed
And to the moon sang the romance of iron

She swam and tore the ermine of the tides
The comet roaming red across black sky
Appeared by mirage to the anchored stars
The mirror-gardens' bloom the anemone

And parallel the double head of hair
Sky blazing waters foaming steel that bleeds
Rise up you ferns from lacerations where
The metal bled and stained the line of reeds

No armour could requite your miseries
Ferns rotting in our memories away
Under our breastplates you shall carbonise
Before the flame where rearing up to neigh

The horse old horse we dream of it once more
Takes our dry bones and sweeps them to the lists
Where the wave rolls our heart along the shore
Where in mild sun the sleeping siren rests

Under the keels bloomed the anemone
Keels ripped on reefs in forest greeneries
In tarnished mirrors floors of ebony
And in our hearts that throb and never cease

C'est le joyau serti au vif des nébuleuses
L'orgueil des voies lactées et des constellations
La prunelle qui met au regard des plus gueuses
Le diamant de fureur et de consolation

Heureuse de nager loin des hauts promontoires
Parmi les escadrons de requins fraternels
La sirène aux seins durs connaît maintes histoires
Et l'accès des trésors à l'ombre des tunnels

Mais ni l'or reluisant dans les fosses marines
Ni les clefs retrouvées des légendes du port
Ne la charment autant que d'ouvrir les narines
Aux vents salés plus lourds des parfums de la mort

C'était par un soir de printemps d'une des années perdues à l'amour
D'une des années gagnées à l'amour pour jamais
Souviens-toi de ce soir de pluie et de rosée où les étoiles devenues comètes tombaient vers la terre
La plus belle et la plus fatale la comète de destin de larmes et d'éternels égarements
S'éloignait de mon ciel en se reflétant dans la mer
Tu naquis de ce mirage
Mais tu t'éloignas avec la comète et ta chanson s'éteignit parmi les échos
Devait-elle ta chanson s'éteindre pour jamais
Est-elle morte et dois-je la chercher dans le chœur tumultueux des vagues qui se brisent
Ou bien renaîtra-t-elle du fond des échos et des embruns
Quand à jamais la comète sera perdue dans les espaces
Surgiras-tu mirage de chair et d'os hors de ton désert de ténèbres
Souviens-toi de ce paysage de minuit de basalte et de granit
Où détachée du ciel une chevelure rayonnante s'abattit sur tes épaules

She is the gem set in the living cloud
Pride of the ordered stars and galaxies
The eye revealing to the ragged crowd
The diamond of rage and solaces

Glad to swim far from cliff-tops thrusting tall
Among fraternal shoals of sharks she'll rove
Hard-breasted siren knows the tales they tell
Where shady tunnels lead to treasure-trove

Not shining gold in trenches of the sea
Not clues to quayside lore would she unearth
She'd rather flare her nostrils joyfully
At the salt winds more fraught with scent of death

It was on a spring evening in one of the years lost to love
One of the years gained to love for ever
Remember that evening of rain and dew when the stars that
turned to comets were falling earthwards
The loveliest and deadliest the comet of fate of tears and of
endlessly getting lost
Was leaving my sky and being reflected in the sea
You were born of that mirage
But you left with the comet and your song died away among
the echoes
Should your song have died away for ever
Is it dead and must I look for it in the tumultuous chorus of
breaking waves
Or will it be reborn deep in the echoes and the spindrift
When the comet will be lost for ever in empty space
Will you rise you mirage of flesh and bone from your desert
of shades
Don't forget this landscape of midnight of basalt and granite
Where detached from heaven a radiant head of hair
descended on your shoulders

Quelle rayonnante chevelure de sillage et de lumière
Ce n'est pas en vain que tremblent dans la nuit les robes de soie
Elles échouent sur les rivages venant des profondeurs
Vestiges d'amours et de naufrages où l'anémone refuse de
    s'effeuiller
De céder à la volonté des flots et des destins végétaux
À petits pas la solitaire gagne alors un refuge de haut parage
Et dit qu'il est mille regrets à l'horloge
Non ce n'est pas en vain que palpitent ces robes mouillées
Le sel s'y cristallise en fleurs de givre
Vidées des corps des amoureuses
Et des mains qui les enlaçaient
Elles s'enfuient des gouffres tubéreuses
Laissant aux mains malhabiles qui les laçaient
Les cuirasses d'acier et les corsets de satin
N'ont-elles pas senti la rayonnante chevelure d'astres
Qui par une nuit de rosée tomba en cataractes sur tes épaules
Je l'ai vue tomber
Tu te transfiguras

Reviendras-tu jamais des ténèbres
Nue et plus triomphante au retour de ton voyage
Que l'enveloppe scellée par cinq plaies de cire sanglante
Ô les mille regrets n'en finiront jamais
D'occuper cette horloge dans la clairière voisine
Tes cheveux de sargasse se perdent
Dans la plaine immense des rendez-vous manqués

Sans bruit au port désert arrivent les rameurs
Qui donc pourrait te voir toi l'amante et la mère
Incliner à minuit sur le front du dormeur
L'anémone du soir fleurie sous tes paupières

Baiser sa bouche close et baiser ses yeux clos
Incliner sur son front l'immense chevelure

What a radiant head of hair of afterglow and of light
Not for nothing do silk dresses tremble in the night
Washed ashore on the beaches coming from the depths
Traces of loves and shipwrecks where the anemone refuses
    to shed its petals
To yield to the will of the waves and the vegetable fates
Alone step by little step she reaches a refuge of high station
And tells the clock it's a thousand pities
No it's not for nothing they throb these wet dresses
Salt crystallises on them in frost-flowers
Drained from loving women's bodies
And the hands that clasped them
They flee from the tuberous gulfs
Leaving to the clumsy hands that laced them
Breastplates of steel and corsets of satin
Have they not felt the radiant hair of stars
Which on a night of dew fell cascading on your shoulders
I saw it fall
You were transfigured

Will you never return from the shades
Naked and more triumphant from your journey
Than the envelope sealed by five wounds of bleeding wax
O the thousand regrets will never cease
To occupy this clock in the nearby clearing
Your sargasso hair is lost
In the enormous rain-shower of missed assignations

Deserted harbour silently they row
Mother and loving woman who could see
You tip at midnight to the sleeper's brow
Your eyelid's bloom the night anemone

Kiss his closed lips and eyes and to his head
Incline your copious hair Siren begone

Bérénice de l'ombre ah! retourne à tes flots
Sirène avant que l'aube ouvre ses déchirures

Une steppe naîtra de l'écume atlantique
Du clair de lune et de la neige et du charbon
Où nous emportera la licorne magique
Vers l'anémone éclose au sein des tourbillons

Tempête de suie nuage en forme de cheval
Ah malheur! Sacré nom de Dieu! La nuit naufrage
La nuit? Voici sonner les grelots! Carnaval
Ferme l'œil! En vérité le bel équipage

Et dans ce ciel suitant des barriques des docks
Soudain brusquement s'interrompent les rafales
Quand la sirène avec l'aurore atteint les rocs
L'anémone du ciel est la fleur triomphale

C'est elle qui dressée au-dessus des volcans
Jette une lueur blafarde à travers la campagne
C'est l'aile du vautour le cri du pélican
C'est le plan d'évasion qui fait sortir du bagne

C'est le reflet qui tremble aux vitres des maisons
Le sang coagulé sur les draps mortuaires
C'est un voile de deuil pourri sur le gazon
C'est la robe de bal découpée dans un suaire

C'est l'anathème et c'est l'insulte et le juron
C'est le tombeau violé les morts à la voirie
La vérole promise à trois générations
Et c'est le vitriol jeté sur les soieries

C'est le bordel du christ le tonnerre de Brest
C'est le crachat le geste obscène vers la vierge

Back to your waves you Bérénice of shade
Before the opening of the wounds of dawn

From the Atlantic foam a steppe is born
Of coal and snow and moonlight We shall be
Mounted aboard the magic unicorn
Wrapped in the storms we'll find the anemone

Soot-storm and horse-shaped cloud! Despair! Dear God!
My Lord! The night is shipwrecked is the night?
Now sobs are heard! The carnival! Eyes shut!
Magnificent ship's company that quite...

And in the sky that oozes with the docks'
Hogsheads the squalls go silent suddenly
Day breaks the siren scrambles on the rocks
Triumphant blooms the sky's anemone

She rears above volcanoes towering
She throws a bleary light across the plain
Call of the pelican and vulture's wing
Plan of escape for convicts on the chain

Reflection flickering in window-glass
Bed-linen in the morgue congealed with blood
A mourning-veil that's rotted on the grass
The ball-gown cut about to make a shroud

Anathema she's insult she's the curse
She's vitriol thrown on a silk brocade
The violated tomb the open hearse
Three generations to the pox betrayed

Christ's house of shame the thunderbolts of Brest
Spit-balls cocked fists for virgins pure and good

C'est un peuple nouveau apparaissant à l'est
C'est le poignard c'est le poison ce sont les verges

C'est l'inverti qui se soumet et s'agenouille
Le masochiste qui se livre au martinet
Le scatophage hideux au masque de gargouille
Et la putain furonculeuse aux yeux punais

C'est l'étreinte écœurante avec la femme à barbe
C'est le ciel reflété par un œil de lépreux
C'est le châtré qui se dénude sous les arbres
Et l'amateur d'urine au sourire visqueux

C'est l'empire des sens anémone l'ivresse
Et le sulfure et la saveur d'un sang chéri
La légitimité de toutes les caresses
Et la mort délicieuse entre des bras flétris

Pluie d'étoiles tombez parmi les chevelures
Je veux un ciel tout nu sur un globe désert
Où des brouillards mettront une robe de bure
Aux mortes adorées pourrissant hors de terre

Adieu déjà parmi les heures de porcelaine
Regardez le jour noircit au feu qui s'allume dans l'âtre
Regardez encore s'éloigner les herbes vivantes
Et les femmes effeuillant la marguerite du silence
Adieu dans la boue noire des gares
Dans les empreintes des mains sur les murs
Chaque fois qu'une marche d'escalier s'écroule un timide
  enfant paraît à la fenêtre mansardée
Ce n'est plus dit-il le temps des parcs feuillus
J'écrase sans cesse des larves sous mes pas
Adieu dans le claquement des voiles
Adieu dans le bruit monotone des moteurs

She's a new people rising pressing west
The dagger and the poison and the rod

She is the invert kneeling to submit
The coprophiliac gargoyle-hideous
The masochist prostrated for the cat
The tart with stinking eyes and boils and pus

Rebarbative the bearded lady's squeeze
Eye of the leper clouds reflected in
The eunuch stripping off beneath the trees
The urine-fancier with viscous grin

The empire of the senses drunkenness
Sulphur blood tasted in a darling's kiss
The rightness of no matter what caress
Anemone bruised arms oblivion bliss

I want a naked sky a trackless world
Rain down you stars to fall on heads of hair
Come fogs and swathe in burlap the adored
Dead beauties rotting in the open air

Goodbye so soon among the porcelain hours
Look the day is going black at the fire catching in the hearth
Look again the living grasses are leaving
So are the women plucking petals from the daisy of silence
Goodbye in the black mud of railway stations
In the print-marks of hands on the walls
Whenever a step on the stairs gives way a shy child appears
    at the mansard window
The season of leafy parks has gone he says
I'm for ever crushing insects as I walk
Goodbye in the clap of sails
Goodbye in the monotonous sound of motors

Adieu ô papillons écrasés dans les portes
Adieu vêtements souillés par les jours à trotte-menu

Perdus à jamais dans les ombres des corridors
Nous t'appelons du fond des échos de la terre
Sinistre bienfaiteur anémone de lumière et d'or
Et que brisé en mille volutes de mercure
Éclate en braises nouvelles à jamais incandescentes
L'amour miroir qui sept ans fleurit dans ses fêlures
Et cire l'escalier de la sinistre descente

Abîme nous t'appelons du fond des échos de la terre
Maîtresse généreuse de la lumière de l'or et de la chute
Dans l'écume de la mort et celle des Finistères
Balançant le corps souple des amoureuses
Dans les courants marqués d'initiales illisibles
Maîtresse sinistre et bienfaisante de la perte éternelle
Ange d'anthracite et de bitume
Claire profondeur des rades mythologie des tempêtes
Eau purulente des fleuves eau lustrale des pluies et des rosées
Créature sanglante et végétale des marées

Du marteau sur l'enclume au couteau de l'assassin
Tout ce que tu brises est étoile et diamant
Ange d'anthracite et de bitume
Éclat du noir orfraie des vitrines
Des fumées lourdes te pavoisent quand tu poses les pieds
Sur les cristaux de neige qui recouvrent les toits
Haletants de mille journaux flambant après une nuit d'encre
   fraîche
Les grands mannequins écorchés par l'orage
Nous montrent ce chemin par où nul n'est venu

Où donc est l'oreiller pour mon front fatigué
Où donc sont les baisers où donc sont les caresses

Goodbye you butterflies crushed in the doors
Goodbye clothes dirtied by days of mucking about

For ever lost in corridors of shade
From echoes deep in earth we call your name
Anemone of light and gold sinister benign
Mercury shivered in one thousand whirls
Love a cracked mirror seven years in bloom
Shall burst out once again in white-hot coals
And wax the staircase of unhallowed doom

Abyss from echoes deep in earth we call your name
Kind mistress of the light and gold and of the fall
In foam of Finistère and deadly spume
Buoying up loving women's supple body
In currents marked with illegible initials
Sinister benign mistress of eternal loss
Angel of anthracite and bitumen
Bright sea-roads' depth mythology of storms
Purulent water of rivers lustral water of rains and dews
Swamp-creature bloody and vegetal

From hammer on anvil to assassin's knife
All that you shatter is star and diamond
Angel of anthracite and bitumen
Shock of blackness osprey of glass cases
Thick smoke wreathes you as you walk
On the snow crystals covering the roofs
That pant with a thousand newspapers aflame from a night
  of fresh ink
The great scarecrows scorched by the storm
Show us this road up which nobody came

Where is the pillow for my weary head
Where is the kiss and where is the caress

Pour consoler un cœur qui s'est trop prodigué
Où donc est mon enfant ma fleur et ma détresse

Me pardonnant si des brouillards bandent mes yeux
Si j'ai l'air d'être ailleurs si j'ai l'air d'être un autre
Me pardonnant de croire au noir au merveilleux
D'avoir des souvenirs qui ne soient pas les nôtres

Pardonnant mon passé mon cœur mes cicatrices
D'avoir parcouru seul d'émouvantes contrées
D'avoir été tenté par des voix tentatrices
Et de ne pas l'avoir plus vite rencontrée

Saurait-elle oublier mes rêves d'autrefois
Les fortunes perdues et les larmes versées
L'étoile sans merci brillant au fond des bois
Et les désirs meurtris en des nuits insensées

Et ces phrases tordues comme notre amour même
Et que je murmurais lorsque minuit blafard
Posait ses maigres doigts sur des visages blêmes
Séchant les yeux mouillés et barbouillant les fards

Dans ces temps-là le ciel était lourd de ténèbres
Le sonore minuit conduisait vers mon lit
Des visiteuses sans pitié et plus funèbre
Que la mort l'anémone évoquait la folie

Les fleurs qui s'effeuillaient sur les fruits de l'automne
Laissèrent leurs parfums aux fleurs des compotiers
Et sur le fût tronqué des anciennes colonnes
Le sel des vents marins mit des lueurs de glaciers

Et longtemps ces parfums orgueil des porcelaines
Flotteront dans la paix des salles à manger

To soothe a heart that wandered far abroad
Where is my child my flower my distress

To pardon me for visions nebulous
Seeming to be another and not there
Believing in the black the marvellous
And having memories we do not share

To pardon me my heart my past my wounds
For some affecting journeys made alone
For being tempted by alluring sounds
For meeting her when too much time was gone

Could she forget my dreams of yesteryear
The waste of fortunes and the wash of tears
Deep in the woods the ruthless shining star
Nights of insanity and slain desires

My words were twisted like our love-affair
I murmured them when bleary midnight smeared
Its bony fingers on pale faces where
It dried moist eyes and left the make-up blurred

The sky was heavy then and shadowy
And chiming midnight guided to my bed
Pitiless women The anemone
Roused madness up more dismal than the dead

Blooms moulted petals on the fruits of fall
Perfumed the buds on compote-bowls below
On broken columns immemorial
The salt sea-breezes threw a glacier-glow

The porcelain's pride these fragrances shall float
Through airy dining-rooms a place of peace

Et les cristaux de sel brilleront dans la laine
Des grands manteaux flottants que portent les bergers

Mes baisers rejoindront les larmes qui vont naître
Ils rejoindront la solitude sans pitié
Les vents marins soufflant sur les chaumes sans maîtres
Et les parfums mourants au fond des compotiers

Je suis marqué par mes amours et pour la vie
Comme un cheval sauvage échappé aux gauchos
Qui retrouvant la liberté de la prairie
Montre aux juments ses poils brûlés par le fer chaud

Tandis qu'au large avec de grands gestes virils
La sirène chantant vers un ciel de carbone
Au milieu des récifs éventreurs de barils
Au cœur des tourbillons fait surgir l'anémone.

L'AVEUGLE

Les yeux clos elle allait dans un pays de nacre
Où la vie assumait la forme d'un croissant
C'était un jour de foire et les jeux de massacre
Retentissaient du rire et des cris des passants

Dans l'eau de l'océan les mines englouties
Recélaient des échos en place de trésors
Les ouvriers lâchant le manche des outils
Incendiaient les forêts et la nouvelle aurore

Persistent too the shining crystal salt
In shepherds' airy overcoats of fleece

My kisses shall rejoin the prophesied
Tears and the solitude implacable
Sea-winds that blow on hearths unoccupied
And perfume dying in the compote-bowl

My loves have made a lasting mark on me
Like a wild horse that slips the gauchos' snares
Regains the pampas and his liberty
Shows off his branded hide to all the mares

The siren singing to a carbon sky
With sweeping virile gestures out at sea
Where reefs rip barrels open, magicks, high
Into the whirlwinds' heart, the anemone.

BLIND

Wall-eyed the land she entered was of pearl
A crescent was life's new morphology
Games of mass killing at a festival
Rang with the merry cries of passers-by

In subterranean mines the ocean pools
Held echoes but no treasure stashed away
While all the workers laid aside their tools
Burnt down the forest and the dawning day

Répandue à grands flots se brisait aux murailles
La terre tressaillait à l'appel des volcans
Les sorciers découvraient dans le corps des volailles
Le mirage du ciel et d'impurs talismans

Chaque nuit éclairée par les aérolithes
Se déchirait sinistre avec un bruit d'accroc
Et les loups en hurlant surgissaient de leurs gîtes
Pour sceller les cailloux des marques de leurs crocs

Sans souci j'ai suivi le chemin de l'aveugle
Ses pieds trébuchaient sur les dalles des perrons
Mais ses doigts déchiffraient les mufles et les gueules
Des fauves effrayés par le bruit des clairons

Sa bouche ne savait ni chanson ni prière
Ses seins qu'avaient mordus d'anonymes amants
Saillaient sous le corsage et sous ses deux paupières
Deux miroirs reflétaient son attendrissement

Il fleurissait dans l'ombre en roses phosphoriques
Dans un parc de granit de flamme et de métal
Où jamais le refrain grotesque des cantiques
Ne troubla le silence immobile et fatal

Je n'oublierai jamais le docteur imbécile
Qui l'ayant délivré des nuits de cécité
Mourut en attendant avec un cœur tranquille
Qu'un archange joufflu vînt l'en féliciter

Mais avant d'évoquer au fond de ses prunelles
Un paysage absurde avec ses monuments
Le fer heurtant le fer en crachats d'étincelles
Et les menteurs levant la main pour les serments

Spilled in great waves and smashed against the walls
The earth was shaking at volcanoes' cries
Magicians found in slaughtered birds' entrails
Disgusting talismans deceitful skies

Night after night lit up by meteors
Burst open with an eerie rending squeal
And howling wolves came surging from their lairs
Scrunched pebbles with their tooth-marks for a seal

Unfazed I tailed the blind one on her course
On flights of flagstone steps her footsteps swerved
Her fingers traced the muzzles and the jaws
Of savage beasts that bugle-calls unnerved

Her lips knew neither songs nor litanies
Blemished by nameless lovers' bites her breasts
Swelled in her bodice while about her eyes
Two mirrors signalled back her tenderness

Phosphorus roses were its blooms in shade
The park was formed of granite metal flame
Where hymns in uncouth chorus never made
A dent in the unmoving deathly calm

I won't forget that doctor what a fool
Who freed her from the dark and sightless place
Died happy waiting for a you've-done-well
From an archangel with a chubby face

Before she summoned up inside her eyes
The spitting sparks the crash of blade on blade
Memorials a land's absurdities
An upraised hand by perjured oath betrayed

Soyez bénis dit-elle au granit de son rêve
Soyez bénis dit-elle aux reflets des cristaux
Le voyage à bon port en cet instant s'achève
Au pied du sémaphore à l'ombre des signaux

Mais aujourd'hui n'est pas mon jour de délivrance
Ce n'est pas moi qu'on rend aux soirs et aux matins
Le rêve prisonnier de mon esprit s'élance
Comme un beau patineur chaussé de ses patins

La terre connaîtra mes cités ténébreuses
Mes spectres minéraux mon cœur sans dimension
Les lilas effeuillés la mort des tubéreuses
La danse que Don Juan et moi-même dansions

Que tous ferment les yeux au temps où mes yeux s'ouvrent
S'il n'est pas tout à moi que me fait l'univers
Avec ses Westminsters ses Kremlins et ses Louvres
Que m'importe l'amour si mon amant voit clair

Et ce soir célébrant notre mariage atroce
Je plongerai l'acier dans ses yeux adorés
Que mon premier baiser soit un baiser féroce
Et puis je guiderai ses pas mal assurés

Je finirai ma vie en veillant sur sa vie
Je le protégerai des maux et des dangers
Je couvrirai son corps contre l'intempérie
Et je prendrai la lettre aux mains du messager

Je lirai l'heure ardente au cadran de l'horloge
J'aurai pour lui des soins hideux et maternels
Je serai l'infirmière à qui vont les éloges
La maîtresse impérieuse aux ordres sans appel

Bless you she murmured to her granite dream
Bless you she murmured now I sail no more
I'm safe in port she told the crystal gleam
Under the signals and the semaphore

But I'm not free I'm not set free today
Restored to dark and light to dusk and dawn
My spirit's captive dream cavorts away
Like a fine skater with her ice-skates on

The earth shall know my towns fuliginous
Mineral ghosts my heart's infinity
The moulted lilacs withered tuberose
The dance we always danced Don Juan and I

All eyes but mine must shut what good is all
The universe unless it's all for me
What good are Louvre Kremlin and Whitehall
What good's my loving if my love can see

Tonight to mark our worthless married bliss
I'll plunge the steel in his beloved eyes
Then my first kiss shall be a savage kiss
And I shall guide his feet's uncertainties

I'll end my life in watching over his
Protect him from all danger and mischance
I'll shield him from the weather's vagaries
Collect the letter from the postman's hands

I'll care for him in vile maternal ways
Let the clock tell the time for us to feel
I'll be the nurse who's given all the praise
Imperious mistress brooking no appeal

Le soir qu'éclaboussaient les étoiles filantes
Se déplia comme un serpent sur les pays
Chaque fleur à son tour a fleuri sur les plantes
Et puis voici la mort qui n'a jamais failli

Lits éventrés nuit éternelle éclair des crimes
Incendie allumé dans la maison des fous
Voici venir l'amour du fin fond des abîmes
Voici venir l'amour lampes éteignez-vous!

MOUCHOIRS AU NADIR

Comme l'espace entre eux devenait plus opaque
Le signe des mouchoirs disparut pour jamais
Eux c'était une amante aux carillons de Pâques
Qui revenait de Rome et que l'onde animait

Eux c'était un amant qui partait vers la nuit
Érigée sur la route au seuil des capitales
Eux c'était la rivière et le miroir qui fuit
La porte du sépulcre et le cœur du crotale

Combien d'oiseaux combien d'échos combien de flammes
Se sont unis au fond des lits de cauchemars
Combien de matelots ont-ils brisé leurs rames
En les trempant dans l'eau hantée par les calmars

Combien d'appels perdus à travers les déserts
Avant de se briser aux portes de la ville
Combien de prêtres morts pendus à leurs rosaires
Combien de trahisons dans les guerres civiles

The dusk was spattered splashed by shooting-stars
On plants each bloom in turn burst into bloom
Dusk snaked its coils across these lands of ours
Hullo here's death inevitable doom

Slit guts of beds and everlasting night
The flash of crimes the madhouse set on fire
Love enters in from the deep infinite
Love enters in. Burn out, you lamps, expire!

HANDKERCHIEFS AT THE NADIR

The space between them getting more opaque
The waving hanky sign was gone for good
They were a sweetheart Easter bells brought back
From Rome, excited by the tidal flood

They were a lover heading for the night
Raised on the road where mighty cities start
They were the mirror and the stream in flight
From cemetery gate and rattler's heart

In depth of nightmare beds how many birds
How many echoes and how many fires
How many sailors dipped and broke their oars
Deep in the watery haunts of calamars

How many deserts lost how many cries
Before they shattered on the city doors
How many priests hanged by their rosaries
How many treasons in the civil wars

Le signe des mouchoirs qui se perd dans les nuages
Aux ailes des oiseaux fait ressembler le lin
Les filles à minuit contemplent son image
Vol de mouette apparue dans le miroir sans tain

Les avirons ne heurtent plus les flots du port
Les cloches vendredi ne partent plus pour Rome
Tout s'est tu puisqu'un soir l'au revoir et la mort
Ont échangé le sel et le vin et la pomme

Les astres sont éteints au zénith qui les porte
Ô Zénith ô Nadir ô ciel tous les chemins
Conduisent à l'amour marqué sur chaque porte
Conduisent à la mort marquée dans chaque main

Ô Nadir je connais tes parcs et ton palais
Je connais ton parfum tes fleurs tes créatures
Tes sentiers de vertige où passent les mulets
Du ciel les nuages blancs du soir à l'aventure

Ô Nadir dans ton lit de torrent et cascades
Le négatif de celle aimée la seule au ciel
Se baigne et des troupeaux lumineux de dorades
Paissent l'azur sous les arceaux de l'arc-en-ciel

Ni vierge ni déesse et posant ses deux pieds
Sur le croissant de lune et l'anneau des planètes
Dans le ronronnement de tes rouages d'acier
Hors du champ tumultueux fouillé par les lunettes

Vieux Nadir ô pavé au col pur des amantes
Est-ce dans ta volière au parc des étincelles
Qu'aboutissent les vols de mouchoirs et la menthe
L'herbe d'oubli dans tes gazons resplendit-elle?

The hanky sign is lost behind the clouds
Linen like birds' wings vanishing from sight
Observed by studious girls through wakeful hours
In the untarnished glass a seagull's flight

The oars no longer lap along the staithe
And Rome no longer gets her Friday bell
It's all gone silent since the night that Death
Swapped wine and salt and apples with Farewell

The stars that ride the Zenith shine no more
O Zenith Nadir sky the paths all tend
Towards the love that's marked on every door
Towards the death that's marked on every hand

Nadir I know your parks your palace too
I know your flowers your creatures and your musk
Your paths of vertigo and derring-do
For mules in heaven for white clouds at dusk

O Nadir in your leaping torrents' bed
The negative of her the sky's one love
Bathes where the shining shoals of bream have fed
On azure blue beneath the rainbows' curve

No virgin and no goddess feet set wide
On crescent moon and planetary disc
Within your steel cogs' purring and outside
The field of strife that lunar lenses frisk

Old Nadir, paving on pure neck of love,
Is it your birdcage on the lawns of sparks
That lures the fluttering hankies while the herb
Mint of forgetfulness gleams in your grass?

Éraillé béant abritant peste et démence
Il arrive il pénètre au port le paquebot
Hors de son flanc comme l'intestin d'une panse
La cargaison étonnement des cachalots
Est partie à la dérive au sommet du mât
Flotte un pavillon noir Écartez-vous voilures
Tout l'équipage mort moisit dans les hamacs
Proie de l'épidémie aux yeux de pourriture
Sur l'épaule inclinant le manche de sa faux
Tout à l'heure à midi des bureaux sanitaires
L'épouvante danseuse étique aux bijoux faux
Paraîtra saluée par les cris des fonctionnaires
Déjà le feu pétille il est trop tard trop tard
Le ciel contemple les gestes des sémaphores
Cependant que le flot ronge le coaltar
Au flanc des bâtiments Qu'apparaisse l'aurore
où les ancres levées aux sanglots des sirènes
Tous ces bateaux prendront la mer en liberté
Qu'ils soient croiseurs chaluts ou trafiquants d'ébène
ou frégate fantôme aux ordres d'Astarté
Mais je crains qu'à leurs proues les moules par milliers
Ne se fixent avant leur départ vers les rades
où l'anneau les attend aux pierres des piliers
où l'on boit le tafia avec les camarades
Que m'importe après tout le sort des matelots
Qu'ils crèvent que le port durant dix quarantaines
Soit affamé tant pis pour le méli-mélo
Tant pis pour les marins et pour les capitaines
Mais au gré des courants flotte la cargaison
La vague la balance et le cap la repousse
La glace et le soleil au gré de la saison
Font péter les caissons où s'accroche la mousse
Où flottent maintenant le poivre et la cannelle
Le café la confiture et les bois précieux
Où sont les essences de fleurs et les flanelles
Les barriques de vin la soie brodée de dieux

Tattered and holed plague-ridden and half-crazed
The ship arrives in harbour On the beam
Like guts hung from a belly it displays
Its cargo an astonishment of sperm
Whales At the masthead a black pennant floats
Out of the way give way you sailing-boats
The crew's all dead and putrid in their berths
Prey to a rot-faced plague that packs its scythe
Just now at noon from some bureau of health
The wondrous phthisic dancer with fake jewels
Will sally forth to office-wallahs' cheers
The fire is crackling it's too late too late
The sky looks on as arms make semaphores
Meanwhile the waves are gnawing at the tar
On flanks of buildings Let the dawn appear
Anchors be weighed as mermaids shed a tear
These ships shall ride the waves at liberty
Cruisers or trawlers traders in ivory
Or phantom frigates of Astarte's fleet
A million whelks might batten on their hulls
Before they sail to roads where bollards wait
Mooring-quoits shipmates quaffing tafia rum
What do I care about the sailors' fate
The captains too I say to hell with them
And may the port starve through ten quarantines
The cargo's drifting at the currents' whim
Bounced by the headlands balanced by the waves
The ice and sun according to the seasons
Extract a farting noise from mossy caissons
Where's all the pepper floating the preserves
Coffee and cinnamon wood chiselled fine
The flower-essences and flannel stuffs
Celestial brocades and casks of wine

Quels poissons ont mangé les viandes et le pain
Et les médicaments et les clous de girofle
La saumure a rempli la gourde des copains
Des épaves se sont échouées au bord des golfes
Mais là n'est pas la mer avec tous ses cadavres
Avec ses tourbillons ses huiles et ses laines
Ses continents déserts ses récifs et ses havres
Ses poissons ses oiseaux ses vents et ses baleines
Non ce n'est pas la mer ni l'eau ni le ressac
Ni l'horizon que brise une explosion d'étoiles
Ni même un naufrageur qui repêche des sacs
ni la reprise mystérieuse sur la voile

La mer ce n'est pas même un miroir sans visage
Un terme de comparaison pour les rêveurs
Un sujet de pensées pour l'engeance des sages
Pas même un lavoir propre à noyer les laveurs

Ce n'est pas un grimoire où dorment des secrets
Une mine à trésor une femme amoureuse
Une tombe où cacher la haine et les regrets
Une coupe où vider l'Amazone et la Meuse

Non la mer c'est la nuit qui dort pendant le jour
C'est un écrin pillé c'est une horloge brève
Non pas même cela ni la mort ni l'amour
La mer n'existe pas car la mer n'est qu'un rêve

Et moi qui l'appelais à l'assaut de la digue
je reste au pied des rocs jonchés de goémon
Tandis que le soleil ouvert comme une figue
saigne sur les tourteaux errant dans le limon

Jamais plus la tempête en sapant les falaises
N'abîmera la ville d'Ys les icebergs

What fish have eaten up the meat and bread
Washed down the medicines and sacks of cloves
The brine is in the shipmates' drinking-gourd
The wrecks have run aground along the coves
But that is not the sea with its cadavers
With all its oils and wools and whirling squalls
Its continents and deserts reefs and harbours
Its fishes and its birds its winds and whales
It's not the sea the water nor the surf
Nor the horizon bombed by stars that burned
Nor yet the wrecker fishing up the stuff
Nor canvas-breadths mysteriously darned

The sea's less than a glass without a face
A dreamer's object of comparison
Theme to be pondered where the sages pace
Less than a wash-house where the washers drown

Not a black book where sleeping secrets lie
A lady-love a miners' treasure-hole
A tomb to hide regrets and enmity
The Amazon's and Meuse's draining-bowl

No it's the night that sleeps throughout the day
A little clock a plundered jewel-chest
Not even that not death not love the sea
Is just a dream the sea does not exist

And I who called on it to storm the wall
Here on the seaweed-spattered rocks I stand
Splayed like a fig the sun is dribbling all
Its blood on turtles lost in soggy sand

No more by sapping undercliffs the storm
Shall damage Lyonesse and harm its walls

Ne dériveront plus à moins qu'il ne me plaise
De recréer les flots les voiles et les vergues

Déjà sentant la mort et la teinture d'iode
Dans la putréfaction qui comblera les mares
Une flore nouvelle apparaît comme une ode
Vers le ciel impalpable où s'éteignent les phares

De Marenne à Cancale
y a un long chemin
L'ai fait à fond de cale
Sur un lit de jasmin

De Marenne à Cancale
y a de bons marins
Des solides des mâles
Et cinq doigts à leurs mains

De Marenne à Cancale
y a du sable fin
y a du vent qui hâle
La gueule des gamins

De Marenne à Cancale
y a morts et vivants
Des moribonds qui râlent
Du soleil et du vent

De Marenne à Cancale
On boit beaucoup de vin
Qui donc qui nous régale
Tout le long du chemin

De Marenne à Cancale
Vogue un fameux lapin

No iceberg drift unless it be my whim
To recreate the waves the stays the sails

Odours of death and iodine arise
From crammed and rotting swamps a novel flower
Spreads like an ode towards unreal skies
And the great lights are quenched in every tower

From Marennes to Cancale
A long voyage I made
Deep down in the hold
On a jessamine bed

From Marennes to Cancale
They are good the deckhands
They are solid and male
With five-fingered hands

From Marennes to Cancale
There is fine powder-sand
Urchins' faces are all
Toasted brown by the wind

From Marennes to Cancale
They may croak moribund
They may live they may fall
In the sun and the wind

From Marennes to Cancale
We have wine to knock back
But who pays for it all
Down the length of the track

From Marennes to Cancale
A big thumper's at large

Un fier luron sans gale
Qui saoula les marins

Où donc est ma négresse
Dit le premier marin
On fit avec sa graisse
Quatre grands cierges fins

Découpée charcutée
On l'a mise en un four
Les moines l'ont mangée
Pendant quarante jours

Où donc est ma gonzesse
Dit le second marin
L'est encore à la messe
à prier tous les saints

Je lui ferai connaître
Mon saint Jean mon saint Louis
Car suis-je ou non le maître
Dans ce sacré bouis-bouis

Où donc le gui Madame
Dit le dernier marin
qui n'avait pas de femme
Et pas de bague aux mains

Le gui le gui silence
vous reviendrez un jour
à l'heure de la danse
Chanter au gui l'amour

Jolly fellow no gall
Fuddles all the jack-tars

Where's my lady of jet
Number One sailor said
They made out of her fat
Four big candles instead

She was cut into chunks
In the oven to roast
She was eaten by monks
In a forty-day feast

Where is my pretty lass
Said the second deck-hand
She is still at the mass
Prays to saint after saint

I shall run johnny past her
And louis I will
Well aren't I the master
In this blamed vaudeville

Where's the mistletoe Ma'am
Said the mizen deckhand
Had no mate on his arm
Had no ring on his hand

The mistletoe silence
Back here you shall rove
At the hour of the dance
Sing your mistletoe love

J'étais aveugle et je croyais qu'il faisait nuit
Est-ce bien toi que je nommais la ténébreuse
Ô nuit sonore et lumineuse quand s'enfuit
L'aigle du cauchemar aimé des nébuleuses

Byron voyageant en Espagne
Habita longtemps à Tolède
Il y rêvait dans la campagne
aux plus belles et aux plus laides
Il y fut aimé d'une folle
Il fut aimé d'une espagnole

Il fut aimé d'une espagnole
La plus belle de la cité
Mais près du lord la tendre folle
Sentait son cœur la tourmenter
Elle mourut d'amour la belle
Comme on fermait la citadelle

Comme on fermait la citadelle
On l'emporta dans son linceul
Et le lord en rêvant aux belles
Derrière elle marchait tout seul
Le long des rues le peuple en foule
Regardait passer la dépouille

Regardaient passer la dépouille
Les lanceurs de malédictions
Et les bigots au cœur de rouille
Et les traîtres à leurs passions
Mais le lord alors sans mot dire
Marcha vers l'insulte et les rires

Marcha vers l'insulte et les rires
Le lord aux yeux lourds d'océans

And I was blind and thought that it was night
Are you the one I surnamed the obscure
Loud shining night-time of the eagle's flight
From nightmare of the blurry nights' allure

Byron passed the Pyrenees
Reached Toledo tarried there
Dreamed amid the olive-trees
Of the fair and not so fair
He was loved by one insane
Lady with no brain in Spain

Lady with no brain in Spain
Quite the fairest in the place
Near milord the lass insane
Felt her heart in turmoil race
Then the beauty died of love
Like a citadel sealed off

Like a citadel sealed off
She was carried in her shroud
There alone but dreaming of
Other beauties walked milord
All the crowds along the way
Watched the last remains go by

Watched the last remains go by
Men were hurling imprecations
Rusty souls spat bigotry
Some were traitors to their passions
Through the jeers without a word
Through the insults came milord

Through the insults came milord
Eyes of heavy ocean swell

Devant lui reculaient les sbires
Les toréros les paysans
Il arriva devant les femmes
Les Pepitas aux lourdes mammes

Les Pepitas aux lourdes mammes
Les gitanes aux noirs cheveux
Les chanteuses les grandes dames
Devant lui baissèrent les yeux
Parvint devant les demoiselles
Bravo Toro! dit la plus belle

Bravo Toro! dit la plus belle
Voici mon cœur voici mon corps
Et voici mon amour fidèle
Mes baisers et mes boucles d'or
Byron fut aimé par deux folles
Fut aimé par deux espagnoles

Est-ce bien toi que je nommais la ténébreuse
avec tes grands flambeaux brûlant au pied des monts
Avec tes rues et tes parvis et fabuleuse
La dame de minuit l'amoureuse sans nom

Son corps qu'eût dessiné en reliant des étoiles
Sur la carte du ciel dans les constellations
Un astronome de jadis son corps sans voile
Est de ceux pour lesquels s'affrontaient les nations

Dans les vergers du ciel faisant sa promenade
Aux arbres sidéraux elle cueille les fruits
Tandis que les soleils dressés en colonnades
Sous leurs piliers de feu la voient marcher sans bruit

Constables and matadors
Country bumpkins back they fell
Till he reached the señoritas
Massively endowed Pepitas

Massively endowed Pepitas
Duchesses and ditty-tweeters
Raven-headed Romany
Lasses all with modest eye
When he reached them up ahead
Bravo Toro! the fairest said

Bravo Toro! the fairest said
Here's my body and my soul
Here's my love unlimited
Hugs and kisses twists of gold
He was loved by two insane
Ladies with no brain in Spain

Are you the one I surnamed the obscure
With your great flares at mountains' foot aflame
Your streets and precincts and that cynosure
The midnight lady-love without a name

Her body sketched perhaps across the skies
By some astronomer who joined the stars
Joined dot to dot on charts of galaxies
Her body goaded nations into wars

In orchards of the sky she promenades
Unheard and plucks the fruit of starry trees
Watched by the suns that rear on colonnades
Beneath their fiery pillars she proceeds

Et le ciel à son tour relégué dans les fables
Retrouve l'océan que je nie à jamais
Les lunes en cristal s'échoueront sur le sable
Où gît l'épave avec ses morts et ses agrès

La peste les marins les étoiles les flots
Les récifs et le bateau fantôme et la peste
La voie lactée et les yeux miteux des hublots
S'enliseront avec les statues au beau geste

Quelle nuit en effet valut nos yeux fermés
Quand visitant les jardins d'or de nos prunelles
Nous écoutions monter l'océan alarmé
Le flux de notre sang battant pour les cruelles.

LE POÈME À FLORENCE

Comme un aveugle s'en allant vers les frontières
Dans les bruits de la ville assaillie par le soir
Appuie obstinément aux vitres des portières
Ses yeux qui ne voient pas vers l'aile des mouchoirs

Comme ce rail brillant dans l'ombre sous les arbres
Comme un reflet d'éclair dans les yeux des amants
Comme un couteau brisé sur un sexe de marbre
Comme un législateur parlant à des déments

Une flamme a jailli pour perpétuer Florence
Non pas celle qui haute au détour d'un chemin
Porta jusqu'à la lune un appel de souffrance
Mais celle qui flambait au bûcher quand les mains

The sky in turn reduced to sailors' lore
Rejoins the sea there's none it shall be said
The crystal moons are stranded on the shore
Where lie the wreck the rigging and the dead

Plague sailors stars and waves and reefs and boat
The phantom boat the plague the milky way
The portholes' shabby eyes shall meet their fate
In quicksands with the statues' fine display

What night was worth the closing of our eyes
We roamed their golden gardens and we heard
The frightened ocean yes our lifeblood rise
Hammering for the cruel ones we loved.

THE POEM TO FLORENCE

Like a blind man with border-posts to pass
And noises of a town that dusk aggrieves
Stubbornly pressing to the carriage glass
His sightless eyes towards winged handkerchieves

Like the rail glinting in the shade of trees
Lightning that lovers' eyes reflect again
Knife trashed on marble sex of effigies
A statesman who addresses the insane

A flame flared up that Florence may live on
Not that which high above the journey's bends
Carried a cry of anguish to the moon
But that which flamed on funeral-pyres when hands

dressées comme cinq branches d'une étoile opaque
attestaient que demain surgirait d'aujourd'hui
Mais celle qui flambait au chemin de saint Jacques
Quand la déesse nue vers le nadir a fui

Mais celle qui flambait aux parois de ma gorge
Quand fugitive et pure image de l'amour
Tu surgis tu partis et que le feu des forges
Rougeoyait les sapins les palais et les tours

J'inscris ici ton nom hors des deuils anonymes
Où tant d'amantes ont sombré corps âme et biens
Pour perpétuer un soir où dépouilles ultimes
Nous jetions tels des os nos souvenirs aux chiens

Tu fonds tu disparais tu sombres mais je dresse
au bord de ce rivage où ne brille aucun feu
Nul phare blanchissant les bateaux en détresse
Nulle lanterne de rivage au front des bœufs

Mais je dresse aujourd'hui ton visage et ton rire
Tes yeux bouleversants ta gorge et tes parfums
Dans un olympe arbitraire où l'ombre se mire
dans un miroir brisé sous les pas des défunts

Afin que si le tour des autres amoureuses
Venait avant le mien de s'abîmer tu sois
Et l'accueillante et l'illusoire et l'égareuse
la sœur de mes chagrins et la flamme à mes doigts

Car la route se brise au bord des précipices
je sens venir les temps où mourront les amis
Et les amantes d'autrefois et d'aujourd'hui
Voici venir les jours de crêpe et d'artifice

Like a dark star's five branches were upraised
Tomorrow rises from today they said
But that which flamed along the milky road
When the nude goddess to the nadir fled

But that which flamed on walls about my gorge
When you love's image fugitive and pure
Rose up and left us and the glowing forge
Cast a red light on palace tower and fir

I carve your name and shun that nameless dirge
For sea-drowned lovers body soul and goods
I mark that night we sloughed our full discharge
And threw our memories like bones to dogs

You melt you sink you vanish but I raise
Beside this haven where no signal glows
No lighthouse blanching vessels in distress
No harbour-lanterns hung on heads of cows

I raise today your laughter and your face
Your stunning eyes your throat your wafting scents
Shade in a mirror smashed by ghosts who pace
On some Olympus of inconsequence

So if the turn of other sweethearts came
Before my own to perish, you shall play
My sorrows' sister and my fingers' flame
Shall welcome and deceive and lead astray

For the road's breaking up on the precipice-rim
The time is at hand when my friends have to die
My loves of the past and my loves of this time
The days of black crepe and contrivance are nigh

Voici venir les jours où les œuvres sont vaines
où nul bientôt ne comprendra ces mots écrits
Mais je bois goulûment les larmes de nos peines
quitte à briser mon verre à l'écho de tes cris

Je bois joyeusement faisant claquer ma langue
le vin tonique et mâle et j'invite au festin
Tous ceux-là que j'aimai. Ayant brisé leur cangue
qu'ils viennent partager mon rêve et mon butin

Buvons joyeusement! chantons jusqu'à l'ivresse!
nos mains ensanglantées aux tessons des bouteilles
Demain ne pourront plus étreindre nos maîtresses.
Les verrous sont poussés au pays des merveilles.

THE NIGHT OF LOVELESS NIGHTS

Nuit putride et glaciale, épouvantable nuit,
Nuit du fantôme infirme et des plantes pourries,
Incandescente nuit, flamme et feu dans les puits,
Ténèbres sans éclairs, mensonges et roueries.

Qui me regarde ainsi au fracas des rivières?
Noyés, pêcheurs, marins? Éclatez les tumeurs
Malignes sur la peau des ombres passagères,
Ces yeux m'ont déjà vu, retentissez clameurs!

Le soleil ce jour-là couchait dans la cité
L'ombre des marronniers au pied des édifices,
Les étendards claquaient sur les tours et l'été
Amoncelait ses fruits pour d'annuels sacrifices.

The time is at hand when these works are in vain
When none can make sense of these readable runes
But I greedily swallow the tears of our pain
Short of breaking my glass on your echoing groans

I am drinking with joy and a smack of the tongue
A manly strong wine I invite to the party
All those whom I loved having broken their kang
Let them come and partake of my dream and my booty

Let's drink up with joy, draining songs to the lees!
The sharp broken bottles have bloodied our hand
So tomorrow we can't give our darlings a squeeze
The gates have been bolted on wonderland.

kang – pillory

THE NIGHT OF LOVELESS NIGHTS

Night of glaciation horrendous night putrescent
Night of febrile phantom rotting greenery
Night of white-hot well-shafts blazing incandescent
Dark without the lightning, lies and trickery

Who gazes on me in the rivers' loud cascades?
Corpses, sailors, fishermen? Burst yourselves, you tumours
Malignant on the skin of transitory shades;
Those eyes have watched me – shout aloud, you clamours! –

They saw me in the city, that day, by setting sun:
Chestnut-trees threw shadows where great edifices rise,
Flags clack-clacked on towers, and summer nearly done
Piled up its harvest-fruits for annual sacrifice.

Tu viens de loin, c'est entendu, vomisseur de couleuvres,
Héros, bien sûr, assassin môme, l'amoureux
Sans douleur disparaît, et toi, fils de tes œuvres,
Suicide, rougis-tu du désir d'être heureux?

Fantôme, c'est ma glace où la nuit se prolonge
Parmi les cercueils froids et les cœurs dégouttants,
Amour cuit et recuit comme une fausse oronge
Et l'ombre d'une amante aux mains d'un impotent.

Et pourtant tu n'es pas de ceux que je dédaigne.
Ah! serrons-nous les mains, mon frère, embrassons-nous
Parmi les billets doux, les rubans et les peignes,
La prière jamais n'a sali tes genoux.

Tu cherchais sur la plage au pied des rochers droits
La crique où vont s'échouer les étoiles marines:
C'était le soir, des feux à travers le ciel froid
Naviguaient et, rêvant au milieu des salines,

Tu voyais circuler des frégates sans nom
Dans l'éclaboussement des chutes impossibles.
Où sont ces soirs? Ô flots rechargez vos canons
Car le ciel en rumeur est encombré de cibles.

Quel destin t'enchaîna pour servir les sévères,
Celles dont les cheveux charment les colibris,
Celles dont les seins durs sont un fatal abri
Et celles dont la nuque est un nid de mystère,

Celles rencontrées nues dans les nuits de naufrage,
Celles des incendies et celles des déserts,
Celles qui sont flétries par l'amour avant l'âge,
Celles qui pour mentir gardent les yeux sincères,

You who vomit serpents, you've come a weary way,
A cold-blooded killer but of course a hero too.
The lover goes out painlessly. You self-made fellow, say,
Self-slayer, do you blush, that bliss entices you?

Ghost, my mirror's glassy-cold, where hearts are dripping blood!
Night drags out its darkness by the frigid cerement:
Love re-cooked, warmed over, like a dubious orange-hood,
And a loving lady with a man who's impotent.

Yet I do not reckon you as one whom I despise.
We shall hug in warm embrace, a handshake too we'll share,
Among love-letters, ribbons, and combs, and fripperies:
Those knees of yours have never been besmirched by prayer.

On the beach you searched below the rampant sea-cliffs there,
Traced the creek where ocean stars go plummeting to ground.
Night had fallen: points of fire careered through frozen air.
Dreamer in the salt-pans, you saw them circle round,

While the sky re-echoed, saw the frigate-birds in flight,
Swooping to their splashdown, unbelievably:
Nameless and tumultuous. Where's that night tonight?
Waves, reload your cannon! Targets crowd the sky.

You were chained in servitude to female martinets,
Women whose bewitching hair can charm the colibri,
Women stony-breasted, a fateful hiding-place,
Women of the downy necks, nests of mystery,

Women swimming naked from a midnight shipwrecked hull,
Women of the firestorm, women of the wild,
Women aged before their time by loves unseasonal,
Women who are liars, though their eyes are undefiled.

Celles au cœur profond, celles aux belles jambes,
Celles dont le sourire est subtil et méchant,
Celles dont la tendresse est un diamant qui flambe
Et celles dont les reins balancent en marchant,

Celles dont la culotte étroite étreint les cuisses,
Celles qui, sous la jupe, ont un pantalon blanc
Laissant un peu de chair libre par artifice
Entre la jarretière et le flot des volants,

Celles que tu suivis dans l'espoir ou le doute,
Celles que tu suivis ne se retournaient pas
Et les bouquets fanés qu'elles jetaient en route
T'entraînèrent longtemps au hasard de leurs pas

Mais tu les poursuivras à la mort sans répit,
Les yeux las de percer des ténèbres moroses,
De voir lever le jour sur le ciel de leur lit
Et d'abriter leur ombre en tes prunelles closes.

Une rose à la bouche et les yeux caressants
Elles s'acharneront avec des mains cruelles
À torturer ton cœur, à répandre ton sang
Comme pour les punir d'avoir battu pour elles.

Heureux s'il suffisait, pour se faire aimer d'elles,
D'affronter sans faiblir des dangers merveilleux
Et de toujours garder l'âme et le cœur fidèle
Pour lire la tendresse aux éclairs de leurs yeux,

Mais les plus audacieux, sinon les plus sincères,
Volent à pleine bouche à leur bouche un aveu
Et devant nos pensées, comme aux proues les chimères,
Resplendit leur sourire et flottent leurs cheveux.

Women ample-hearted, or poised on shapely limbs,
Women of nefarious and subtly smiling lips,
Women of sweet nature whose diamond never dims,
Women promenading with undulating hips,

Women with tight trousers clinging to their thighs,
Women with white panties underneath a skirt
Leaving free a little flesh, purposeful surprise,
In between the garter and the frills that float and flirt,

Women that you followed, in hope, or diffident,
Women that you followed, not a glance was offered back:
While the wilting posies they threw you as they went
Led you on for ages, to follow in their track.

You will follow doggedly till you or they are dead,
Bleary-eyed from staring into harsh obscurities,
Seeing how the dawn lights the heaven of their bed,
Sheltering their shadow in the closing of your eyes.

Roses between their teeth, doe-eyes of caresses,
With cruel hands they shall attack without remorse,
Torture your core, get your blood in bloody messes,
Seemingly to punish you for fighting in their cause.

Happy could it only be enough, to win their love,
Not to weaken faced with peril's mysteries,
Keeping heart and soul with fortitude to prove,
To discern the love-light in their flashing eyes,

But the most audacious, never the sincerest,
Plunder, gobble-mouthed, mouthing pledges to the air:
Their smiles entice our thoughts, as prows pursue chimeras,
Those bright resplendent smiles, that bobbing hair.

Car l'unique régit l'amour et ses douleurs,
Lui seul a possédé les âmes passionnées
Les uns s'étant soumis à sa loi par malheur
N'ont connu qu'un bourreau pendant maintes années.

D'autres l'ont poursuivi dans ses métamorphoses:
Après les yeux très bleus voici les yeux très noirs
Brillant dans un visage où se flétrit la rose,
Plus profonds que le ciel et que le désespoir.

Maître de leur sommeil et de leurs insomnies
Il les entraîne en foule, à travers les pays,
Vers des mers éventrées et des épiphanies...
La marée sera haute et l'étoile a failli.

Quelqu'un m'a raconté que, perdu dans les glaces,
Dans un chaos de monts, loin de tout océan,
Il vit passer, sans heurt et sans fumée, la masse
Immense et pavoisée d'un paquebot géant.

Des marins silencieux s'accrochaient aux cordages
Et des oiseaux gueulards volaient dans les haubans
Des danseuses rêvaient au bord des bastingages
En robes de soirée et coiffées de turbans.

Les bijoux entouraient d'étincelles glaciales
Leur gorge et leurs poignets et de grands éventails
De plumes, dans leurs mains, claquaient vers des escales
Où les bals rougissaient les tours et les portails.

Les danseurs abîmés dans leur mélancolie
En songe comparaient leurs désirs à l'acier.
C'était parmi les monts, dans un soir de folie,
De grands nuages coulaient sur le flanc des glaciers.

For love and its pangs have a tyranny all their own:
Uniquely possessed is a passion-driven soul.
Many years of torture, that's all that some have known,
Some who by misfortune accepted love's control.

Others chase it, see how it metamorphoses:
Baby-blue eyes that become a death-black pair,
Glinting from a face full of wilting roses,
Deeper than the heavens, and deeper than despair.

Master of their sleeping and their sleepless reveries,
Love has dragged the lot of them through countries by the score,
Disembowelled oceans and epiphanies…
High tide, the water's up, the star is bright no more.

Once a person told me that, lost among the floes,
In a mountain cauldron where the ocean was remote,
He was watching, smokeless and steady as she goes,
Hung about with flags, an enormous packet-boat.

High in the rigging the seabirds were screaming,
Jack-tars in the shrouds shinned silent up and down.
All along the stowage there were dancing-girls dreaming:
Each wore a turban and an evening gown.

At their throats were necklaces of icy brilliance,
Wrists all bejewelled waving ostrich-feather fans
Click-clacked to go ashore where masquerade cotillions
Blushed red on portals and on barbicans.

Male dancers, melancholy, broken and grieving,
Likened their desires in their dreams to steel.
High in the mountains, on a night of raving,
The glaciers were guiding great clouds downhill.

Un autre découvrit, au creux d'une clairière,
Un rosier florissant entouré de sapins.
Combien a-t-il cueilli de roses sanguinaires
Avant de s'endormir sous la mousse au matin?

Mais ses yeux ont gardé l'étrange paysage
Inscrit sur leur prunelle et son cœur incertain
A choisi pour cesser de battre sans courage
Ce lieu clos par l'odeur de la rose et du thym.

Du temps où nous chantions avec des voix vibrantes
Nous avons traversé ces pays singuliers
Où l'écho répondait aux questions des amantes
Par des mots dont le sens nous était familier.

Mais, depuis que la nuit s'écroule sur nos têtes,
Ces mots ont dans nos cœurs des accents mystérieux
Et quand un souvenir parfois nous les répète
Nous désobéissons à leur ordre impérieux.

Entendez-vous chanter des voix dans les montagnes
Et retentir le bruit des cors et des buccins?
Pourquoi ne chantons-nous que les refrains du bagne
Au son d'un éternel et lugubre tocsin?

Serait-ce pas Don Juan qui parcourt ces allées
Où l'ombre se marie aux spectres de l'amour?
Ce pas qui retentit dans les nuits désolées
A-t-il marqué les cœurs avec un talon lourd?

Ce n'est pas le Don Juan qui descend impassible
L'escalier ruisselant d'infernales splendeurs
Ni celui qui crachait aux versets de la Bible
Et but en ricanant avec le commandeur.

Down in a clearing, someone else discovered,
Hemmed about by fir-trees, a rose-bush in flower.
How many blood-red roses had he gathered,
Till he slept on mosses in the night's last hour?

That uncanny landscape on his eyes was leaving
Imprints of a vision and his failing heartbeat chose
This place to cease from its chicken-hearted heaving,
Sequestered in the essences of wild thyme and rose.

Since the days we sang, when our voices all resounded,
Through these peculiar lands we've made our way.
Loving women questioned us and echoes responded
In words of simple meanings that we used every day.

But, now that night has come crumbling down around us,
In our hearts these words acquire an eerie resonance.
Sometimes repetitive in memory they hound us,
Then we disobey their imperious commands.

Can you hear those voices that sing in the sierras,
Sounds of battle-trumpet and of hunting-horn?
Why is our only song the chain-gang's chorus,
While forever blaring the dismal sirens warn?

Might it be Don Juan on the prowl in every alley
Where the shadows mingle with love's spectral revenants:
Footfall that goes echoing through nights of melancholy,
Did it stamp on human hearts a bruising dominance?

Never the Don Juan of uncaring haughty mettle,
Striding down the stairways where the hellfire splendours run,
Not the one who used to spray the Bible with his spittle,
Sneering as he quaffed with the Governor of stone.

Ses beaux yeux incompris n'ont pas touche les cœurs,
Sa bouche n'a connu que le baiser du rêve,
Et c'est celui que rêve en de sombres ardeurs
Celle qui le dédaigne et l'ignore et sans trêve

Heurte ses diamants froids, ses lèvres sépulcrales,
Sa bouche silencieuse à sa bouche et ses yeux,
Ses yeux de sphinx cruels et ses mains animales
À ses yeux, à ses mains, à son étoile, aux cieux.

Mais lui, le cœur meurtri par de mortes chimères,
Gardant leur bec pourri planté dans ses amours,
Pour un baiser viril, ô beautés éphémères,
Vous sauvera sans doute au seuil du dernier jour.

Le rire sur sa bouche écrasera des fraises,
Ses yeux seront marqués par un plus pur destin.
C'est Bacchus renaissant des cendres et des braises,
Les cendres dans les dents, les braises dans les mains.

Mais pour un qui renait combien qui, sans mourir,
Portent au cœur, portent aux pieds de lourdes chaines.
Les fleuves couleront et les morts vont pourrir...
Chaque an reverdira le feuillage des chênes.

J'habite quand il me plaît un ravin ténébreux au-dessus duquel le ciel se découpe en un losange déchiqueté par l'ombre des sapins, des mélèzes et des rochers qui couvrent les pentes escarpées.

Dans l'herbe du ravin poussent d'étranges tubéreuses, des ancolies et des colchiques survolés par des libellules et des mantes religieuses et si pareils sans cesse, le ciel la flore et la faune où succèdent aux insectes les corneilles moroses et les rats musqués, que je ne sais quelle immuable saison s'est abattue sur ce toujours nocturne ravin, avec son dais en losange constellé que ne traverse aucun nuage.

Hearts are all untouched, for they've misread his pretty eyes,
Only in dreams has his mouth the taste of kisses,
Dreams that are dreamed in her sombre fantasies
By one, relentless, who ignores him and despises,

Buffets him with jewels of ice, with lips cadaver-cold,
Thrusting her unspeaking mouth against his mouth and eyes,
Her deadly sphinx's eyes, her two hands' feral hold
On his eyes and hands, on his star and on the skies.

Though his heart is brutalised by dead and monstrous creatures,
Though they pierce his passions with their rotting pointed snout,
For just a single manly kiss, you perishable sweethearts,
On the Last Day's threshold he will save you, pluck you out.

Laughter on his lips will conjure strawberry crushes;
Purer is the destiny, the stamp his gaze proclaims.
His hands full of embers and his teeth full of ashes,
He's the reborn Bacchus, who surges from the flames.

Yet, for each one born again, how many who, undying,
Round their hearts and ankles must wear a heavy chain.
Rivers will be flowing and the dead will be decaying...
Every year in springtime the oaks are green again.

I live when I choose in a dark ravine above which the sky is a jagged diamond cut up by the shade of the fir-trees, larches and rocks that cover the steep slopes.

In the grass of the ravine grow strange tuberous plants, columbine and meadow-saffron; above them circle praying mantises and dragonflies; insects give way to muskrats and melancholy crows. So unceasingly constant are sky, flora and fauna that some immutable season must have descended on this ever nocturnal ravine with its star-studded diamond-shaped canopy, not crossed by any cloud.

Sur les troncs des arbres deux initiales, toujours les mêmes, sont gravées. Par quel couteau, par quelle main, pour quel cœur?.

Le vallon était désert quand j'y vins pour la première fois. Nul n'y était venu avant moi. Nul autre que moi ne l'a parcouru.

La mare où les grenouilles nagent dans l'ombre avec des mouvements réguliers reflète des étoiles immobiles et le marais que les crapauds peuplent de leur cri sonore et triste possède un feu follet toujours le même.

La saison de l'amour triste et immobile plane en cette solitude.

Je l'aimerai toujours et sans doute ne pourrai-je jamais franchir l'orée des mélèzes et des sapins, escalader les rochers baroques, pour atteindre la route blanche ou elle passe à certaines heures. La route où les ombres n'ont pas toujours la même direction.

Parfois il me semble que la nuit vient seulement de s'abattre. Des chasseurs passent sur la route que je ne vois pas. Le chant des cors de chasse résonne sous les mélèzes. La journée a été longue, parmi les terres de labour, à la poursuite du renard, du blaireau ou du chevreuil. Le naseau des chevaux fume blanc dans la nuit.

Les airs de chasse s'éteignent. Et je déchiffre difficilement les initiales identiques sur le tronc des mélèzes qui bornent le ravin.

Nulle étoile en tombant n'a fait jaillir l'écume,
Rien ne trouble les monts, les cieux, le feu, les eaux,
Excepte cet envol horizontal de plumes
Qui révèle la chute et la mort d'un oiseau.

Et rien n'arrêtera cette plume envolée,
Ni les cheveux luisants d'un cavalier sauvage,
Ni l'encre méprisable au fond d'un encrier,
Ni la vague chantante et le grondant orage,

Ni le cou séduisant des belles misérables,
Ni la branche de l'arbre et le tombeau fermé,
Ni les bateaux qui font la nuit grincer des câbles,
Ni le mur où des cœurs par des noms sont formés,

On the trunks of the trees two initials, always the same, are engraved. What knife put them there, held by what hand and with whom in mind?

The valley was deserted when I first came here. No-one had set foot in it before I did. No-one but myself has explored it.

The pond where frogs swim rhythmically in the shade reflects stars that never move, and the marsh, alive with the sad sonorous cries of toads, has a will-o'-the-wisp that is always the same.

The season of sad and stalled love hovers over this solitude.

I will always be in love with it and will surely never manage to pass the fringe of larches and fir-trees, to climb the contorted rocks so as to reach the white road where at certain times she passes. The road where shadows do not always point the same way. Sometimes it seems to me that night has only just fallen. Hunters go by on the road, a thing I cannot see. The song of hunting horns echoes under the larches. It has been a long day in among the ploughed fields chasing foxes, badgers or roe-deer. The horses' nostrils steam white in the night.

The music of the hunt fades away. And I can just decipher the matching initials on the trunks of larches at the edge of the ravine.

No star has plunged to send foam spurting from the ocean,
Nothing disturbs the mountains, the heavens, fire and sea,
Only these feathers flying in horizontal motion
Revealing a bird's fast fall, a small fatality.

And nothing will stop this single flying feather,
Not the glistening hair of a savage on his horse,
Nor ink in an inkwell, hateful altogether,
Nor the song of waves, nor the tempest's angry curse,

Nor the sweet necks of women, lovely losers,
Nor the branches of trees and the sealed-up tombs,
Nor the ships with creaking of their midnight hawsers,
Nor the wall where hearts are crafted out of names,

Ni le chant des lépreux dans les marais austères,
Ni la glace qui dort au fond des avenues
En reflétant sans cesse un tremblant réverbère
Et jamais, belle neige, un corps de femme nue,

Ni les monstres marins aux écailles fumeuses,
Ni les brouillards du nord avec leurs plaies d'azur,
Ni la vitre où le soir une femme rêveuse
Retrace en sa mémoire un amour au futur,

Ni l'écho des appels d'un voyageur perdu,
Ni les nuages fuyards, ni les chevaux en marche,
Ni l'ombre d'un plongeur sur les quais et les arches,
Ni celle du pavé a son cou suspendu,

Ni toi Fouquier-Tinville aux mains de cire claire:
Les étoiles, les mains, l'amour, les yeux, le sang
Sont autant de fusées surgissant d'un cratère.
Adieu! C'est le matin blanchi comme un brisant.

Ô mains qui voudriez vous meurtrir à l'amour
Nous saurons vous donner le plus rouge baptême
Près duquel pâliront le feu des hauts fourneaux
Et le soleil mourant au sein des brouillards blêmes.

Les plus beaux yeux du monde ont connu nos pensées,
Nous avons essayé tous les vices fameux,
Mais les baisers et les luxures insensées
N'ont pas éteint l'espoir dans nos cœurs douloureux.

Je vis alors s'ouvrir des portes de cristal
Sur le cristal plus pur d'un fantôme adorable:
«Jetez dans le ruisseau votre cœur de métal
«Et brisez les flacons sur le marbre des tables!

Nor the songs of lepers in the grim bog's quaking,
Nor the sleeping mirror down along the avenue
Reflecting at all times a streetlamp shaking,
With never, snowy beauty, a woman's limbs to view;

Nor the sea-monsters with their soot-blackened scales,
Nor the northern hazes with their deep blue scars,
Nor the twilit window where a woman recalls
Dreamily the memory of future love-affairs,

Nor the cries that echo from a wayfarer lost,
Nor the scudding clouds nor horses at the trot,
Nor on quays and arches the shadow someone cast,
Plunging, with a paving-stone dangling at his throat,

Nor you, Deadly Accuser, with hands of waxen lustre:
The stars in heaven, hands and eyes and blood and love,
Are so many rockets fired and bursting from a crater.
Goodbye! Here's morning, bone-white like a breaking wave.

You hands that long for love on which to bruise yourselves,
We'll know how to give you the tint of blood's baptism:
Beside it the brightness of furnace-fires dissolves,
The sun pales, moribund in sea-fog's dismal bosom.

They knew all our thinking, the world's most lovely eyes,
There was no famous vice we did not essay,
But for all the kisses and insensate lecheries
Hope within our grieving hearts was never snuffed away.

Then I saw swing open two gates of crystal
On the purer crystal of a phantom most adorable:
"Fling it in the stream, fling down your heart of metal,
Shatter the jugs on the table-tops of marble!

«Crevez vos yeux et vos tympans; et que vos langues
«Par vos bouches crachées soient mangées par les chiens,
«Dites adieu à vos désirs, bateaux qui tanguent,
«Que vos mains et vos pieds soient meurtris par des liens!

«Soyez humbles, perdez au courant de vos transes
«Votre espoir, votre orgueil et votre dignité
«Pour que je puisse encore augmenter vos souffrances
«Instituant sur vous d'exquises cruautés.»

C'est elle qui parla. C'est aussi l'amoureuse,
C'est le cœur de cristal et les yeux sans pitié,
Les plus beaux yeux du monde, ô sources lumineuses,
La belle bouche avec des dents de carnassier.

Enfonce tes deux mains dans mon cerveau docile,
Mords ma lèvre en feignant de m'offrir un baiser,
Si la force et l'orgueil sont des vertus faciles,
Dure est la solitude à 1'amour imposée.

Je parlais d'un fantôme et d'un oiseau qui tombe,
Mon rêve perd les mots que ma bouche employait.
La prairie où je parle est creusée par les tombes
Et 1'écho retentit du bruit clair des maillets.

On dresse l'échafaud dans la prison prochaine.
Le condamné qui dort dans un lit trop étroit
Rêve des grands corbeaux qui survolaient la plaine
Quand il y rencontra le désir et l'effroi.

Ces deux spectres zélés cheminaient côte à côte
Déchirant leur manteau et leur face aux branchages,
De faux amants frappés sans merci par leur faute
À leur suite faisaient un long pèlerinage.

"Burst your eyes and eardrums, and let your tongues
Be spat out of your mouths for hungry dogs to eat;
Desires are boats in heavy seas: give them your So Longs.
Let cords tightly knotted bruise your hands and feet.

"Be humbled! Lose in the flooding of your terror
Your hope and your pride and your specious dignity.
I shall increase your suffering and horror,
I shall practise on you exquisite cruelty."

She it was who spoke: the woman, the amorous,
Her heart and eyes of crystal, her pitiless nature.
The loveliest eyes of all, o well-springs luminous!
Beautiful mouth, teeth of a prowling creature.

Thrust both your hands into my compliant brain!
Bite my lip pretending to love me with a kiss.
Strength and pride are virtues easy to attain:
What's hard when foisted on love is loneliness.

I spoke of a falling bird and a spectral shadow
My dream mislays the words of my mouth's uttering
Hollowed out with graves as I speak is the meadow
Brightly rings an echo, sound of hammering.

A gallows is erected in the prison next door.
The condemned man sleeping in a too narrow bed
Dreams of the giant crows that winged across the moor
The day he encountered enchantment and dread.

Side by side these two zealous phantasms walked,
The brambles ripping at their coats and faces,
False lovers mercilessly punished by their fault
Following on pilgrimage to no end of places.

Des incendies sifflaient sur les toits des hameaux.
Les poissons attirés par de célestes nasses
Montaient avec lenteur à travers les rameaux.
Des bûcherons sortaient de leurs chaumières basses.

Le condamné qui dort parlait avec 1'un d'eux,
Plus spectral que le chêne où se plantait la hache:
«Ecoutez, disait-il, mugir au loin les bœufs,
Le vent qui souffle ici brisera leur attache.»

Écoute jusqu'au jour la voix de la cruelle,
Sa bouche à la saveur d'un fruit empoisonné,
Le ciel et la montagne ou les troupeaux s'appellent
Viennent de se confondre à nos yeux étonnés.

Charmé par les oiseaux, et par 1'amour trompé,
Dans de noirs corridors, sous de sombres portiques
L'amant recherchera la marque de 1'épée
Qu'Isis au cœur de feu dans son cœur a trempée...
Ô lame au fil parfait, sœur des fleuves mystiques!

L'oiseau qui chantait pour elle
Dans sa cage ne chante plus
Et la reine des hirondelles
Ne tourne plus, ne tourne plus.

Un jour j'ai rencontré le vautour et l'orfraie.
Leur ombre sur le sol ne m'a pas étonné.
J'ai déchiffré plus tard sur des remparts de craie
L'initiale au charbon d'un nom que je connais.

Un vampire a frappé ma vitre de son aile:
Qu'il entre, couronné des algues de l'étang,
Avec son beau collier de vives coccinelles
Qui prédisent l'amour, la pluie et le beau temps.

Village thatches sizzled with conflagrations.
Fish that were drawn to the dragnets far aloft
Slowly ascended through ramifications.
Woodcutters sprang from every humble croft.

Sleeping the condemned man addressed one of the pair,
Axe was laid to spectral oak, more spectral still was he:
"Far away the cattle is lowing, can you hear,
This wind breaks their tethers (he said) and sets them free."

Cruel woman! All through the night her voice is heard.
Her lips are a fruit that is poison to the taste.
Heaven and the mountains where herd calls out to herd
All are one confusion we contemplate amazed.

Whom the birds bewitched, the one who love has cheated,
In black labyrinths under sombre portico,
The lover will search for the brand-mark of the sword-blade
Tempered in her very heart by Isis fire-hearted...
Perfect steel, you sister of rivers' mystic flow!

Songbird in a birdcage once
Sang for her, it sings no more
And the queen of swallows turns
Nevermore, turns nevermore.

Once I encountered the vulture and the osprey.
They cast shadows on the ground that failed to frighten me.
Scrawled on chalk sea-ramparts I later on deciphered
Charcoaled initials of a name well-known to me.

A vampire with its wing brushed against my window-pane:
It has a crown of lake-weed, welcome guest come hither,
Round its neck live ladybirds make a pretty chain,
Harbingers of love and of splendid summer weather.

Coucher avec elle
Pour le sommeil côte à côte
Pour les rêves parallèles
Pour la double respiration

Coucher avec elle
Pour l'ombre unique et surprenante
Pour la même chaleur
Pour la même solitude

Coucher avec elle
Pour l'aurore partagée
Pour le minuit identique
Pour les mêmes fantômes

Coucher coucher avec elle
Pour l'amour absolu
Pour le vice pour le vice
Pour les baisers de toute espèce

Coucher avec elle
Pour un naufrage ineffable
Pour se prostituer l'un à l'autre
Pour se confondre

Coucher avec elle
Pour se prouver et prouver vraiment
Que jamais n'a pesé sur l'âme et le corps des amants
Le mensonge d'une tache originelle

Toujours avoir le plus grand amour pour elle
N'est pas difficile
Mais tout est douteux pour les cœurs de feu, pour les cœurs fidèles

to take her to bed
to sleep side by side
for parallel dreaming
breath doubled on breath

to take her to bed
for the one magic shadow
the one single warmth
the one isolation

to take her to bed
one daybreak two sharing
one midnight the same
identical phantoms

to take her to take her to bed
for absolute love
for vice for vice
for all kinds of kisses

to take her to bed
for awe-stricken shipwreck
for mutual whoring
for melding together

to take her to bed
to prove us and prove to us truly
this thing never weighed on two lovers' body and soul
the lie of original blemish

having always the greatest love for her
is quite easy
yet there is doubt for fiery hearts, faithful hearts

Toujours avoir le plus grand amour
Y a-t-il des trahisons involontaires
Non la chair n'est jamais menteuse
Et le corps du plus vicieux reste pur

Pur comme le plus grand amour pour elle
Dans mon seul cœur il fleurit sans contrainte
Nulle boue jamais n'atteignit l'image de celle
La seule aimée dans le cœur de l'amant.

Nulle boue jamais n'atteignit le plus grand amour pour elle
C'est pour sa pureté qu'on admire le diamant
Nulle boue ne tache le diamant ni le cœur de celle
La plus aimée dans le cœur de l'amant

Le plus sincère amant capable du plus grand amour
N'est pas un chaste ni un ascète ni un puritain
Et s'il éprouve le corps des plus belles
C'est qu'il sait bien que le plus beau est celui de l'aimée

Le plus sincère amant est un débauché
Sa bouche a connu et éprouvé tous les baisers
Se livrerait-il à tous les vices
Il n'en vaudrait que mieux

Car le plus sincère amant s'il n'est pas aimé par celle qu'il aime
Peu lui importe, il l'aimera
Eternellement désirera d'être aimé
Et d'aimer sans espoir deviendra pur comme un diamant.

Tout son corps ne sera qu'une proie décevante
Pour les fausses amantes et pour les faux amours
Et sans pitié
L'amant le véritable sacrifiera tout pour celle qu'il aime

having the greatest love always
are there betrayals unwilled
no the flesh never lies
and no matter how vicious the body is pure

pure as the greatest love for her
in my heart uniquely it flourishes free
no stain has touched the image of her
the only-beloved in the heart of the lover

no stain touched the greatest love for her
for purity we admire the diamond
no stain on the diamond nor on the heart of her
the most-beloved in the heart of the lover

the genuine lover adept of the greatest love
is no abstainer ascetic or puritan
if he tries the loveliest bodies of women
it is knowing the loveliest is his beloved

the genuine lover that rake
his mouth has known and checked out all the kisses
let him surrender to every vice
he'd be all the better

for the genuine lover unloved by her
what does he care he will love her
eternally he will long to be loved
hopeless love will make him pure as a diamond

his body will just be a scrap and a morsel
for false loving women false loves
having no pity
the genuine lover will sacrifice all for the woman he loves

Qu'importe s'il a toujours le plus grand amour pour elle
Au jour de la rencontre désirée
Il sera plus pur que l'aube et le feu
Et prêt pour l'extase

Toujours avoir le plus grand amour pour elle
Il n'y a pas de trahison corporelle
Et que ton cœur batte toujours pour elle
Que tes yeux se ferment sur son unique image.

Être aimé par elle
Nul bonheur nulle félicité
Désir pas même
Mais volonté ou plutôt destin

Être aimé par elle
Non pas une nuit de toutes les nuits
Mais à jamais pour l'éternel présent
Sans paysage et sans lumières

Être aimé par elle
Écrit dans les signes du temps
Malgré tout contre antan et futur
À jamais

Mais pour être aimé par elle
Faut-il perdre jusqu'a l'amour
La vie n'en parlons pas
L'amour l'amour non plus

Être aimé par elle
C'est inévitable
Pas de chants pas de cris
Nul sentiment

why not if he still has the greatest love for her
on the day of the longed-for encounter
he will be beyond sunrise beyond fire
ready for ecstasy

always having the greatest love for her
the body cannot betray
may your heart always beat for her
your eyes close on her image alone

to be loved by her
not happiness joy
not even desire
it's will no it's fate

to be loved by her
not for one night of many
but endless the present for ever
no landscape no light

to be loved by her
inscribed in the waymarks of time
regardless of bygones and future
no end

and yet to be loved by her
all must be lost even love
no talk please of life
nor of love nor of love

to be loved by her
it's unavoidable
no songs no shouts
no emotion

Être aimé par elle
Marbre impassible Mers figées Ciels implacables
Mais attendre attendre longtemps attendre encore
Attendre? nié par l'éternité.

Mourir après elle
Est le rôle dévolu à l'amant
À lui seul le droit suprême
De graver un nom sur une pierre périssable

De graver un nom sur un arbre périssable
Et de s'éteindre pour jamais
S'éteindre lui après elle
Mais l'amour le plus grand amour
Brûlera comme une flamme éternelle.

Depuis de si longs mois, ma chère, que je t'aime
Pourquoi ne pas vouloir connaître mes travaux?
Si mes jours sont soumis à de mornes systèmes
Mes nuits sont escortées par de nobles prévôts.

Dois-je veiller encore un bûcher renaissant,
Si vif que le Phénix ne pourrait y survivre,
Ou dois-je, naufragé, vers les vaisseaux passant
Effeuiller sans raison les pages de ce livre?

Dois-je m'anéantir pour éteindre ma foi?
L'univers de mon rêve exalte ton image
Mais les pays fameux que j'ai créés pour toi
Seront-ils traversés mieux que par ton mirage?

S'il faut mourir au pied des idoles rivales,
Je suis prêt. Confessant ta cruelle grandeur
Je mourrai si tu veux pour n'être en tes annales
Que l'écho faiblissant d'une inutile ardeur.

to be loved by her
impassive marble frozen seas implacable skies
to wait and to wait on and on to be waiting
to wait denied by eternity

to die after she does
this role devolves on the lover
his alone is the ultimate right
to carve a name on a mouldering stone

to carve a name on a mouldering tree
to be snuffed out for ever
snuffed out him after her
but the love the greatest
will burn an unquenchable flame.

Darling these many months of love you've been
Incurious that I am working hard
My days are governed by a grim routine
My nights escorted by an honour-guard.

Must I still tend and stir a beacon-glow
More fierce than any phoenix might endure,
A castaway, my pages torn to show
To every passing ship, a futile chore?

To quench my faith, is life to be laid down?
My dream-world holds your image high aloft
I conjured for you countries of renown
What may traverse them better than your ghost?

If I must die at rival idols' feet
I'm ready. You excel in cruelty.
The merest echo of a futile heat
Abating in your annals I shall be.

Je donne tout pour toi, jusqu'au cœur des fantômes,
Soumis à mon fatal et délicieux tourment
Quitte pour disparaître en deux lignes d'un tome
Et sans être invoqué le soir par les amants.

Je suis las de combattre un sort qui se dérobe,
Las de tenter l'oubli, las de me souvenir
Du moindre des parfums émanant de ta robe,
Las de te détester et las de te bénir.

Je valais mieux que ça mais tu l'as méconnu.
Un jour d'entre les jours de soleil sur les roches
Souviens-toi de l'amant dont le cœur était nu
Et qui sut te servir sans peur et sans reproche.

Attends-tu que j'aborde à de lointains rivages
Pour dire en regardant tes genoux désertés:
«Qui donc s'en est allé, j'ignore son visage
«Mais pourquoi s'en va-t-il seul vers sa liberté?

«Il faut le retrouver, serviteur infidèle,
«L'enchaîner à mon bagne après l'avoir châtié
«Et qu'il me serve encore avec un cœur modèle
«Sans même pour sa peine éprouver ma pitié.

«Car je suis impérieuse et veux qu'on m'obéisse,
«Nul ne doit me quitter sans être congédié.
«Tant pis pour celui-là qui rentre à mon service
«Si son orgueil hautain ne l'a pas répudié.

«Je connais pour les cœurs des prisons fantastiques:
«Que l'amant fugitif y retourne au plus tôt
«Car il me faut ce soir de nombreux domestiques
«Pour cirer mes souliers et m'offrir le manteau.»

I give my heart and all, turn bloodless spook
Submissive to delight of deadly pain
Just for the briefest mention in a book
Never on twilit lovers' lips again.

I'm tired of wrestling with fate's waywardness,
Tired of expunging and recalling too
Each perfume-wisp emerging from your dress,
Tired of detesting and of blessing you.

I was not so little worth, but you were not aware.
One sunny day of days on the rocky shore
Remember your lover with his heart stripped bare
Fearless and without reproach, your faithful servitor.

Must I drop my anchor in some far distant place
Before you notice no-one is fawning at your knee?
You'll say: 'Who's gone missing? I don't recall his face:
Why's he made a lonely dash for liberty?

"He must be recaptured, my disloyal slave,
Chained in my penal camp, properly chastised.
With a model heart he must diligently serve,
Meet with no compassion, condignly penalised.

"For I am imperious, I must be obeyed.
No-one may be absent unless I grant release.
Once again subjected to service, woe betide
One too proud and haughty to mumble penances.

"Prisons for hearts, I know of some, fantastic!
Better show up soon, that lover on the run.
Tonight I have a number of vacancies domestic,
Wipe and shine my shoes, get my overcoat on."

À quoi bon? L'évadé connaît bien sa prison.
Sans doute a-t-il choisi de trop précieux otages
Pour vouloir à nouveau te payer sa rançon:
Les trésors d'un cœur pur ne souffrent pas partage.

Évade-toi de l'eau, des prisons, des potences,
Adieu, je partirai comme on meurt un matin.
Ce ne sont pas les lieues qui feront la distance
Mais ces mots: Je l'aimais! murmurés au lointain.

Adorable signe inscrit dans les eaux mortes
Profondeurs boueuses
Ô poissons qui rôdez autour des algues
Où est la source que j'entends couler depuis si longtemps et que je n'ai jamais rencontrée
Qui ferme sans cesse des portes lourdes et sonores?
Eaux mortes Source invisible.
Criminel attends-moi au détour du sentier parmi les grandes ciguës.

Pareilles aux nuages les soirées sans raison naissent et meurent avec ce tatouage au-dessus du sein gauche: Demain
L'eau s'écoule lentement par une fêlure de la bouteille où les plus fameux astrologues viennent boire l'élixir de vie
Tandis que l'homme aux yeux clos ne sait que répéter: «Une cigogne de perdue deux de retrouvées»
Et que les ciguës se fanent dans l'ombre du rendez-vous
Et que demain ponctuel mais masqué en costume de prud'homme ouvre un grand parapluie rouge au milieu de la prairie où sèche le linge des fermières de l'aube.
Blêmes effigies fantômes de marbre dressés dans les palais nocturnes

Une lame de parquet craque
Une épée tombe toute seule et se fiche dans le sol
Et je marche sans arrêt à travers une succession

But what's the good? The escaper knows his prison.
Holding precious hostages, he is not prepared
(So it seems) to pay you a second time his ransom:
Treasures of a pure heart never can be shared.

Get away from water, from gallows and from gaols
Farewell! I shall leave like a death at dawn of day.
What will keep us distant won't be weary miles
But the words: I loved her! murmured far away.

Adorable sign writ in stagnant water
Muddy depths
You fishes skirting the seaweed
Where is the spring I have heard burbling so long but never
found
That ceaselessly closes heavy clanging doors?
Stagnant waters Invisible spring.
Criminal! Wait for me where the path goes curving through
tall hemlock.

Like clouds evenings are born and die at random, with this
tattoo above the left breast: 'Tomorrow'
Water seeps slowly from a cracked bottle from which
renowned astrologers come to drink the elixir of life
While a man with his eyes shut can only repeat:
'Lose one stork, find two'
And hemlock wilts in the rendezvous' shadow
And Tomorrow, punctual but disguised as a magistrate,
opens a great red umbrella right out in open country
where the farmers'-wives of dawn dry their washing.
Livid effigies marble phantoms erect in night-palaces

A floorboard creaks
A sword falls of its own accord and sticks in the ground
And I walk straight through a series

De grandes salles vides dont les parquets cirés ont le reflet de l'eau.
Il y a des mains dans cette nuit de marais
Une main blanche et qui est comme un personnage vivant
Et qui est la main sur laquelle je voudrais poser mes lèvres et
où je n'ose pas les poser.

Il y a les mains terribles
Main noircie d'encre de l'écolier triste
Main rouge sur le mur de la chambre du crime
Main pâle de la morte
Mains qui tiennent un couteau ou un revolver
Mains ouvertes
Mains fermées
Mains abjectes qui tiennent un porte-plume
Ô ma main toi aussi toi aussi
Ma main avec tes lignes et pourtant c'est ainsi
Pourquoi maculer tes lignes mystérieuses
Pourquoi? plutôt les menottes plutôt te mutiler plutôt plutôt

Écris écris car c'est une lettre que tu écris à elle et ce moyen
impur est un moyen de la toucher
Mains qui se tendent mains qui s'offrent
Y a-t-il une main sincère parmi elles
Ah je n'ose plus serrer les mains
Mains menteuses mains lâches mains que je hais
Mains qui avouent et qui tremblent quand je regarde les yeux
Y a-t-il encore une main que je puisse serrer avec confiance
Mains sur la bouche de l'amour
Mains sur le cœur sans amour
Mains au feu de l'amour
Mains à couper du faux amour
Mains basses sur l'amour
Mains mortes à l'amour
Mains forcées pour l'amour
Mains levées sur l'amour

Of big empty rooms whose polished floors reflect like water.
There are hands in this marshy night
A white hand that's like a living person
It's the hand I'd like to put my lips to
    and I don't dare.

There are terrible hands
Inky black hand of a sad schoolboy
Red hand on the wall of a room of crime
Pale hand of a dead woman
Hands holding a knife or a revolver
Hands open
Hands closed
Abject hands clutching a pen-holder
My own hand you as well yes you
My hand with your lines and yet that's it
Why stain your mysterious lines
Why? Rather handcuffs rather self-harm rather rather

Write write it's a letter to her and this impure way
    is a way to move her
Hands extended hands proffered
Is there one sincere hand among them
Oh I no longer dare shake hands
Lying hands craven hands hands I hate
Hands that confess that tremble when I look into eyes
Is there any hand I can still shake with confidence?
Hands on lips of love
Hands on a heart lacking love
Hands at the fire of love
Hands to cut off for false love
Hands low on love
Hands dead to love
Hands forced for love
Hands raised over love

Mains tenues sur l'amour
Mains hautes sur l'amour
Mains tendues vers l'amour
Mains d'œuvres de l'amour
Mains heureuses de l'amour
Mains à la pâte hors l'amour horribles mains
Mains liées par l'amour éternellement
Mains lavées par l'amour par des flots implacables
Mains à la main c'est l'amour qui rôde
Mains liées par l'amour éternellement
Mains pleines c'est encore l'amour
Mains armées c'est le véritable amour
Mains de maître mains de l'amour
Main chaude d'amour
Main offerte à l'amour
Main de justice main d'amour
Main forte à l'amour!
Mains Mains toutes les mains
Un homme se noie une main sort des flots
Un homme s'en va une main s'agite
Une main se crispe un cœur souffre
Une main se ferme ô divine colère
Une main encore une main
Une main sur mon épaule
Qui est-ce?
Est-ce toi enfin?
Il fait trop sombre! quelles ténèbres!
Je ne sais plus à qui sont les mains
Ce qu'elles veulent
Ce qu'elles disent
Les mains sont trompeuses
Je me souviens encore de mains blanches dans l'obscurité
    étendues sur une table dans l'attente
Je me souviens de mains dont l'étreinte m'était chère
Et je ne sais plus

Hands held over love
Hands high over love
Hands reaching to love
All hands on love
Hands happy with love
Hands kneading outside love horrible hands
Hands linked by love eternally
Hands washed by love by implacable waves
Hands by hand it's love at large
Hands full it's love again
Hands bearing weapons it's true love
Masterful hands hands of love
Hand hot with love
Hand offered to love
Hand of justice hand of love
Strong hand in love!
Hands Hands every hand
A man drowns a hand comes out of the sea
A man leaves a hand is waved
A hand clenches a heart suffers
A hand closes o wrath divine
A hand another hand
A hand on my shoulder
Who is it?
Is it you at last?
It's too dark! What shadows!
Whose hands I don't know any more
What they want
What they're saying
Hands deceive
I still remember white hands in the gloom
    stretched on a table waiting
I remember hands whose grasp was dear to me
And now I don't know

Il y a trop de traîtres trop de menteurs
Ah même ma main qui écrit
Un couteau! une arme! un outil! Tout sauf écrire!
Du sang du sang!

Patience! Ce jour se lèvera.

Églantines flétries parmi les herbiers
Ô feuilles jaunes
Tout craque dans cette chambre
Comme dans l'allée nocturne les herbes sous le pied.
De grandes ailes invisibles immobilisent mes bras et le
    retentissement d'une mer lointaine parvient jusqu'à moi.
Le lit roule jusqu'à l'aube sa bordure d'écume et l'aube ne paraît pas
Ne paraîtra jamais.
Verre pile, boiseries pourries, rêves interminables, fleurs flétries,
Une main se pose à travers les ténèbres toute blanche sur mon front,
Et j'écouterai jusqu'au jour improbable
Voler en se heurtant aux murailles et aux meubles l'oiseau de
    paradis, l'oiseau que j'ai enfermé par mégarde
Rien qu'en fermant les yeux.

Jamais l'aube a grands cris bleuissant les lavoirs,
L'aube, savon trempé dans l'eau des fleuves noirs,
L'aube ne moussera sur cette nuit livide
Ni sur nos doigts tremblants ni sur nos verres vides.
C'est la nuit sans frontière et fille des sapins
Qui fait grincer au port la chaîne des grappins
Nuit des nuits sans amour étrangleuse du rêve
Nuit de sang nuit de feu nuit de guerre sans trêve
Nuit de chemin perdu parmi les escaliers
Et de pieds retombant trop lourds sur les paliers
Nuit de luxure nuit de chute dans l'abîme
Nuit de chaînes sonnant dans la salle du crime
Nuit de fantômes nus se glissant dans les lits

Too many traitors too many liars
Even my own hand as it writes
A knife! a weapon! An instrument! Anything but writing!
Blood, blood!

Be patient! that day will dawn!

Withered dog-roses pressed in albums
Yellow leaves
Everything creaks in this bedroom
Like herbs underfoot in a night alley.
Great invisible wings pin my arms and the boom
  of a distant sea reaches my ears.
My bed rolls its foam fringe till dawn and dawn does not appear
Will never appear.
Broken glass, rotten woodwork, endless dreams, withered flowers,
Through the dark a white white hand is laid on my brow,
And I will listen till the unlikely dawn of day
To a bird of paradise flying into walls and furniture, the bird
  I caged by mistake
Just by closing my eyes.

Dawn the loud shouts the wash-place turning blue
Dawn the soap wetted in black rivers' flow
Never this bruised night dawn's ebullience
On empty glasses and our trembling hands
Night dark trees' daughter uncontainable
That makes the grappling-chains in harbours squeal
The night of loveless nights dream-suffocator
The night of blood of fire of war no quarter
The night of feet that lost their way on stairs
And tramped on landings, night of lewd affairs,
Of fallings into depths, of shackles clanking
In halls of crime, of naked spectres sneaking

Nuit de réveil quand les dormeurs sont affaiblis.
Sentant rouler du sang sur leur maigre poitrine
Et monter à leurs dents la bave de l'angine
Ils caressent dans l'ombre un vampire velu
Et ne distinguent pas si le monstre goulu
N'est pas leur cœur battant sous leurs côtes souillées.
Nuit d'échos indistincts et de braises mouillées
Nuit d'incendies étincelant sur les miroirs
Nuit d'aveugle cherchant des sous dans les tiroirs
Nuit des nuits sans amour, où les draps se dérobent,
Où sur les boulevards sifflent les policiers
Ô nuit! cruelle nuit où frissonnent des robes
Où chuchotent des voix au chevet des malades,
Nuit close pour jamais par des verrous d'acier
Nuit ô nuit solitaire et sans astre et sans rade!

Dans tes yeux, dans ton cœur et dans le ciel aussi
Vois s'étoiler soudain l'univers imprécis,
La fissure grandir étroite et lumineuse
Comme si quelque fauve aux griffes paresseuses
Avait étreint la nuit et l'avait déchirée
(Mais la lueur sera pâle et lente la marée)
Des nervures courir dans le cristal fragile
Des fêlures mimer des couleuvres agiles
Qui rouleraient et se noueraient dans la lueur
Pâle d'une aube étrange. Ainsi lorsque le joueur
Fatigué de tourner les cartes symboliques
Voit le matin cruel éclairer les portiques
Maintes pensées et maints désirs presque oubliés
Maints éventails flétris tombent sur les paliers.

Tais-toi, pose la plume et ferme les oreilles
Aux pas lents et pesants qui montent l'escalier.
La nuit déjà pâlit mais cette aube est pareille
À des papillons morts au pied des chandeliers.

Between the sheets, of weakened sleepers waking.
On scrawny chests they feel the hot blood froth
Angina-foam comes rising to their teeth
Black shade a hairy vampire is caressed
They are indifferent if the ravening beast
Is their own heartbeat in their sullied chest.
Night of dim echoes and of coal-fires doused
Bright blaze in mirrors to destruction roused
Blind hands that grope for pennies in a chest
The night of loveless nights absconding sheets
Night of policemen's whistles in the streets
Night! cruel night when evening dresses quail
When voices whisper at the sick bedside
Night closed for evermore by bolts of steel
Night solitary night no star no guide!

See in your eyes and heart and in the sky
The blurry cosmos flaring suddenly
The fissure swelling tight and luminous
As if some tawny beast with idle claws
Had crushed the night and shredded it (although
Dawn will be watery, the flood-tide slow)
The brittle crystal's shot with nerves and veins
Fault-lines that mime the serpent's writhing turns
That roll and intertwine in a strange dawn's
Pale glimmer. Likewise when the player tired
Of turning over each symbolic card
Sees cruel daybreak light the portico
Then half-forgotten thoughts and yearnings go
Like torn fans dropped in upstairs corridors.

So hush put down your pen and close your ears
To slow and heavy steps that mount the stairs
The night grows pallid but the dawn appears
Like moths dead at the base of chandeliers.

Une tempête de fantômes sacrifie
Tes yeux qui les défient aux larmes du désir.
Quant au ciel, plus fané qu'une photographie
Usée par les regards, il n'est qu'un long loisir.

Appelle la sirène et l'étoile à grands cris
Si tu ne peux dormir bouche close et mains jointes
Ainsi qu'un chevalier de pierre qui sourit
À voir le ciel sans dieux et les enfers sans plainte.

Ô Révolte!

A phantom storm gives your defiant eyes
To passion's tear-drops as a sacrifice.
Heaven's a faded photo, worn away
By scrutiny, a mere long holiday.

Cry out call up the mermaid and the star
If you can't sleep hands clasped lips closed as well
A knight in stone observing debonair
A godless sky an uncomplaining hell.

RISE UP!

LOVER

YOUKI FOUJITA

FONTAINE

La fontaine brisée m'a dit quelle était sa vie
Toujours mouillée toujours pleurant
Et les terrifiantes histoires que raconte l'eau
Quand elle sort de terre
Les poissons monstrueux qu'elle a portés
Et patati et patata
Ce n'est pas une vie rose
Que la vie d'une fontaine brisée.

SOIR

Jadis un cœur battait dans cette poitrine
Il ne battait que pour elle
Le cœur bat toujours mais on ne sait plus pourquoi

Celui-là a clos ses lèvres à jamais
Il ne dit plus Il ne dira jamais plus
le mot amour

Peut-être le cœur bat-il toujours pour elle
Il bat sûrement encore pour elle
Mais il bat dans le silence

Ce doit être une triste nuit
Que la nuit de celui-là
Qui écoute battre son cœur

FOUNTAIN

The shattered fountain told me about its life
Always wet always weeping
And the terrifying tales that water tells
When it comes out of the ground
The monstrous fishes it has had in it
Di da di da
It's no bed of roses
The life of a shattered fountain.

EVENING

A heart used to beat in this breast
Beating only for her
The heart still beats but no-one knows why

He has closed his lips for ever
He never says He will never say again
the word love

Perhaps the heart still beats for her
Surely it still beats for her
But it beats in silence

It must be a sad night
This night of his
Listening to his heart beating

Il l'écoute il bat comme aux grands jours
Comme aux jours délicieux
Comme aux jours d'illusion

Mais l'amour n'a plus le droit de se révéler
Par la parole de ce veilleur acharné
Obstiné à aimer et à souffrir

Et si elle aussi a un cœur
Un soir elle viendra à pas de loup
Fermer ces yeux qui fixent son image dans l'obscurité

Et mettre sur le silence de cet amour
Le silence immense et sifflant du sommeil
Mais alors elle apparaîtra dans un rêve
Et tout sera à recommencer.

À L'AUBE

Le matin s'écroule comme une pile d'assiettes
En milliers de tessons de porcelaine et d'heures
Et de carillons
Et de cascades
Jusque sur le zinc de ce bistro très pauvre
Où les étoiles persistent dans la nuit du café

Elle n'est pas pauvre
Celle-là dans sa robe de soirée souillée de boue
Mais riche des réalités du matin
De l'ivresse de son sang
Et du parfum de son haleine que nulle insomnie ne peut altérer

He listens it beats like in the great days
Like in the delicious days
Like in the days of delusion

But love is no longer allowed to show itself
By order of this desperate insomniac
Hell-bent on loving and suffering

And if she too has a heart
One evening she'll come tiptoeing up
To close these eyes that pinpoint her image in the dark

And to cap the silence of this love
With the immense whistling silence of sleep
But then she will re-appear in a dream
And it'll all have to start over again.

AT DAWN

Morning shatters like a pile of dishes
Into thousands of shards of china and of hours
And peals of bells
And waterfalls
Down to the zinc counter of this beggars' bar
Where the stars persist in the coffee-cup night.

She is no beggar
That one in her mud-soiled evening gown
But rich with the morning's realities
The intoxication of her blood
And the scent of her breath that no insomnia can alter

Riche d'elle-même et de tous les matins
Passés présents et futurs
Riche d'elle-même et du sommeil qui la gagne
Du sommeil rigide comme un acajou
Du sommeil et du matin et d'elle-même
Et de toute sa vie qui ne se compte
Que par matinées, aubes éclatantes
cascades, sommeils,
Nuits vivantes

Elle est riche celle-là
Même si elle tend la main
Et doit dormir au frais matin
Dans sa robe crottée
sur un lit de désert.

NUITS

Femmes de grand air
Femmes de plein vent
Est-ce que la nuit est douce pour vous

Femmes de plein vent
Rôdeuses rencontrées à l'aube
Est-ce que la nuit ne vous déchire pas

Femmes de grand air
Laboureuses perdues dans les plaines
Est-ce que la nuit est une moisson pour vous

Rich with herself and all the mornings
Past present and future
Rich with herself and the sleep that overtakes her
Sleep stiff as mahogany
Sleep and morning and herself
And her whole life which is reckoned only
In mornings, brilliant dawns
Waterfalls, sleeps,
Living nights

She's rich, that one
Even if she holds out her hand
And must sleep in morning chill
In her muddy dress
On a folding bed.

NIGHTS

Women of great airs
Women of fresh winds
Is the night kind for you

Women of fresh winds
Rovers met at dawn
Doesn't the night hurt you

Women of great airs
Labourers lost in the plains
Is night your harvest-time

Femmes de plein vent
Marchandes de poissons aux mains crevassées
Est-ce que la nuit coule vite pour vous

Femmes réveillées au petit jour
Femmes traînant au travail des pieds meurtris
Est-ce que la nuit est sans écho pour vous

La nuit est-elle douce?
La nuit vous déchire-t-elle?
Moissonnez-vous la nuit?
La nuit coule-t-elle vite pour vous?

Femmes de grand air
Femmes de plein vent
Femmes de la nuit de l'aube et du jour
Rôdeuses laboureuses poissonnières
Aimez-vous le plein air
Aimez-vous le grand vent?

LE LOUP

Le loup n'a plus les dents longues
au temps des aubépines
Les yeux lueurs de brasier
Éclatantes étoiles
Figures de lac et de torrent
Neige forêt
Et sur tout cela comme dans les images
La zébrure d'un ruisseau de sang
Un traîneau fuyant au loin vers les forêts

Women of fresh winds
Fishmongers with chapped hands
Does night go fast for you

Women woken before dawn
Women dragging bruised feet to work
Has night no echo for you

Is the night kind?
Does the night hurt you?
Do you harvest at night?
Does night run fast for you?

Women of great airs
Women of fresh winds
Women of night of dawn and of day
Rovers labourers fishmongers
Do you like the fresh air?
Do you like the great wind?

THE WOLF

The wolf no longer has long teeth
In the time of hawthorns
Brazier-glow eyes
Flashing stars
Forms of lake and torrent
Snow forest
And on all of that as in images
The zebra-stripe of a stream of blood
A sleigh fleeing far off to the forests

La voix d'une petite fille
Loup y es-tu n'y es-tu pas
au temps des aubépines
au temps des pommes de pin.

MOURIR

Pour mourir sans regret il faut être si lasse
Pour mourir sans regret des désirs oubliés
Pour mourir sans chagrin pour mourir sans pitié
Faut-il détruire aussi les mains les yeux les faces

Celles-là qui sont nées choisies parmi les races
avec un cœur violent par nul amour plié
avec des membres durs que rien ne peut lier
Savent chercher la mort parmi les tombes basses

Mais celles qui aimaient celles qui dans leurs bras
surent garder parfois dans la froideur des draps
L'amant ou le mari jusqu'à défier les ombres

Fermeront leurs deux yeux par une nuit sans feux
Et jetant leur amour comme un dernier enjeu
Connaîtront le repos creux comme les décombres.

The voice of a little girl
Wolf are you there aren't you there
In the time of hawthorns
In the time of pinecones.

DYING

To die without regret means being so soft
Regretting no desires that slipped away
To die with neither pity nor dismay
Must hands eyes faces all be written off

Those women born elect among the races
With heart so violent no love can fold
With limbs so hard no tying-down can hold
Know to seek death in the low burial-places

But those who loved who many times embraced
Lover or husband often mounting guard
In the cold bed-sheets to defy the shades

In fireless night shall close their two eyes shut
And throwing down their love like one last bet
Shall know repose as deep as tips of waste.

LE BEL APRÈS-MINUIT

Plus blanche que la neige et les cristaux de sel
La flore de la nuit épanouit ses pétales
Et grandit remplissant les espaces du ciel
Où tel cheval d'azur hennit rue et détale

Vers des prairies semées de récentes étoiles
à travers des moissons d'astres et de reflets
Du feu de quatre fers éclaboussant les voiles
Il plonge au plus profond des ténèbres de lait

Déroulant le ruban des cycles abolis
Les plus courts fléchissant au poids des crépuscules
Pour avoir de trop près soleils aux feux pâlis
approché ta rougeur de la Lyre et d'Hercule

Mais la lune à cette heure en robe de mariée
Traîne à ses talons blancs la nébuleuse et blanc
blanc comme le matin sur la mer pétrifiée
Le bélier de l'aurore apprête son élan

La comète à son front a mis ses étincelles
Belle négresse ô lune où vas-tu d'un pas lent
Retrouver ton époux aux yeux de mirabelle
Dont Vénus bassina le lit d'un corps galant

Champagnes ruisselez dans les constellations
Si les vins sont pareils aux étoiles liquides
Retrouvons ô Bourgogne en toi la création
Des monstres fabuleux de l'éther et du vide

Nous ferons apparaître en pressant les raisins
Mercure et Jupiter et le Cancer et l'Ourse
En dépit des flambeaux reflétés dans le vin
Et du soleil baigné dans la fraîcheur des sources

BEAUTIFUL AFTER-MIDNIGHT

Whiter than the snow or the crystals of salt
Flowers of night are spreading wide their petals
Growing in the sky to fill the spaces of the vault
Where a blue horse neighs, kicks, heads for meadows

And grasslands sown with newly minted stars
Through harvests of pinpoints and reflected light
Spattering the sails with its four horseshoes' flares
Plunging in deepest shadows milky-white

Rolling out the ribbon of rhythms long since dead
The shortest buckling with the weight of day's last fire
Suns paled and faded that went too near the red
Glow of the constellations Hercules and Lyre

Even now the moon who is robed as a bride
Drags in her white claws the misty one and white
White as the morning on ocean petrified
The ram of the dawn prepares his dashing flight

The comet is wearing its sparklers on its brows
You moon black and beautiful moving slow ahead
Where do you meet your golden-plum-eyed spouse?
With a splendid body Venus warmed his bed

You champagnes go streaming through the constellations
If wines are similar to liquid stars
Then Burgundy in you let's recover the creation
Of fairytale monsters, the ether, empty spheres.

Cancer and the Bear, Mercury and Jupiter,
As we press the vintage we shall make them shine
Never mind the sun bathed in fresh spring-water
Never mind the torches reflected in the wine

Toi bel après-minuit escorté de légendes
Entraîne encore un couple aux valses du désir
afin que le buveur lassé te redemande
D'emplir son verre avec le sang des souvenirs.

LA ROSE AU BORD DE SEINE

La rose qui fleurit
aux berges de la Seine
Fleurit après minuit
sur les pelouses naines

Sur les pelouses naines
où danse le sommeil
où chantent les sirènes
Près Pontoise et Corbeil

Près Pontoise et Corbeil
à la pêche à la ligne
Près Thommery et Creil
où chantent les vieux cygnes

où chantent les vieux cygnes
où s'échouent les noyés
Si l'amour est indigne
et se fait monnayer

Et se fait monnayer
Là où fleurit la rose
Faudra bien la payer
Si l'on aime sans cause

Beautiful after-midnight with the legends in your train
Draw another couple to the waltzes of desire
Till the weary drinker shall ask you once again
To fill up his glass with blood of memory's fire!

THE ROSE BY THE SEINE

There's a rose that flowers
All along the Seine
In the wee small hours
On each tiny lawn

On each tiny lawn
Where the slumbers play
To the siren song
By Pontoise and Corbeil

By Pontoise and Corbeil
Fishing rods fishing lines
By Thommery and Creil
And the crooning swans

And the old swans crooning
Where the drowned go down
If love is demeaning
And cashed in for coin

And cashed in for coin
Where the rosebush flowers
You must pay for the rose
If you love without cause

Si l'on aime sans cause
Sans cause elle a fleuri
Elle a fleuri la rose
En Seine près Paris

En Seine près Paris
Flottez joyeux cadavres
Doux amants et maris
Jusqu'en rade du Havre

Jusqu'en rade du Havre
où s'arment les vapeurs
C'est l'amour qui vous navre
C'est la mort qui fait peur.

PAS VU ÇA

Pas vu la comète
Pas vu la belle étoile
Pas vu tout ça

Pas vu la mer en flacon
Pas vu la montagne à l'envers
Pas vu tant que ça

Mais vu deux beaux yeux
Vu une belle bouche éclatante
Vu bien mieux que ça.

If you love without cause
Without cause it flowers
The flowering rose
On the Seine by Paris

On the Seine by Paris
Float you blithe cadavers
Sweet husbands and lovers
To the wharves of Le Havre

To the wharves of Le Havre
Where the warships berth
You are wounded in love
And our fear is death.

DIDN'T SEE THAT

Didn't see the comet
Didn't see the lovely star
Didn't see all that

Didn't see the sea in a bottle
Didn't see the mountain inside-out
Didn't see that much. But...

Saw two lovely eyes
Saw a lovely gorgeous mouth
Saw much better than that.

LE RÊVE DANS UNE CAVE

Tant de flacons étaient brisés dans cette cave
que l'odeur du vin bu par le sable montait
Comme un brouillard d'octobre au-dessus des vieux quais
Et les murs salpêtrés étaient jaunes de lave

L'araignée en filant sa toile balançait
son ventre de goulaffe enflé par ces fumées
ainsi qu'une frégate à l'heure où la marée
clapote et crève en l'ombre avec un bruit d'abcès

Belle frégate au nom fabuleux d'amoureuse
Ta sirène à la proue aux cheveux bien peignés
T'aurait-elle livrée aux crocs des araignées
que tu parus soudain dans la toile et nombreuses

Tes voiles que gonflaient d'infimes aquilons
Te poussaient toute blanche à l'assaut des ténèbres
noires comme une mer agitée et que zèbre
L'écume qui s'enroule au cou des tourbillons

Belle frégate blanche autant qu'une chemise
Par une lavandière oubliée dans un champ
Par une nuit sans astre et sur un fil séchant
Belle frégate vogue aux merveilles promises

Car on n'entend nul autre bruit dans ce cachot
que l'eau qui pleure au sein des conduites sonores
Et que le bruit des pas montant montant encore
D'un attardé qui rêve aux douceurs d'un lit chaud.

THE DREAM IN A CELLAR

So many bottles shattered in this cellar.
The wine-soaked sand gave off a rising smell,
Like fog above old quaysides in the fall,
And the saltpetred walls were lava-yellow.

The spider span its thread and poised its greedy
Paunch that these aromatics magnified,
Just as a ship does, when the clacking tide
Is popping like an abscess in the shadow.

Fine ship, that sleek-haired siren on your prow
(Your name in legend is a loving lady's) –
Would she have left you in the jaws of spiders?
Abruptly you were in the web – and how

Crowding, and swelled by base north winds, your sails
Pushed you, white ship, to wrestle the tenebrous
Black of an angry sea whipped up to zebras
By foam that twists about the neck of squalls.

Fine ship, as white as any shirt a laundress
Left hanging on the line, abandoned careless,
Out in the meadow when the night was starless:
Set sail, fine ship, towards the promised wonders!

No sound inside the dungeon. Just that tread.
Water sobs on the bosom of the plumbing.
Someone, kept late, is climbing, climbing, coming,
Dreaming the sweetness of a well-warmed bed.

L'OISEAU MÉCANIQUE

L'oiseau tête brûlée
Qui chantait la nuit
Qui réveillait l'enfant
Qui perdait ses plumes dans l'encrier

L'oiseau pattes de 7 lieues
Qui cassait les assiettes
Qui dévastait les chapeaux
Qui revenait de Suresnes

L'oiseau l'oiseau mécanique
A perdu sa clef
Sa clef des champs
Sa clef de voûte

Voilà pourquoi il ne chante plus.

LA CHANSON DU PETIT JOUR

La bague au doigt
que vous m'aviez donnée
Je ne sais si je dois
si je dois pardonner.

Dans la ville de Lille
Ils s'étaient séparés
Adieu! et par la ville
Tous deux étaient allés

Au labeur de la mine
Il noircissait ses mains

THE MECHANICAL BIRD

The burnt-head bird
That sang in the night
That woke up the child
That lost its quills in the ink

The bird with the 7-league feet
That broke the plates
That ruined the hats
Came back from Suresnes

The bird the mechanical bird
Has lost its key
The key of the fields
The key of the vault

That's why it stopped singing.

DAYBREAK SONG

The ring on my finger
The one you had given
I wonder I wonder
Must that be forgiven?

In Lille they broke up
In the city of Lille
Went this way and that way
And parted, farewell

A labouring miner
Hands black to the bone

Du poussier pour l'angine
Du caillou pour la faim.

La bague au doigt
que vous m'aviez donnée
Je ne sais si je dois
si je dois pardonner.

Beaucoup souffraient pour elle
Elle avait de beaux yeux
Et qu'elle était donc belle
Avec ses blonds cheveux

Si belle que pour elle
Beaucoup aimaient pleurer
amour à la cruelle
Vous nous réunirez

La bague au doigt
que vous m'aviez donnée
Je ne sais si je dois
si je dois pardonner

Il est mort en Décembre
noirci par le charbon
à l'heure où dans la chambre
auprès du feu fait bon

Il pourrit dans la terre
quelque part dans le nord
où l'on boit de la bière
Et tant pis pour les morts

La bague au doigt
que vous m'aviez donnée

He had dust for angina
For hunger a stone

The ring on my finger
The one you had given
I wonder I wonder
Must that be forgiven?

For her many suffered
Her face was so fair
And she was so pretty
The gold of her hair

And she was so pretty
They all loved to blubber
Dear love you are haughty
You'll bring us together.

The ring on my finger
The one you had given
I wonder I wonder
Must that be forgiven?

He died in December
All blackened with grime
Warm fire in the parlour
The welcoming time

It was somewhere up north
Where they sup the brown ale
He rots in the earth
Let the dead go to hell

The ring on my finger
The one you had given

Je ne sais si je dois
si je dois pardonner

Eh bien tant mieux pour elle
Et bien tant pis pour lui
Sachez vivre pucelles
Une vie sans ennui

Soyez riches méchantes
Et laissez dans vos cœurs
tomber des larmes lentes
En gardant les yeux rieurs

La bague au doigt
que vous m'aviez donnée
Je ne sais si je dois
si je dois pardonner

LE BEAU JARDIN

au milieu du jardin se dresse la volière
où des toucans criards raillent les perroquets
et dans la tour en ruine accablée sous le lierre
Les yeux ronds d'un hibou allument des quinquets

Quand il fait jour dans les allées un éléphant
Mécanique s'agite avec des pas d'homme ivre
La biche avec audace y précède son faon
Et l'heure sur l'horloge est lente à se survivre

I wonder I wonder
Must that be forgiven?

So she was in clover
His fortunes were failing
Girls, here's how to go for
A life of plain sailing

Be rich be disgraceful
Weep deep slow and long
But keep up a face full
Of laughter and song

The ring on my finger
The one you had given,
I wonder I wonder
Must that be forgiven?

THE BEAUTIFUL GARDEN

Right in the middle's the aviary.
Mobbing the parrots, toucans howl.
The old tower crumbles under ivy.
Flaring, the round eyes of an owl.

Like a drunk by day in the tree-lined walks
A mechanical elephant sways and shakes.
The doe goes boldly ahead of her fawn
The hour on the clock lives tardily on.

L'arôme du café flotte dans la cuisine
où le feu ronfle et chante au ventre du fourneau
où le couteau planté dans le beurre s'incline
vers l'oignon parfumé et le pain de gruau

C'est une carte postale
qui arrive de très loin
Voyageur boucle ta malle
Et repars sur ton chemin

adieu volière jardin
que l'on parcourut en rêve
Redonnez-moi mon gourdin
Il est l'heure, marche ou crève

Chantant la gloire des blondes
s'en vont les gais chemineaux
Les trains sifflent par le monde
Sur la mer vont les bateaux

Mais vous en verrez bien d'autres
Des villes aux toits d'acier
Des vins qui vaudront le nôtre
Flatteront votre gosier

Mais quel est donc votre nom
Ce nom est celui d'une autre
ne disant ni oui ni non
vous ne saurez pas le nôtre

En arrivant à l'étape
Demandez à l'hôtelier
De vous mettre sur la nappe
Le bon vin de son cellier

In the kitchen smelling of coffee-beans
The fire in the stove's belly snores and sings.
The knife that's stuck in the butter leans
To the wheat-loaf and pungent onion-rings.

From a far distant place
Here's a postcard today
Time to pack up your case
To be on your way

Goodbye cage and park
In a dream we have passed
Once again my stout stick
Get going or bust

Jolly tramps sing refrains
To the glory of blondes
The globe whistles with trains
Ships are crossing the ponds

You'll see lots more cities
Of steel roofs and towers
Soothe your epiglottis
With wines good as ours

But what is your name
Here's the name of another
Don't deny or confirm
You shan't know ours either

While pausing from travel
You'll ask the hotelier
To place on your table
Good wine from his cellar

Si vous renversez le verre
vous en boirez un second
Et quitte à rouler par terre
vous viderez le flacon

Tandis que le jardin peuplé de beaux oiseaux
Dormira sous la lune et l'ombre des glycines
En mêlant au parfum des fleurs sous les arceaux
L'arôme du café sortant de la cuisine.

CHANT DES CENT MILLE

au temps des Tournesols
au temps des Rosalies
Pierre Jacques et Paul
ont bu jusqu'à la lie
chante le rossignol

Le rossignol est imbécile
De chanter à perdre l'haleine
après une viennent cent mille
sur la grand'route de la plaine

Mais à la cent mille et unième
se terminera le cortège
Le vin est bu mais je vous aime
Il est trop tard voici la neige
au revoir cent mille et unième
Tu fus semblable à la première
Et l'on sait bien que ce qu'on sème
Fera le pain pour ceux derrière

If you knock back the glass
You'll drink a glass more
You'll drink the whole flask
If you don't hit the floor

The garden stocked with feathered swells
Sleeps in the moon's wistaria-shade.
To notes of flowers from the arcade
The kitchen adds its coffee-smells.

SONG OF THE MILLION

in the Sunflower spell
with the sweet Rosalies
Jack Peter and Paul
drank down to the lees
sings the nightingale

silly nightingale fellow
sings his breath all away
there's a million to follow
one along the wide way

But the millionth and one
shall be last in the queue
too late snow's coming on
wine's all drunk I love you
goodbye millionth and one
you're just like her who led
sure the seed that we've sown
gives the hindmost their bread

Pour ceux derrière qui s'en viennent
Les cent mille au nom de vengeance
chacun son jour chacun la sienne
Et sur qui venger vos souffrances

> au temps des Tournesols
> au temps des Rosalies
> Meure le rossignol
> Et meurent de folie
> Pierre Jacques et Paul

Il reviendra d'autres cent mille
jouant encore à pile ou face
Dites-leur face et tombe pile
Et reprenez votre besace

Et reprenez votre chemise
Et reprenez votre folie
Fermez la porte des églises
Et pourtant elle était jolie

jolie et folle et désirable
Mais de ses lèvres sans sourire
ne tombaient que mots raisonnables
comme des sous en tirelire

Trop riche enfant de solitude
Endormez-vous hors de vos songes
Cœur sec cœur mort sans inquiétude
votre sagesse était mensonge

> Pierre Jacques et Paul
> ont bu jusqu'à la lie
> Le vin dur à plein bol
> au temps des Rosalies
> au temps des Tournesols

hindmost coming this way
million eager for vengeance
each his own each his day
who's your mark for comeuppance

in the Sunflower spell
with the sweet Rosalies
you can die nightingale
die crazily please
Jack Peter and Paul

Million others will come
heads and tails will flip
you call tails it falls heads
and you take up your scrip

and you take up your shirt
and your weird craziness
you shut tight every church
she was lovely oh yes

lovely crazy loveable
but her smiles were never frank
all her words were sensible
pennies in the piggy-bank

too rich child of loneliness
sleep beyond your reverie
dry heart dying no distress
your good manners told a lie

Jack Peter and Paul
drank down to the lees
hard wine in full bowl
with the sweet Rosalies
in the Sunflower spell

PIERRE À PIERRE

Pierre à pierre et pied à pied
Et cœur à cœur et tête à tête
Les beaux jours sont passés

Fil à fil et feuille à feuille
Et un à un et seul à seul
Les jours sont beaux et ne passent pas

Grain à grain corps à corps
Et côte à côte et main à main
Bien malin qui gagnera la bataille

Pierre à grain et seule à un
Et main à cœur et tête à cœur
L'amour est vaste comme le monde.

SUR LA ROUTE

Sur la route parfois on rencontre des vignes
Dont les raisins mûris sont à portée de main
Qu'ils sont bons! Et partons où serons-nous demain?
Car la feuille ressemble à la main par les lignes.

Mais chérissons le vin où se lisent les signes
sacrés de la jeunesse et des désirs humains
Le verre est bu, partons reprenons le chemin
qui naît au chant du coq et meurt au chant du cygne

Il reste cependant l'empreinte de nos verres
sur la nappe tracée. Aux mains des lavandières
La tache partira bientôt au fil de l'eau.

STONE TO STONE

Stone to stone and foot to foot
And heart to heart and head to head
The good days are past

Thread by thread and leaf by leaf
And one by one and lone by lone
The days are good they do not pass

Seed to seed body to body
And side by side and hand in hand
Cunning is the one who'll win the battle

Stone to seed and lone by one
And hand on heart and head to heart
Love is enormous as the world.

ON THE ROAD

On the road now and then we may come across vines
And the grapes are all ripe, just an arm's length away
Aren't they good! Let's be off, who knows where in a day?
For the leaf's like a hand, with the same little lines.

But let's cherish the vine with its numinous signs
Runes of youth and of human desire on display
Now the glass is drunk dry let's get back on our way
At the cockcrow it blooms, in the swan-song declines

Yet the mark of our glasses imprinted remains
On the tablecloth. Under the laundresses' hands
Running water will rapidly banish the stains.

Ainsi vont les serments belle fille qui chantes
Pour trinquer à plaisir en l'honneur des méchantes
Remplissez notre verre aux bondes des tonneaux.

LE MORT QUI PARLE

Quand j'ai perdu ma bien-aimée
Elle était si fraîche
que j'admirais d'avance son visage
Sous les voiles de deuil

je perdis du même coup
mes trois enfants
mon buffet directoire
mon salon Louis XV
Et ci et ça et bien d'autres choses
Et toute ma fortune
Voilà ce qu'il a dit le mort
En somme il avait perdu la vie
De quel droit parlait-il ainsi
Qui l'avait autorisé à prendre la parole?
on se demande de quoi les morts se mêlent maintenant
Pourquoi parlait-il
oui pourquoi
De quel droit
Quel insolent ce mort!

That's how promises vanish my lovely who stands
At the bung with a song come and fill up our glass
We shall drink as we choose to each mischievous lass

DEAD MAN SPEAKING

When I lost my darling
She was so fresh
that I admired her face in advance
Under her funeral veil

I lost at the same moment
my three children
my directoire sideboard
my Louis Quinze drawing-room
And this and that and much more
And my entire fortune
That's what he said the dead man
In short he had lost his life
By what right did he talk like that
Who gave him leave to make a speech?
The things the dead get up to these days
Why did he speak
yes why
By what right
The insolence of this dead man!

DANS UN PETIT BATEAU

Dans un petit bateau
Une petite dame
Un petit matelot
Tient les petites rames

Ils s'en vont voyager
Sur un ruisseau tranquille
Sous un ciel passager
Et dormir dans une île

C'est aujourd'hui Dimanche
Il fait bon s'amuser
Se tenir par la hanche
Échanger des baisers

C'est ça la belle vie
Dimanche au bord de l'eau
Heureux ceux qui envient
Le petit matelot.

LA BELLE QUE VOILÀ

quand l'âge aura flétri ces yeux et cette bouche
quand trop de souvenirs alourdiront ce cœur
quand il ne restera pour bercer dans sa couche
ce corps aujourd'hui beau que des spectres moqueurs

quand la poussière infecte en recouvrant les choses
vêtira d'un linceul les désirs abolis
quand l'amour plus fané qu'en un livre une rose
ne sera plus qu'un nom sous des portraits pâlis

IN A LITTLE BOAT

In a little boat
Sits a little lady
At the little oars
Sits a little sailor

See them take a trip
On a quiet stream
In the sunlight sleep
On an island dream

One of those Sundays
Do as one pleases
Hold the love-handles
Give and get kisses

Life lived on Sundays
Down by the water
Happy who envies
That little sailor.

THAT LOVELY WOMAN

When age shall make those lips and eyes grow pale
When the heart's burdened down by memories
And when to lull those limbs now beautiful
None shall be left but ghosts that jeer and tease,

When filthy dust that covers all shall clothe
And fold in shrouds desire's abolished flame
When love as wilted as a dry-pressed rose
Shall hook on faded photographs its name

quand il sera trop tard pour n'être plus cruelle
quand l'écho des baisers et l'écho des serments
Décroîtront comme un pas la nuit dans une ruelle
ou le sifflet d'un train vers le noir firmament

quand sur les seins pendants le ventre qui se ride
Les mains aux doigts séchés durcies par les passions
Et lasses d'essuyer trop de larmes acides
Referont le bilan de leur dégradation

quand nul fard ne pourra mentir à ce visage
S'il se penche au miroir jadis trop complaisant
Pour se désaltérer comme au lac d'un mirage
Aux rêves du passé revécus au présent

La belle que voilà restera belle encore
Par la vertu d'un feu reflété constamment
aux vitres d'un château dont les salles sonores
seront hantées par ceux qui furent ses amants

La belle que voilà ainsi qu'une fontaine
Dont le flot toujours pur sur les marbres disjoints
S'écoule en entraînant d'ineffables sirènes
Pour perdre sa splendeur ne renoncera point

Rien ne disparaîtra des ciels qui se reflètent
Malgré la peau fripée et malgré les reins plats
Restera jalousée et présente à la fête
Jeune éternellement la belle que voilà

Tant de cœurs ont battu jadis à son attente
qu'une flamme est enclose en ce corps sans raison
qu'indigne de ces feux elle reste éclatante
Ainsi qu'à l'incendie survivent les tisons.

When it will be too late to make us kind
When echoes of each kiss and vow shall die
Like footsteps dwindling in a darkened wynd
Or a train whistling to the midnight sky

When hands that passion rendered dry and hard
By wrinkled abdomen and dangling teat
Weary of wiping all those acid tears
Shall check their degradation's balance-sheet

When no cosmetic can deceive this face
That leans towards a long-complaisant glass
As if to drink from a cool mirage-lake
Dreams that the present borrows from the past

That lovely woman shall be lovely still
By virtue of a fire that plays and plays
On windows of great echoing rooms, that will
Be haunted by her loves of bygone days

That lovely woman like a fountainhead
Streaming on slabs of marble always pure
By all her siren-train accompanied
Shall not renounce her glory evermore

Nor shall she vanish from reflected skies
Though loins are flattened skin is loosely hung
She shall go feasting, watched by envious eyes
That woman lovely and for ever young

So many hearts once in attendance beat
That in her limbs an unreal flame is sheathed.
Rising above its fires she dazzles yet,
A poker in a burnt-out house, unscathed.

MA SIRÈNE

Ma sirène est bleue comme les veines où elle nage
Pour l'instant elle dort sur la nacre
Et sur l'océan que je crée pour elle
Elle peut visiter les grottes magiques des îles saugrenues
Là des oiseaux très bêtes
conversent avec des crocodiles qui n'en finissent plus
Et les oiseaux très bêtes volent au-dessus de la sirène bleue
Les crocodiles retournent à leur boire
Et l'île n'en revient pas
ne revient pas d'où elle se trouve
où ma sirène et moi nous l'avons oubliée

Ma sirène a des étoiles très belles dans son ciel
Des étoiles blondes aux yeux noirs
Des étoiles rousses aux dents étincelantes
et des étoiles brunes aux beaux seins
Chaque nuit trois par trois
alternant la couleur de leurs cheveux
Ces étoiles visitent ma sirène
Cela fait beaucoup d'allées et venues dans le ciel
Mais le ciel de ma sirène n'est pas un ciel ordinaire

Ma sirène a sept bateaux sur son océan
Lundi Mardi Mercredi Jeudi Vendredi
Samedi et Dimanche
Les uns à vapeur les autres à voiles
Les uns rapides les autres lents
Mais tous beaux mais tous charmants
avec des marins connaissant leur métier

Ma sirène a des savons de toutes formes et de toutes couleurs
C'est pour laver sa jolie peau

MY MERMAID

My mermaid is blue as the channels she swims in
Just now she's asleep on the mother-of-pearl
And on the ocean I create for her
She can visit the superb grottoes of the Ludicrous Islands
Where some very silly birds
Chat to crocodiles who never leave off
And the very silly birds fly over the blue mermaid
The crocodiles turn back to their drinking
And the island never comes back
never comes back from where it is
where my mermaid and I have forgotten it

My mermaid has beautiful stars in her sky
Blonde stars with black eyes
Redhead stars with shining teeth
and brunette stars with lovely breasts
Every night three by three
alternating their hair colour
These stars call on my mermaid
Which makes a lot of coming and going in the sky
But my mermaid's sky is no ordinary sky

My mermaid has seven boats on her ocean
Monday Tuesday Wednesday Thursday Friday
Saturday and Sunday
Some steamboats some sailing-boats
Some fast some slow
But all beautiful and delightful
with sailors who know their business

My mermaid has soaps of every shape and colour
To wash her pretty skin

Ma sirène a beaucoup de savons
L'un pour les mains
L'autre pour les pieds
Un pour hier
Un pour demain
Un pour chacun des yeux
Et celui-là pour sa queue d'écailles
Et cet autre pour les cheveux
Et encore un pour son ventre
Et encore un pour ses reins

Ma sirène ne chante que pour moi
J'ai beau dire à mes amis de l'écouter
Personne ne l'entendit jamais
Excepté un, un seul
Mais bien qu'il ait l'air sincère
Je me méfie car il peut être menteur.

LITTÉRATURE

Je voudrais aujourd'hui écrire de beaux vers
Ainsi que j'en lisais quand j'étais à l'école
Ça me mettait parfois les rêves à l'envers
Il est possible aussi que je sois un peu folle

Mais compter tous ces mots accoupler ces syllabes
Me paraît un travail fastidieux de fourmi
J'y perdrais mon latin mon chinois mon arabe
Et même le sommeil mon serviable ami

My mermaid has so many soaps
One for her hands
Another for her feet
One for yesterday
One for today
One for each eye
And that one for her fish-tail
That one for her hair
Another for her belly
Another for her loins

My mermaid sings only for me
No use telling my friends to listen
No-one ever hears her
Except only one
But though he seems sincere
I mistrust him as he may be a liar.

LITERATURE

I'd like to pen the finest verse to-day
The sort of thing I used to read at school
It sometimes turned my dreams the other way
Call me a soppy thing perhaps a fool

But joining syllables in twos and threes
Word-counts the mincing labour of an ant
I'd lose my latin arabic chinese
Even my sleep my valued confidant

J'écrirai donc comme je parle et puis tant pis
Si quelque grammairien surgi de sa pénombre
Voulait me condamner avec hargne et dépit
Il est une autre science où je puis le confondre.

SECONDE CHANSON DE LA FLEUR DE SOUCI

Ayant dit ayant fait
Ce qui me plaît
Je vais à droite je vais à gauche
Et j'aime la fleur de souci

Je vais à droite je vais à gauche
Je bois du vin je bois de l'eau
Chantant faux mais chantant fort
Et j'aime la fleur de souci

Chantant faux mais chantant fort
Quand le diable y serait
Je l'inviterais
S'il aime la fleur de souci

Je l'inviterais
Comme j'invite tous les bons camarades
à partager mon verre et ma chanson
Et à vider nos verres sur la fleur de souci.

In fact I'll write the way I speak so there
If any lurking jumped-up pedant scouted
My work with spiteful sneers I'd bring to bear
Another science and he'd soon be routed.

SECOND SONG OF THE WORRYGOLD

I did and I said
What entered my head
I go left I go right
I love the worrygold

I go left I go right
I drink wine drink water
Sing wrong but sing strong
I love the worrygold

Sing wrong but sing strong
If Old Nick were about
I'd call him out
If he loves the worrygold

I'd call him out
And all my good friends
To join in my glass and my song
Drain our glasses over the worrygold

Souci *means 'Worry' but also 'Marigold'*

SOYONS SÉRIEUSE

Quand la mort sur mes seins posera ses balances
J'espère, jours d'amour que vous l'emporterez
Sur les jours où mon cœur battant dans le silence
n'éveille que l'écho pour me désespérer

J'espère que ma bouche à tels baisers soumise
En vain n'aura jamais affronté ces baisers
que les nuits où l'amour déchira ma chemise
se déchiraient aussi pour nous éterniser

Mais les jours de tristesse où le branle des cloches
Du donjon de mon cœur résonne à mon poignet
Comme une pièce fausse au fond de quelque poche
Se rouille et tinte encore un agaçant regret

Je débarque en un port sans phare et sans vigie
Où je découvre au fond d'un boulevard venteux
Mes éternels désirs brûlant en effigie
Sans étincelles sans chaleur presque sans feu

Et je pénètre alors dans les châteaux farouches
Où des miroirs d'oubli semblent se refléter
De corridor en corridor et si ma bouche
veut boire c'est aux flots magiques du Léthé

Autour des hauts parloirs ainsi que des armures
Mes beaux jours alignés rêvent aux anciens temps
Et soudain surgissant des sombres encoignures
Des cloches par milliers agitent leurs battants

Et parallèlement le bronze heurtant le bronze
Entoure la rêveuse avec de durs barreaux
Tels que pour La Ballue en eût rêvé Louis onze
ou Bostock pour ses lions Lili pour ses oiseaux

WOMAN, BE SERIOUS

When death upon my breasts shall set his balance,
I hope, you days of love, you will triumph there
Over those days when my heart as it beats in silence
Wakes only the echo that brings me to despair

I hope that my lips which received and have undergone
Such kisses shall never have kissed to no purpose, never;
That the nights of love when my shirt was rent and torn
Were rent and torn themselves so we'd live for ever

But the days of sadness when the swing of the bells
Of my heart's inner keep resounds to the stroke of my wrist,
Just as, deep in a pocket, a coin that's minted false
Still rusts and discolours a chance regrettably missed

Gone ashore in a port with no watch and no harbour-light,
At the end of a windy street I discover a pyre:
My eternal desires have been torched on a bonfire-night
With no sparks and no heat and hardly any fire

Then I find my way into strongholds perhaps accursed
Where the mirrors of forgetting reflect each other
From one corridor to the next, and if I've a thirst
Then it's for the river Lethe's magic water

Ranged round the castle's parlours and armouries
Are my days of splendour, dreaming of former times
And suddenly rising from dark corners and crannies
Bells in their thousands busily stir their chimes

And in parallel the clanging of bronze on bronze
Surrounds the dreaming girl with such solid bars
As were dreamed up for La Ballue by Louis Onze
By Lili for birds, Bostock for his big-cat stars.

Infranchissable cage aux murailles sonores
Je trouve en mon tourment son remède et l'éther
bourdonne moins que ce royaume sans aurore
Cette forêt de sons et ce bruyant désert

Et défiant la mort sa faux et ses balances
Bien sûre jours d'amour que vous l'emporterez
sur les jours où mon cœur vibre dans le silence
mon propre cœur est seul à me désespérer.

BONJOUR BONSOIR

Il est nuit sois la flamme
Et la rougeur qui colore les nuages
Bonjour monsieur Bonsoir
Madame Vous ne paraissez pas votre âge

Qu'importe si vos étreintes
Font saigner les astres jumeaux
Qu'importe si ta face est peinte
si le givre brille aux rameaux

De granit ou de marbre
Votre âge paraîtra
Et l'ombre des grands arbres
sur vos tombeaux se promènera.

Cage of the echoing walls, impassable barrier,
In my torment I find its cure, and the ether is humming
Less than this kingdom of no dawn, this area
That's a forest of sounds, a sparsely inhabited thrumming

And defying death and his swinging scythe and his balance
Of course, you days of love, you will triumph there
Over the days when my heart vibrates in silence
It's only my own heart brings me to despair.

GOOD MORNING GOOD EVENING

It is night. Be the flame
Be the clouds' blush of rouge
Morning Sir, Evening Ma'am
You do not look your age

So what if each time you embrace
Blood oozes from the heavenly twins?
So what if you've a painted face
And on the branches hoar-frost shines?

Of granite or of marble
Your age shall seem to be
And on your tombs shall stroll the shade
Of many a mighty tree.

HISTOIRE DE FOLFANFIFRE

Folfanfifre à l'école ne savait rien
À l'école n'apprenait rien
Son maître étant un sot
Folfanfifre fut un sage
De ne rien apprendre de faux
Folfanfifre eut ce courage

Folfanfifre au bistro ne buvait rien
au bistro ne mangeait rien
Le patron étant un empoisonneur
Folfanfifre eut ainsi la chance
de ne pas mourir avant l'heure
Et de pouvoir encore danser une danse

Folfanfifre au bal dansa cette danse
se brisa un bras un pied une dent et la panse
Folfanfifre mourut à son heure
au même instant que ses compagnons
qui moururent empoisonnés par malheur
et par de mauvais champignons

Folfanfifre avait une maîtresse
Folfanfifre aimait ses caresses
Il avait beau n'être pas beau
Il était aimé mieux qu'un autre
Il s'en souvient en son tombeau
Ferez-vous de même en le vôtre?

Folfanfifre n'avait pas l'air heureux
Peut-être était-il heureux
Mais au point où il en est
Qu'est-ce que ça peut bien faire
Vous souvenez-vous qui il était
vous sa maîtresse et vous son frère?

TALE OF FOL-FAN-FIFER

Fol-Fan-Fifer went to school
Learning nothing there at all.
Blame the master he was plastered
Fol-Fan-Fifer was no fool
Learning anything untrue?
Not for him the cocky bastard

Fol-Fan-Fifer at the diner
Took no food nor drink at all
These were poisoned by the owner
Fol-Fan-Fifer's lucky chance
No untimely funeral
He survived to dance the dance

Fol-Fan-Fifer shimmied but
Broke his arm foot tooth and gut
Time for death his moment comes
In the same hour as his chums
Dying poisoned by mischance
Mushrooms evil champignons

Fol-Fan-Fifer's girlfriend gave
Him caresses he adores
No good being no good-looker
Loved him well her fancy took her
Looks back fondly from his grave
Will you do the same from yours?

Fol-Fan-Fifer looked unhappy
But consider where he's at
Just supposing he was happy
What would be the good of that?
You his girlfriend you his brother
Can you tell him from another?

Folfanfifre aimait l'arc-en-ciel
aimait aussi les hirondelles
Il aimait les feux d'artifice
Sans doute aussi le vieux bourgogne
l'argent l'or et le pain d'épices
Mais il n'aimait pas la besogne

Folfanfifre aurait voulu toujours dormir
Pour gagner son pain il se privait de dormir
Il est bien avancé à cette heure
Maintenant qu'il est au cercueil
Mais peut-être dort-il à cette heure
Peut-être même ne dort-il que d'un œil?

Folfanfifre qui n'apprit rien
Savait tout ne sachant rien
Nous non plus ne savons pas grand-chose
Si l'on nous aime et si nous aimons
Si c'est au rosier que fleurit la rose
Si plus que Folfanfifre nous existons

Folfanfifre ne se posait pas de questions
Et ne répondait jamais aux questions
Tout compte fait je puis le dire
Je crois bien qu'il avait raison
Moi j'ai raison de rire
Et vous de pleurer sans raison.

He loved rainbows in the sky
Loved the way the swallows fly
Loved the fireworks in July
Burgundy mature and red
Silver gold and gingerbread
Wasn't fond of penury

He'd have liked a life of sleep
Lost his sleep to earn his bread
Which has put him well ahead
Swaddled in his shroud below
Mightn't he be sleeping now
One eye open for a peep?

Fol-Fan-Fifer learning nothing
Knew it all and still knew nothing
Which of us can say he knows
If we're loved and if we're lovers
If the rose-bush bears the rose
If we are more real than he was?

Fol-Fan-Fifer never queried
Never answered any query
All in all I can declare it
I believe he had good reason.
I have reason to be merry,
You, to weep, for no good reason.

MON AMOUR PARLE-MOI

Quand tu m'aimes, qu'à tes étreintes
Je m'abandonne avec émoi
Pour calmer mes tourmentes mes craintes
   Mon amour parle-moi

Il faut peupler les nuits hostiles
Avec les cris de nos émois
Il faut charmer les nuits tranquilles
   Mon amour parle-moi

Dans la nuit vouée aux mauvais sorts
Des fantômes jettent l'effroi
Et toi si tu es un mort?
   Mon amour parle-moi

Si tu m'aimes il faut le dire
Il faut me prouver tes émois
Il faut me prouver ton délire
   Mon amour parle-moi

Même si tu dis des mensonges
Si tu simules ton émoi
Pour que le songe se prolonge
   Mon amour parle-moi

LOU LA REQUINE

I

Tu n'es ni beau ni riche,
Ton amour est un faix,

MY LOVE SPEAK TO ME

When we love and in your arms
I find ecstasy
Soothe my terrors and alarms
  My love speak to me

We must crowd the nights of threat
Shout our ecstasy
Must enchant the nights of rest
  My love speak to me

In the night of evil doom
Phantoms frighten me
What if you are dead and gone
  My love speak to me

If you love me then confess
Prove your ecstasy
Prove to me your wantonness
  My love speak to me

Even if you tell me lies
Faking ecstasy
Dream a dream that never dies
  My love speak to me

SHARK-WOMAN LOU

I

Not pretty nor rich
Your love is a drag

Par le mal qu'il me fait
Ton amour m'est fétiche

Laisse se rassir la miche
Dans le fond du buffet
Trop sincère en effet
Tu perds tout quand tu triches

Tu souffres sans le dire
Tu pleures dans ton rire
Tu es bien mon amant

Je suis Lou la rouquine
Je suis Lou la requine
Je t'aime éperdument

II

Pour le mal qu'il me fait
Ton amour m'est fétiche
Laisse rassir la miche
Dans le fond du buffet

Dans la nuit du café
La nébuleuse biche
Fuit dans le ciel en friche
Aux lueurs d'autodafé

Quand tu viens nuitamment
Rôder tel un dément
Près de Lou la coquine

It's done me such harm
It's a witch-doctor's charm

Let the last bit of bread
In the cupboard go stale
You're a touch too sincere
When you cheat you lose all

In silence you suffer
You laugh when you blubber
You're truly my lover

I'm ginger-top Lou
I'm super-shark Lou
I love you I do

II

It's done me such harm
It's a witch-doctor's charm
Let the last of the loaf
In the cupboard go off

In the coffee-bar night
The nebulous fawn
Flees to fallow-field dawn
By the flames' cruel light

When you come in the night
Like a madman you'll go
Round rascally Lou

Si tu lis l'avenir
Dis-moi quand va mourir
L'amour plus hérissé qu'un buisson d'églantines

III

Si la mort me coiffait
avec son peigne d'ambre
Le ciel serait défait
Juillet serait Décembre

Si la mort m'appelait
Elle deviendrait muette
Les murs de son palais
Tomberaient sur sa tête

Je ne veux pas mourir
De mon sang je suis ivre
aux autres de pourrir
à nous de leur survivre

Et nous pourrons chanter
Lou la douce requine
Son cœur et sa beauté
L'amour et l'églantine

La rose au bec de l'aigle
Exhalant ses parfums
et la saveur du seigle
et nos soifs et nos faims

Et que nos soifs ardentes
nos faims et nos désirs bel amant
chère amante ne puissent s'assouvir

If you have second sight
Tell me when will it die
This love no wild rose so pernickety grows

III

If death did my hair
With his comb of amber
The sky would despair
July'd be December

If death ever called me
He'd find he was mute
The walls of his palace
Would fall on his pate

I don't want to die
My blood sets me raving
Let others decay
We'll carry on living

We'll sing of the shark
The gentle shark Lou
Her beauty her heart
Wild rose and love too

In the beak of an eagle
A rose rides and wafts
The taste of the rye-grain
Our hungers and thirsts

Let our thirst that is burning
Dear soul-mate dear lover
Our hunger our yearning
Keep blazing for ever.

IV

Après moi mon amour, avec tant d'insistance
Tu appelles en rêve et désires me voir
que ton rêve m'atteint à travers la distance
Et que tu m'apparais à la chute du soir

J'admire ton amour et chéris ta constance
Ce n'est pas pour sept ans, comme un bris de miroir
Mais pour l'éternité qu'un regard sans prudence
a marqué ton destin du sceau de mon pouvoir

Je sais ce que je puis ordonner à ton cœur
Que ce cœur m'appartient et que jamais ne meurt
Le feu qui m'illumine autant qu'il te consume

Mais je suis ta victime autant que ton vainqueur
Et notre amour gagna, comme un fer, sa vigueur
Des chocs d'un lourd marteau sur une dure enclume.

CONTE DE FÉE

Il était un grand nombre de fois
Un homme qui aimait une femme
Il était un grand nombre de fois
Une femme qui aimait un homme
Il était un grand nombre de fois
Une femme et un homme
Qui n'aimaient pas celui et celle qui les aimaient

IV

Love, you call after me with such insistence,
Dreaming: a sight of me is your desire.
And so I read your dream across a distance:
as evening falls I see you, by me, here.

Awed by your love, I cherish your persistence.
Not just the seven years of a broken mirror,
But for all time, one look that knew no prudence
stamped on your fate the hallmark of my power.

I know what I can tell your heart to do:
your heart is mine and deathless is the flame
shining on me, no less consuming you.

I am your victor but no less your victim.
Our love has gained its strength like iron from
great hammer-blows on a hard anvil pounding.

FAIRY TALE

Once upon many many times
A man loved a woman
Once upon many many times
A woman loved a man
Once upon many many times
A woman and a man
Didn't love the man and woman who loved them

Il était une fois
Une seule fois peut-être
Une femme et un homme qui s'aimaient.

CHANSON-CAILLOU

J'arrive en chantant
Visage de bois visage de bois
Je pars en rêvant
Ô mon amour ô mon roi

Viennent les Printemps
Odeurs des bois odeurs des bois
à nous deux tuons le temps
Pour qu'il renaisse avec la joie

Eh quoi je suis toute seule
Cercueil de bois cercueil de bois
Ô mon amour ma chère gueule
Te souviens-tu de moi parfois?

Ô JEUNESSE

Ô jeunesse voici que les noces s'achèvent
Les convives s'en vont des tables du banquet
Les nappes sont tachées de vin et le parquet
Est blanchi par les pas des danseurs et des rêves

Once upon one time
Once upon perhaps only one time
A woman and a man loved each other.

PEBBLE-SONG

I arrive I'm singing
Wooden face wooden face
When I leave I'm dreaming
O my love my king my ace

Comes another may-time
Woody smells woody smells
Time to kill our playtime
Soon reborn with peal of bells

Hey I'm all alone now
Wooden coffin wooden coffin
O my love my own now
Think of me remember often

DAYS OF YOUTH

Days of youth the wedding is over
The guests are leaving the banquet
There's wine on the cloths, and the parquet
Is whitened by dancers and dreams.

Une vague a roulé des roses sur la grève
quelque amant malheureux jeta du haut du quai
Dans la mer en pleurant reliques et bouquets
Et les rois ont mangé la galette et la fève

Midi flambant fait pressentir le crépuscule
Le cimetière est plein d'amis qui se bousculent
que leur sommeil soit calme et leur mort sans rigueur

Mais tant qu'il restera du vin dans les bouteilles
qu'on emplisse mon verre et bouchant mes oreilles
J'écouterai monter l'océan dans mon cœur.

BAGATELLES

BAGATELLES

Vous reviendrez me voir, dit-elle
Quand vous serez riche à millions
Quand les roses de Bagatelle,
Sous la neige s'épanouiront.

Lavant le sable des rivières,
Brisant le quartz, ouvrant le tronc
Des caoutchoucs à la lisière
D'un enfer d'arbres aux fûts ronds,

Libérant des nids de pétrole,
Ou labourant les Alaskas,
Quatre-vingts ans, la terre molle
Cacha le trésor des Incas.

A wave strewed the foreshore with roses
Love's victim has hurled off the quayside
Weeping wretchedly keepsakes and posies
The kings ate the cake and the bean.

Flaming noon foreshadows the twilight
Friends jostle in graveyards to slumber
In peace and for death without stiffness

But while there's still wine in the bottles
Fill my glass and with ears stopped I'll listen
To my heart where the ocean is rising.

BAGATELLES

BAGATELLES

You'll come back to me, she said,
Rich as Croesus, when the rose
Down at Bagatelle shall spread
Buds and blossoms in the snows.

Washing loads of river-sand,
Breaking quartz to smithereens
Tapping rubber from a stand
Of infernal round-boled trees

Freeing up the beds of oil
Heavy work in the Alaskas
Eighty years in yielding soil
Hidden treasure of the Incas

Quand il revint, elle était morte,
Il était bête, il était vieux,
Mais les amants de cette sorte
Ne sont pas tellement nombreux.

Que fleurissent à Bagatelle
Les roses de poudre et frimas,
Mais que fleurissent surtout celles
Que l'on aime jusqu'au trépas.

LE NUAGE

Le nuage dit à l'indien:
«Tire sur moi tes flèches,
Je ne sentirai rien.»

«C'est vrai, rien ne t'ébrèche,
Répond le sauvage,
Mais vois mes tatouages!
Rien de pareil sur les nuages.»

CHANSONS BRÈVES

I

Depuis si longtemps que tu chantes
N'as-tu pas soif? N'as-tu pas faim?

He came back but she'd passed over.
He was old and cretinous.
Even so, this type of lover,
They are hardly numerous.

May there bloom at Bagatelle
Roses of the snow and frost
May those darlings bloom as well
That we love till life is lost.

THE CLOUD

Said a cloud in the sky
To a warlike brave
Let your arrows go zing
I won't feel a thing

Said the brave so bold
You cannot be holed
But here's where you lose
You have no tattoos.

SHORT SONGS

I

Aren't you hungry? Thirsty too?
You interminably croon.

J'ai soif! mais la fontaine est lente
J'ai faim! M'aimeras-tu demain?

II

Vous n'aviez pas ces yeux ma chère
Tout cet avril qui fut le nôtre
J'y lis une phrase étrangère
J'y vois le souvenir des autres

III

Ma jalousie est semblable à la neige
Elle est monotone et pourtant
Elle recouvre, elle protège
Toute la gloire du printemps.

CHANSON

De bon cœur, la bonne aventure,
Chante colombe, au fond du bois;
L'étoile baigne aux sources pures,
Trois par trois sont partis les mois,
De bon cœur, la bonne aventure.

Qu'elle était douce à son amant.
De bon cœur, la bonne aventure,
Allons à son enterrement;
Et qu'elle avait belle figure,
Qu'elle était douce à son amant.

Yes I am! The fountain's slow
Will you love me very soon?

II

All this April-time of ours,
Those were not my darling's eyes!
There I scanned a stranger's phrase,
Someone else's memories.

III

Like the snow, my jealousy
Is a tiresome, dreary thing.
Yet it cloaks protectively
All the glory of the spring.

SONG

In good heart, the future's fair,
Sing, you dove, deep in the wood,
Pure spring waters bathe a star,
Three times three the months have fled,
In good heart, the future's fair.

To her darling she was good,
In good heart, the future's fair,
Now in earth we'll see her laid;
And her face and form were fair,
To her darling she was good.

Il en aima bien mieux les autres,
Chante colombe au fond des bois;
Meurent prophète et ses apôtres,
On s'oubliera selon les lois.
On en aimera mieux les autres.

Vienne le jour des vieux bilans,
L'étoile baigne aux sources pures.
Qu'elle était douce à son amant,
De bon cœur, la bonne aventure.
Vienne le jour des vieux bilans.

Trois par trois sont partis les mois,
Qui se souvient encore d'elle?
Après trois fois trois ans, ma foi,
À la sienne reste fidèle,
Chante colombe, au fond des bois.

MINOTAURE
[Révue Littéraire]

À manger son propre sang
En tartine sur du pain

À boire l'eau de l'étang
Où les morts prennent leur bain

À prononcer des paroles
Nées de cœurs empoisonnés

Others more than her he'd cherish,
Sing, you dove, deep in the wood;
Prophets and apostles perish,
We'll forget, by rights we should.
Others more than her we'll cherish.

Check the figures, how they stood,
Pure spring waters bathe a star.
To her darling she was good,
In good heart, the future's fair.
Check the figures, how they stood.

Three times three the months have fled,
Who remembers her today?
Three times three years now, dear God,
Faithful to your darling stay,
Sing, you dove, deep in the wood.

MINOTAUR

[A literary magazine.]

He ate his own gore
On buttered sliced bread

He drank from the mere
Where wallow the dead

He uttered the phrases
Of hearts that were poisoned

À fréquenter les écoles
Des esprits emprisonnés

À marcher sur le chemin
Où l'on marche avec les mains

Le Minotaure a vieilli
Loin des siens et du pays

Il va retrouver les sphinx
Les licornes et les lynx

Qui lui disent il est tard
Déjà l'on ferme l'enceinte

L'homme salera ton lard
Dans un coin du labyrinthe

Mugis encore si tu peux
Minotaure de rien, Minotaure de peu.

LA REINE COUCHÉE DANS SON LIT

La Reine couchée dans son lit
Écoute un rossignol chanter
Écoute aussi la sentinelle
Qui fait les cent pas dans la cour

Enrolled in the classes
Of spirits imprisoned

He strolled on the strands
Where you stand on your hands

The minotaur's senile
A lonely old exile

He searches for sphinxes
For unicorns lynxes

Who tell him it's late
The labyrinth's barred

Behind its back gate
They'll pickle your lard

Won't you venture to roar
Little Minus-o-taur?

QUEEN IN BED

Queen in bed is listening
Nightingale she hears it sing
Hears the sentry pacing hard
Ten by ten one hundred yard
Loudly pacing palace guard

Cent pas par-ci, cent pas par-là
Une reine et un rossignol
Et le soldat qui sent le rhum
Dans la cour du royal palais

Le soldat couché dans son lit
N'écoute pas chanter la Reine
N'écoute pas le rossignol
Qui fait les cent pas dans la cour

Et le rossignol dans son nid
N'écoute pas la sentinelle
N'écoute pas même la Reine
Qui fait les cent pas dans la cour

Cent pas par-ci, cent pas par-là
Voilà bientôt quatre cents pas
Avec les cent pas du passant
Dans ce palais extravagant

SIRAMOUR

Semez, semez la graine
Aux jardins que j'avais.
Je parle ici de la sirène idéale et vivante,
de la maîtresse de l'écume et des moissons de la nuit
Où les constellations profondes comme des puits grincent
de toutes leurs poulies et renversent à pleins seaux sur
la terre et le sommeil un tonnerre de marguerites et
de pervenches.
Nous irons à Lisbonne, âme lourde et cœur gai,

Ten by ten one hundred yard
One queen and one nightingale
Sentry in the palace yard
Pacing pungent red rum smell

In his bed the sentinel
Heeds no singing queen at all
Listens to no nightingale
Pacing ten by ten the yard

In her nest the nightingale
Heeds no sentinel at all
Listens to no singing queen
Pacing ten by ten the yard

Hundred here a hundred there
Hundred more as someone passes
Very soon four hundred paces
Palaces are lavish places

SIREN-AMOUR

Sow seed in my garden
Sow seed it was thriving.
I speak of the ideal and living siren,
Mistress of the foam and the night harvests
Where the constellations as deep as wells creak in all
their pulleys and pour by the bucket-load on earth
and on sleep a thunder of pearls and of periwinkles.
To Lisbon we journey, soul sings and heart hardens

Cueillir la belladone aux jardins que j'avais.
Je parle ici de la sirène idéale et vivante,
Pas la figure de proue mais la figure de chair,
La vivante et l'insatiable,
Vous que nul ne pardonne,
Âme lourde et cœur gai,
Sirène de Lisbonne,
Lionne rousse aux aguets.
Je parle ici de la sirène idéale et vivante.
Jadis une sirène
À Lisbonne vivait.
Semez, semez la graine
Aux jardins que j'avais.

Que Lisbonne est jolie.
La fumée des vapeurs
Sous la brise mollie
Prend des formes de fleurs.

Nous irons à Lisbonne
Âme lourde et cœur gai,
Vous que nul ne pardonne,
Lionne rousse aux aguets.

Semez, semez la graine,
Je connais la chanson
Que chante la sirène
Au pied de la maison.

Nous irons à Lisbonne
Âme lourde et cœur gai,
Cueillir la belladone
Aux jardins que j'avais.

To pluck belladonna where once I had gardens.
I speak of the ideal and living siren,
Not the figure of the prow but the figure of flesh,
Living and insatiable,
You siren of Lisbon,
That nobody pardons,
Sharp lioness auburn,
Soul sings and heart hardens.
I speak of the ideal and living siren.
There once was a siren
In Lisbon was living.
Sow seed in my garden
Sow seed it was thriving.

Lisbon knows how to please.
The puffs and the steams
Are pulped by the breeze
And shaped into blooms.

We journey to Lisbon
Soul sings and heart hardens,
Sharp lioness auburn
That nobody pardons.

The seed's to be sown,
The siren's old ditty
She sings as I've known
Near a house in the city.

To Lisbon we journey
Soul sings and heart hardens,
To pluck belladonna
Where once I had gardens.

Il est minuit très noire,
La nuit toutes les fleurs,
Versez, versez à boire,
Sont de même couleur.

Je connais la sirène
Je connais sa chanson
Voyez sa robe traîne
Et charme les poissons.

Mais la graine qui germe
Connaîtra pas ses fleurs.
Chaque jour a son terme,
Chaque amour ses douleurs.

Tout en elle est semblable à l'eau, son élément,
Mais à l'eau de montagne et qui glace les membres
Du nageur qui s'y risque et devient son amant:
Il souffre. Il sombre. Il meurt dans ces flots de décembre.

Allongée dans son lit, le tain de son miroir,
Elle épouse docile un corps et son image,
Quitte à rendre à la terre un cadavre le soir.
Les oiseaux de sa rive ont un charmant ramage.

Cette eau qui désaltère est fatale au buveur.
On le retrouve mort auprès de quelque borne
Et d'un plus sûr poignard poignardé en plein cœur
Que celui que l'on trempe en cette onde qui s'orne

Des cristaux de la lune et de l'azur polaire
Et qui chante en coulant sur les fonds de cailloux
Et qui rugit au fond des gorges solitaires
Ainsi qu'une putain battue par son voyou.

At night all the flowers
Have only one hue
In the black midnight hours
Let's drink, me and you.

O siren I've known
Both you and your ditty:
That sweep of your gown
the fish think it pretty.

But the seed and the germ
Shall never bear flowers.
Each day has its term,
Each love has its tears.

She entirely resembles her element, water,
But it's high-mountain water that freezes the swimmer
Who plunges in deep and ends up as her lover:
He sinks and he dies in the waves of December.

Stretched long in her bed that's the black on her mirror
She marries quite meekly a corpse and its image;
The earth as dusk falls will receive a cadaver.
The birds on her banks sing a sweet tirra-lirra.

This thirst-quenching water brings death to the drinker
They find him again he is dead in some gully
And stabbed to the heart by a deadlier dagger
Than ever was dipped in this glittering water

That wears the moon-crystals and blue of the pole-star
And sings as it runs on the deep bed of pebbles
And roars in the deep inaccessible gorges
Like a whore beaten up by her cheap trashy fellow.

Mais celui-là qui peut, plongeur au cœur robuste,
Atteindre l'autre rive et sécher au soleil
Les gouttes scintillant sur ses reins et son buste
Et la boue des bas-fonds collée à ses orteils,

Est désormais trempé comme un poignard de mort,
Une lame de crime aux touches sans remède,
Un estoc de jadis pour redresseur de torts,
Plus dur que les aciers de Sheffield et Tolède.

Honneur à toi, Sirène, honneur à toi torrent,
Ô femme dont l'amour trempe une âme solide.
Qu'importe si ta bouche aux baisers effarants
Fut salée par les pleurs de tes amants avides.

Don Juan te rencontra avant les mille et trois.
C'est toi qui lui donnas son tourment et son charme,
C'est l'écho de tes chants qu'écoutaient dans sa voix
Celles qu'il abîmait dans l'amour et les larmes.

Les deux fils de Don Juan apprirent par tes lèvres,
Lord Byron le destin, le courage et l'orgueil,
Et Nerval où trouver le philtre d'outre-fièvres
Pour te ressusciter dans ses rêves en deuil.

Il est minuit au pied du château qui n'est ni celui de la Belle au bois dormant, ni le seul en Espagne, ni le roi des nuages mais celui dont les murailles dressées au sommet d'une montagne dominent la mer et la plaine et maints autres châteaux dont les tours blanchissent au loin comme les voiles perdues sur la mer. Il est minuit dans la plaine et sur la mer, il est minuit dans les constellations vues d'ici et voici que l'étoile, la tantôt noire, la tantôt bleue, surgit au-delà de l'écume éclatée comme un orage bas dans les ténèbres liquides. À ses rayons, la bouteille abandonnée dans l'herbe et les ajoncs s'illumine des voies lactées qu'elle paraît contenir et ne contient pas car, bien bouchée, elle

But one who jumps in with a spirit robust and
Dries out in the sun (having got right across)
All the glistening drops on his kidneys and chest and
The mud from the stream-bed that sticks to his toes,

Is annealed from now on like a murderous dagger,
A criminal blade for whose touch there's no healing,
A thrust from the past by a righteous avenger,
Steel solid as Sheffield and tough as Toledo.

All hail to you, Siren, and fast-flowing river,
You woman whose love is a strong soul's immersion!
Who cares if your mouth of the terrible kisses
Was salted by tears of importunate lovers?

A thousand and three were the trysts of Don Juan:
But first you endowed him with charms and with torment
Your lilting was heard (for his voice was an echo)
By the women he ruined with loving and weeping.

Don Juan's two sons from your lips took their lessons:
Lord Byron learnt courage, magnificence, destiny;
Nerval discovered the draught beyond fever
To bring you to life in his funeral reverie.

It's midnight below the castle which isn't Sleeping Beauty's or the only one in Spain or king of the clouds, but the one whose walls rise on a mountain peak and dominate the sea and the plain and many other castles whose towers shine far off like sails lost on the sea. It's midnight on plain and sea, midnight in the constellations to be seen from here, and look! the star, now black, now blue, is rising above the foam that splashes like a low storm in the dark waters. By its light, the bottle left in reeds and greenery shines with the milky ways it seems to contain and doesn't contain, since it is well stoppered and

recèle en ses flancs la sirène masquée, la captive et redoutable sirène masquée, celle qu'on nomme l'Inouïe dans les mers où jamais elle ne daigne chanter et la Fantomas dans les rêves. Et, vrai, vêtue du frac et du haut de forme, on l'imagine parcourant un bois de mauvais augure tandis que les musiques d'une fête lointaine somment vainement les échos de ramener à elles ce charmant travesti. On l'imagine encore, amazone, dans ce même bois, à l'automne, serrant contre elle un bouquet de roses trop épanouies dont les pétales s'envolent sous les efforts combinés du vent et du trot de son cheval.

Pour l'instant captive elle attend la délivrance dans sa prison bien bouchée par une main amoureuse, tandis qu'une lettre, non remise à son destinataire, moisit sur le sol. C'est l'heure où les dés et les horloges font des bruits singuliers qui étonnent les veilleurs. C'est l'heure où l'amant qui déshabille sa maîtresse s'étonne du crissement musical et inaccoutumé de la soie et du linge. Pâles et rêveurs, tous écoutent ces manifestations de l'invisible qui n'est que leurs pensées et leurs rêves et, ceux-là, sur les chiffres fatidiques et, ceux-ci, sur l'heure qui marqua jadis le rendez-vous manqué et, les derniers, sur l'éclat de la chair admirable éternisent quelques secondes leurs regards qui, soudain, voient loin, très loin au-delà des enjeux et des changements de date, au-delà des caresses et des serments, au-delà même des chants indéchiffrables des sirènes. Il est minuit sur le château, sur la plaine et sur la mer.

Il est minuit sur les jeux et les enjeux.
Il est minuit au cadran des horloges.
Il est minuit sur l'amour et sur les lettres égarées et la sirène chante, mais sa voix ne dépasse pas les parois de verre, mais le buveur survient et boit la chanson et libère la sirène, celle qu'on nomme l'Inouïe et qu'on nomme aussi la Fantomas.

Cigogne étoile aimée du silence et des sens
Baisers défunts des rois la lance désirée
Le cercle tracé sous les toits du ciel assassin
Par le sang sans vergogne et les roses et les fourrés

holds the masked mermaid, the formidable captive masked mermaid called Unheard-of in the seas where she declines to sing, and Fantomas in dreams. Indeed one pictures her in top hat and tails, moving through a wood of ill omen while distant festive music re-echoes but cannot coax back the cross-dressed charmer. One pictures her too, an amazon in the same wood, in autumn, clutching blown roses whose petals are scattered by the wind and by her horse's rhythmic trot.

Captive for now, she awaits release from the prison a loving hand has firmly sealed, while an undelivered letter rots on the ground. It's the time of night when dice and clocks make odd, surprising noises; when the lover undressing his mistress is surprised by the unaccustomed musical rustling of silk and linen. The pallid and the dreamers all listen to these revelations of the invisible which is merely their thoughts and dreams and, for those, the fateful numbers, for these,the hour of the missed rendezvous and for them all, the impact of the splendid flesh that for some seconds eternises their gaze, who suddenly see far, far beyond the hazards and changes of plan, beyond the caresses and promises, beyond even the indecipherable siren songs. It's midnight on castle, plain and sea.

It's midnight on gaming and gambling.
It's midnight on the dials of clocks.
It's midnight on love and lost letters and the siren sings, but her voice does not pass the glass partitions, but the drinker comes up and drinks the song and sets the siren free, the siren who is called Unheard-of and also Fantomas.

Stork star loved by silence and sense
Defunct kisses of kings the longed-for lance
Circle traced under roofs of assassin sky
By shameless blood and roses and thickening

Bourgogne naissante à l'aube d'un baiser
Bateaux encerclés intelligibles paroles du cercle
En trois segments martyrisé
Du signe plus reliant l'amant à sa maîtresse
L'hippocampe à la sirène
Et que nul ne les atteigne ni ne les sépare.
Que ceux qui le tenteraient
Soient confondus s'ils sont de mauvaise foi
Réduits à l'impuissance s'ils sont de bonne foi.
Que rien par ce cercle qui les isole
Ne sépare la sirène de l'hippocampe
L'hippocampe de la sirène
Et que dit-il lui:
Que rien ne l'atteigne elle
Dans sa beauté dans sa jeunesse dans sa santé
Dans sa fortune dans son bonheur et dans sa vie.

Que le buveur, ivre de la chanson, parte sur un chemin biscornu bordé d'arbres effrayants au bruit de la mer hurlant et gueulant et montant la plus formidable marée de tous les temps, non hors de son lit géographique, mais coulant d'un flux rapide hors de la bouteille renversée tandis que, libre, la sirène étendue sur le sol non loin de cette cataracte, considère l'étoile, la tantôt noire, la tantôt bleue, et s'imagine la reconnaître et la reconnaît en effet.

Ceci se passe, ne l'oublions pas, dans une véritable plaine, sur un véritable rivage, sous un véritable ciel. Et il s'agit d'une véritable bouteille et d'une véritable sirène, tandis que s'écoule une mer véritable qui emporte la lettre et monte à l'assaut du château.

Écoulement tumultueux du contenu de l'insondable bouteille. C'était pourtant une bouteille comme les autres et elle ne devait pas contenir plus de 80 centilitres et, pourtant, voilà que l'Océan tout entier jaillit de son goulot où adhèrent encore des fragments de cire.

Burgundy born in the daybreak of a kiss
Boats encircled intelligible words of the circle
martyred in three segments
Of the plus sign linking the lover to his mistress
The sea-horse to the mermaid
And let nothing injure them nor separate them
Let those who would try
Be confounded if in bad faith
Rendered impotent if in good faith
Let nothing in this circle that sets them apart
Separate the mermaid from the sea-horse
The sea-horse from the mermaid
And what does he say:
Let nothing injure her
In her beauty in her youth in her health
In her fortune in her happiness in her life.

May the drinker, drunk with the song, set off on a two-horned path lined by frightening trees to the sound of the howling roaring sea mounting the most fearsome surge that ever was, not out of its geographical bed, but swiftly flowing out of the overturned bottle while the mermaid, prostrate on the ground near this cataract, considers the star, now black now blue, imagines she recognises it, and does indeed recognise it.

This happens let's not forget on a real plain, on a real shore, under a real sky. And it's a real bottle and a real mermaid, and a real flooding sea that carries off the letter and rises to attack the castle.

Tumultuous outpouring of the contents of the fathomless bottle. Yet it was an ordinary bottle that shouldn't have held more than 80 centilitres, and yet, here was the entire Ocean bursting from its neck, to which bits of wax still clung. Roaring of hills and of the castle's

Frémissement des monts et des fondations du château sous l'assaut de l'eau, déplacement de l'étoile, rien ne peut distraire la sirène de sa rêverie en proie à sa propre respiration, dans l'odeur de violette de la nuit. Monte, monte Océan, roule tes vagues et reflète en les déformant les monstres inscrits dans les constellations et joyeux de se mesurer avec les terribles créatures de tes cavernes et de tes gouffres, monte, monte, emporte les buissons de thym et de prunelliers et fais, l'un sur l'autre, ébouler les tumulus de glaise et d'argile et les tas de cailloux, renverse la tombe oubliée par un criminel d'autrefois et un fossoyeur paresseux à l'aube d'un jour d'été où les diamants de la vie résonnaient formidablement dans les verres du cabaret et s'étalaient en cartes d'îles inconnues sur la nappe blanche.

Monte, monte et roule ton écume en fourrures élégantes puisque la sirène se plonge en toi, se roule en toi et monte avec toi vers le porche obscur du château, citadelle d'ombre et de fantômes, béant sur la ligne d'horizon qu'il engloutit interminablement.

Et voici que la sirène pénètre dans le château et s'égare dans un long corridor de draperies et de toiles d'araignées à l'issue duquel, lance et flamme et épée dans les mains, dans son armure de fer l'attend un chevalier.

Long combat, mêlée où le cliquetis de l'armure se mêle au cliquetis des écailles, éclairs des épées dans l'ombre, ahan des combattants, reflets des étoiles du ciel sur la cuirasse et les cuissards et de l'Océan sur la queue de la sirène, sang s'insinuant dans les jointures des dalles, souffle qui fait vibrer les toiles d'araignées. L'une de celles-ci s'agite sur le mur et son ombre en fait une créature abominablement géante.

Quand la sirène s'éloigne, les pièces de l'armure baignent, pêle-mêle, dans le sang, sur le sol, tandis qu'à son tour la tantôt noire, la tantôt bleue, pénètre à son tour dans le corridor, s'empare de l'épée du chevalier, attaque la sirène.

foundations under the waters' assault, shifting of the star, nothing can distract the mermaid from her reverie in thrall to her own breathing, in the aroma of night violet. Rise, rise, Ocean, roll your waves, reflect and distort the monsters inscribed in the constellations whose joy is to vie with the fearsome creatures of your gulfs and caverns, rise, rise, carry off the shrubs of thyme and sloe, tumble in a heap the cairns and the mounds of clay and loam, overturn the tomb forgotten by an old-time criminal and a lazy gravedigger at a summer day's dawn when life's diamonds rang out loud in the glasses on the bar and stacked up on maps of unknown islands on the white tablecloth.

Surge, surge and roll your foam in elegant furs, for the mermaid is plunging, rolling into you and surging with you to the dark portal of the castle, a citadel of shade and phantoms, gaping at the skyline which it engulfs without end.

And now the mermaid enters the castle and is lost in a long corridor of drapes and spider-webs, at whose far end a knight awaits her, lance and flame and sword in hand.

Long combat, hand-to-hand, the rattle of armour mingling with the rattle of scales, swords flashing in the gloom, exertions of combatants, sky stars reflected on cuirasses and greaves, Ocean stars on the mermaid's tail, blood seeping between the flagstones, wind shaking the spider-webs. One of these trembles on the wall and its shadow makes a horribly gigantic creature.

As the mermaid moves on, the pieces of armour swim pell-mell in blood, on the floor, while in its turn the one now black, now blue, enters the corridor, seizes the knight's weapon, attacks the mermaid.

Escrime fabuleuse, ce spectacle je le vois, il se déroule sous mes yeux, escrime fabuleuse que celle de l'étoile dont les branches se rétractent et s'allongent tour à tour. Zigomar du ciel, astucieuse duelliste, étoile, ton dernier reflet est parti vers des planètes distantes de millions et millions de kilomètres et, demain, dans des millions d'années, les astronomes surpris de ne plus voir ton fanal parmi les récifs sidéraux publieront qu'un grand naufrage vient d'avoir lieu dans les espaces célestes et qu'il faut noter ta disparition sur la liste déjà longue des phénomènes inexplicables et je doute que l'on donnerait créance à qui dirait que c'est une sirène qui, te frappant dans ton cœur à cinq branches, a supprimé ton éclat de l'écrin des comètes, des soleils, des planètes, des nébuleuses et de tes sœurs, les autres étoiles, parmi lesquelles te regretteront tes compagnes préférées, l'étoile du Nord et l'étoile du Sud.

Ô sirène! je te suivrai partout. En dépit de tes crimes, compte tenu de la légitime défense, tu es séduisante à mon cœur et je pénètre par ton regard dans un univers sentimental où n'atteignent pas les médiocres préoccupations de la vie.

Je te suivrai partout. Si je te perds, je te retrouverai, sois-en sûre et, bien qu'il y ait quelque courage à t'affronter, je t'affronterai car il ne s'agit de souhaiter ici ni victoire ni défaite tant est beau l'éclat de tes armes et celui de tes yeux quand tu combats.

Marche dans ce château désert. Ton ombre surprend, c'est sûr, les marches des escaliers. Ta queue fourchue se prolonge longuement d'étage en étage. Tu étais tout à l'heure au plus profond des souterrains. Te voici maintenant au sommet du donjon.

Soudain tu t'élèves, tu montes, tu t'éloignes en plein ciel. Ton ombre, d'abord immense, a diminué rapidement et ta minuscule silhouette se découpe maintenant sur la surface de la lune. Sirène tu deviens flamme et tu incendies si violemment la nuit qu'il n'est pas une lumière à subsister près de toi dans des parterres de fleurs inconnues hantées par les lucioles.

Wonderful swordplay, this spectacle unfolding before my eyes, wonderful swordplay of the star, its branches retracting and extending. Zigomar of the sky, crafty dueller, your last reflection has set off toward planets millions and millions of miles away, and tomorrow, in millions of years' time, astronomers puzzled not to see your beacon among the astral reefs, will announce a great shipwreck in heavenly space, and say your disappearance must be added to the already long list of unexplained phenomena, and I doubt if anyone will say a mermaid struck you in your five-branched heart and snuffed out your gleam of comets'-manes, suns and planets and nebulæ and your sisters the other stars. Among these, you will be missed by your preferred companions, the North star and the South star.

O mermaid! I shall follow you everywhere. In spite of your crimes, given your legitimate defence, you are seductive to my heart and by your gaze I come through to a universe of sentiment, impervious to life's mundane preoccupations.

I shall follow you everywhere. If I lose you, I'll find you again, be sure of it, and although it takes courage to confront you, I shall confront you, for it's not a case of wishing for victory or defeat, so splendidly do your weapons flash, and your eyes too, when you fight.

Go into this deserted castle. Your shadow is certainly a surprise for the staircases. Your forked tail grows much longer on every floor. Just now you were deep, deep underground. Now you are at the top of the keep.

Suddenly erect, you surge and soar away into the sky. Your shadow, immense at first, quickly shrinks and your tiny silhouette is outlined on the surface of the moon. Mermaid you become flames and you blaze so violently in the night that no light can exist near you in the unknown flower-beds haunted by fireflies.

Bonjour la flamme.
Elle me tend ses longs gants noirs.
Et c'est le matin le feu l'aube et les ténèbres et l'éclair. Bonjour la flamme.
Tu ne me brûles pas.
Tu me transportes.
Et je ne serais plus que cendre, ô flamme, si tu m'abandonnais.

Alors, comme les astres tombaient du ciel sur le lac invisible dans lequel je m'enfonçais avec délices,
Elle mit ses mains à mon cou et, me regardant dans les yeux de ce regard que mes yeux absorbent, elle dit:
«C'est toi que j'aurais dû aimer.»
Souviens-toi de cette parole pour les années futures, toi seule digne d'incarner l'inégalable amour que je portais à une autre à jamais disparue,
Et puisses-tu ne jamais la prononcer de nouveau
Dans un carrefour de rides, sous un ciel de jours fanés et de désirs abolis.

Je baise tes mains,
Tu as le droit de ne pas m'aimer
Insensé celui qui le méconnaît
Je baise tes mains.
Très haut dans le ciel montent les fumées calmes et le chant d'un oiseau si difforme que les nuages n'osent l'accueillir et que le ciel est plus clair et plus pur quand vole cet oiseau solitaire.
Je baise tes mains.
Je baise tes mains avant le départ pour la nuit, à l'arrivée des cauchemars, quand tu dors et quand tu rêves et quand tu penses à moi et quand tu n'y penses pas. Je baise tes mains, tu as le droit de ne pas m'aimer.

Et toi,
Te souviens-tu de cette sirène de cire que tu m'as donnée?

Good morning flame.
She reaches me her long black gloves.
And it's day fire dawn and shadows and lightning.
Good morning flame.
You don't burn me.
You transport me.
And I'd be nothing but ashes, flame, if you abandoned me.

So, as when stars fell from the sky on the invisible lake where with delight I immersed myself,
She put her hands to my neck and, gazing into my eyes with the gaze that my eyes drink down, she said:
"You are the one I should have loved."
Remember those words for the years to come, you who alone can worthily incarnate that incomparable love I bore another who is gone forever,
And may you never be able to say them again
In a crossroads of wrinkles, under a sky of wilted days and discontinued yearnings.

I kiss your hands.
You are entitled not to love me.
Deranged is the one who mistakes that.
I kiss your hands.
Up, up in the sky go the calm plumes of smoke and the song of a bird so misshapen that the clouds dare not receive it and the sky is brighter and purer when this lonely bird is flying.
I kiss your hands.
I kiss your hands before we part for the night,
    when nightmares come, when you sleep and you dream and you think of me and you don't think of me. I kiss your hands, you are entitled not to love me.

And you.
Do you remember that wax mermaid you gave me?

Tu te prévoyais déjà en elle et dans celle qui te ressemble.
Tu ne meurs pas de la transfiguration de mon amour,
mais tu en vis, elle te perpétue.
Car c'est l'amour qui prévaut même sur toi, même sur elle.
Et tu ne seras vraiment morte
Que le jour où j'aurai oublié que j'ai aimé.

Cette sirène que tu m'as donnée, c'est elle.
Sais-tu quelle chaîne effrayante de symboles m'a conduit
de toi qui fus l'étoile à elle qui est la sirène?
Ô sœurs parallèles du ciel et de l'Océan!
Mais toi.
Je t'ai rencontrée l'autre nuit,
Une fameuse nuit d'orages, de larmes, de tendresse et de colère.
Oui, je t'ai rencontrée, c'était bien toi.
Mais quand je me suis approché et que je t'ai appelée et que je
t'ai parlé,
C'est une autre femme qui ma répondu:
«Commenr savez-vous mon nom?»

Regarde ton nouveau visage, car tu n'es pas morte.
Par la grâce de l'amour regarde ton nouveau visage.
Regarde, il est aussi beau que fut le premier.
Tu n'as guère changé.
Tes yeux de pervenche, tes yeux désormais éteints ne
brillent plus dans un visage douloureux et ironique.
Non, deux yeux plus sombres dans un visage à la fois
plus sévère et plus gai.
Elle aime comme toi les petits bistros, les zincs à l'aube
dans les quartiers populaires, la joie des ouvriers
quand ils sont joyeux.
Te rappelles-tu une nuit d'abîmes?
Nous avons passé devant le Trocadéro et au-delà, sur un
boulevard où passe le métro aérien, non loin du Vel'
d'Hiv'.

You already foresaw yourself in her, and in one who is like yourself.
You don't die by my love's transfiguring, but you live by it, it perpetuates you.
For it's love that prevails, even over you, even over her.
And you'll never be truly dead
Till the day I forget that I loved.

This mermaid you gave me: she's the one.
Do you know what frightening chain of symbols led me from you, once the star, to her, now the mermaid?
O parallel sisters of sky and Ocean!
But you.
I met you the other night,
A famous night of storm, of tears, of tenderness and of anger.
Yes, I met you, it was definitely you.
But when I went to you and called to you and spoke to you,
Another woman answered me:
"How do you know my name?"

Look at your new face, for you're not dead.
By the grace of love look at your new face.
Look, it's as beautiful as the first one was.
You've hardly changed.
Your periwinkle eyes, your eyes from now on are quenched, and shine no more in a pained ironical face.
No, two eyes more gloomy in a face both more stern and more merry.
Like you, she's fond of little bistros, zinc counters at dawn in the working-class districts, the gladness of working people when they are glad.
Do you remember a night of mystery?
We'd gone past the Trocadéro and beyond it, on a boulevard where the metro goes overhead, not far from the Vélodrome d'Hiver,

Nous avons bu de la bière au «Rendez-vous des camioneurs».
Il était six heures du matin.
Un plombier plaisanta longtemps avec nous.

Et, une autre fois, dans ce café où l'on sert du faro et de la gueuse lambik, te souviens-tu de Marie de la gare de l'Est?
Elle fut jadis belle, aimée, riche.
Elle se lave maintenant aux fontaines Wallace.
Mais, comme elle a gardé un certain goût de luxe,
Une fois par mois elle va se faire épouiller dans un hôpital.
Il me semble parfois que ce n'est pas avec toi mais avec ton nouveau corps, ton nouveau visage, que j'ai vu toutes ces choses.
Regarde, regarde ton nouveau visage.
Il est aussi beau que fut le premier.
Regarde, regarde ton nouveau corps.
Je me souviens de la rencontre entre ces deux visages de mon amour, de mon unique amour.
C'est peut-être de cela que tu es morte.
Mais tu vis, vous vivez,
Amantes bien nommées, insoumises à mon amour,
Visages bien nommés, corps bien nommés.
Je pleure sur la mémoire que tu perdis en mourant, mais la mort m'est indifférente.
Moi, je me souviens.
Je te trouve semblable à toi-même,
Aussi cruelle et aussi douce,
Et ne m'accordant tellement
Que pour me faire plus violemment regretter le peu que tu me refuses.

Nous voici vieux déjà tous deux.
Nous avons trente ans de plus qu'aujourd'hui,
Nous pouvons parler de jadis sans regret, sinon sans désir.
Tout de même nous aurions pu être heureux,

We drank beer at the "Truckers' Corner".
It was six o'clock in the morning.
A plumber swapped jokes with us, for quite a while.

And another time, in that cafe where they serve sweet Belgian beers, do you remember Marie of the Gare de l'Est?
Once she was loved, rich, beautiful.
Now she washes in the Wallace fountains.
But having kept a certain taste for luxury,
Once a month she has herself deloused in a hospital.
Sometimes I think it wasn't with you but with your new body, your new face that I saw all this.
Look, look at your new face.
It's just as beautiful as the first one was.
Look, look at your new body.
I remember the meeting of these two faces of my love, my one and only love.
Perhaps that's what you died of.
But you're alive, both of you,
Lovers well named, not subjected to my love,
Faces well named, bodies well named.
I weep for the memory you lost when you died, but death is all the same to me.
I do remember.
I find I resemble you,
as cruel and as sweet,
And only allowing me so much
So as to make me regret more violently the little you refuse me.

Here we are both old already.
We're thirty years older than today,
we can talk of old times without regret, if not without desire.
All the same we could have been happy,

S'il était dit qu'on puisse l'être
Et que les choses s'arrangent dans la vie.
Mais du malheur même naquit notre insatiable, notre funeste, notre étonnant amour.
Et de cet amour le seul bonheur que puissent connaître deux cœurs insatiables comme les nôtres.

Écoute, écoute monter les grandes images vulgaires que nous transfigurons.
Voici l'Océan qui gronde et chante et sur lequel le ciel se tourmente et s'apaise semblable à ton lit.
Voici l'Océan semblable à notre cœur.
Voici le ciel où naufragent les nuages dans l'éclat triste d'un fanal promené à tour de rôle par les étoiles.
Voici le ciel semblable à nos deux cœurs.
Et puis voici les champs, les fleurs, les steppes, les déserts, les plaines, les sources, les fleuves, les abîmes, les montagnes
Et tout cela peut se comparer à nos deux cœurs.
Mais ce soir je ne veux dire qu'une chose:
Deux montagnes étaient semblables de forme et de dimensions
Tu es sur l'une
Et moi sur l'autre.
Est-ce que nous nous reconnaissons?
Quels signes nous faisons-nous?
Nous devons nous entendre et nous aimer.
Peut-être m'aimes-tu?
Je t'aime déjà.
Mais ces étendues entre nous, qui les franchira?
Tu ne dis rien mais tu me regardes
Et, pour ce regard,
Il n'y a ni jour ni étendue
Ma seule amie mon amour.

Je n'ai pas fini de te dire tout.
Mais à quoi bon…

if that were said to be possible
and if things get sorted out in life.
But it's actually misfortune that gives birth to our insatiable, deadly, amazing love.
And from this love comes the only happiness that two insatiable hearts like ours can know.

Listen, listen to the great vulgar images rising as we transfigure them.
Here's Ocean growling and singing as the sky above writhes and smoothes like your bed.
Here's Ocean like our heart.
Here's the sky where clouds are shipwrecked in the sad flash of a beacon that the stars parade in turn.
Here's the sky like our two hearts.
Then here are the fields, flowers, steppes, deserts, plains, springs, rivers, chasms, mountains,
And all of that can be compared to our two hearts.
But this evening I've just one thing to say:
Two mountains were alike in shape and size
I'm on one
You're on the other.
Do we recognise each other?
What signs do we make?
We should understand and love each other.
Perhaps you love me?
I love you already.
We have these understandings between us. But who will go further?
You say nothing but you look at me
And for this look,
There is no when, no duration.
My one darling my love.

I have more to tell you.
But what's the use…

L'indifférence en toi monte comme un rosier vorace qui, détruisant les murailles, se tord et grandit,
Étouffe l'ivrogne de son parfum...
Et puis, est-ce que cela meurt?
Un clair refrain retentit dans la ruelle lavée par le matin, la nuit et le printemps.
Le géranium à la fenêtre fermée semble deviner l'avenir.
C'est alors que surgit le héros du drame.
Je ne te conte cette histoire qui ne tient pas debout que parce que je n'ose pas continuer comme j'ai commencé.
Car je crois à la vertu des mots et des choses formulées.

Nul jeu, ce soir, sur la table de bois blanc.
Un ciel creux comme une huître vide
Une terre plate
La demoiselle sans foudre apparaîtra-t-elle?
Un peu de poisson abandonné sur le carrelage d'une cuisine n'en peut plus d'ennui.
Il se gonfle
Près de lui dans la boîte à ordures luit l'arête.
Corridor sombre traversé par les chats
Une porte de saltimbanque s'ouvre et se ferme alternativement sur une femme, sur un homme, sur un homme, sur une femme.
Et la demoiselle sans foudre dit qu'au carrefour d'aubépines et de sainfoin elle perdit un bas
Qu'elle perdit l'autre au pied du chêne fendu
Et sa chemise sur la berge.
La demoiselle sans foudre est nue toute nue
Elle tient un cœur palpitant de poisson dans la main
Elle regarde vaguement devant elle
Elle se mord les lèvres jusqu'au sang et parfois s'arrête et chantonne.
La demoiselle sans foudre est seule toute seule.
Le cœur de poisson palpite dans sa main
L'ombre tombe sur son corps nu et le fait étinceler

Indifference in you climbs like a devouring rosebush that destroys walls, twists and spreads,
Befuddles and stifles with its perfume...
And then does it die?
A bright melody rings out in the lane washed by morning, night and springtime.
The geranium at the closed window seems to guess the future.
That's the cue for the hero of the drama.
I only tell you this tale which doesn't stand up because I daren't go on as I started.
Because I have faith in the goodness of words and formulations.

No game this evening on the white wood table.
A sky hollow as an empty oyster.
A flat landscape
The young lady with no thunderclap: will she appear?
A fish-heart abandoned on a tiled kitchen floor can take no more tedium
It swells up
Near it in the rubbish-bin is the shining backbone.
Dark corridor, thoroughfare of cats
A clown's door opens and shuts on a woman, then a man, then a man, then a woman.
And the young lady with no thunderclap says that at the hawthorn and sanfoin crossroads she lost a stocking
That she lost the other under the blasted oak
And her shirt on the riverbank
The young lady with no thunderclap is nude quite nude
She holds a throbbing fish-heart in her hand
She gazes vaguely in front of her
She bites her lips enough to draw blood and sometimes stops and croons
The young lady with no thunderclap is alone quite alone
The fish-heart throbs in her hand
Shade falls on her nude body and makes it glitter

C'est ainsi que naissent les constellations
C'est ainsi que naît le désir
C'est alors que se souvenant de lui-même un noctambule s'arrête sous un réverbère au coin d'une rue, regarde rougeoyer la lumière.
Et avant de reprendre son chemin s'imagine tel qu'il était des années auparavant avec son regard vif et sa bouche sanglante.
À l'heure où la demoiselle sans foudre venait tendrement le border dans son lit.

La sirène rencontre son double et lui sourit.
Elle s'endort alors du sommeil adorable dont elle ne s'éveillera pas.
Elle rêve peut-être. Elle rêve certainement. Nous sommes au matin d'un jour de moissons lumineuses et de tremblements de terre et de marées de diamants, les premières retombant sur tes cheveux et surgissant de tes yeux, les seconds signalant ta promenade et les troisièmes montant à l'assaut de ton cœur.
Il est cinq heures du matin dans la forêt de pins où se dresse le château de la sirène, mais la sirène ne s'éveillera plus car elle a vu son double, elle t'a vu. Désormais ton empire est immense.
D'un sentier sort un bûcheron sur lequel la rosée tremble et s'étoile.
Au premier arbre qu'il abat surgit un grand nombre de libellules!
Elles s'éparpillent dans des territoires de brindilles. Au second arbre se brisent les premières vagues. Au troisième arbre tu m'as dit «Dors dans mes bras.»

Tu diras au revoir pour moi à la petite fille du pont
à la petite fille qui chante de si jolies chansons
à mon ami de toujours que j'ai négligé
à ma première maîtresse
à ceux qui connurent celle que tu sais
à mes vrais amis et tu les reconnaîtras aisément
à mon épée de verre
à ma sirène de cire
à mes monstres à mon lit
Quant à toi que j'aime plus que tout au monde

That's how constellations are born
That's how desire is born
That's how a sleepwalker comes to himself, stops under the lamp on a street-corner and watches the light redden
And before going on his way, pictures himself as he was years ago with his bright eyes and bleeding lips
At the time when the young lady with no thunderclap came to tuck him up tenderly in bed.

The mermaid meets her double and smiles at her.
Then she falls asleep, in that adorable sleep, never to awaken.
She may dream. She does dream. We're in the morning of a day of gleaming harvests, of earthquakes, of diamond tides, the first falling back on your hair and springing from your eyes, the second marking your movement and the third surging to assail your heart.
It's five in the morning in the pine-forest where the mermaid's castle rears up, but the mermaid will not wake again, for she has seen her double, she has seen you. From now on, your empire is immense.
A wood-cutter comes out of a path. The dew on him trembles and makes starry patterns.
He fells a tree and up fly a great many dragon-flies.
They disperse among the twigs. He fells another tree and the first waves break against it. He fells a third tree and you said to me:
"Sleep in my arms."

You said goodbye for me to the little girl at the bridge
the little girl who sings such pretty songs
to my lifelong friend I neglected
to my first mistress
to those who knew you-know-who
to my real friends who you'll easily recognise
to my glass sword
to my wax mermaid
to my monsters to my bed
as for you the one I love more than anything in the world

Je ne te dis pas encore au revoir
Je te reverrai
Mais j'ai peur de n'avoir plus longtemps à te voir.

Amer destin celui de compter la feuille et la pierre blanche
Malice errant le premier du mois de mai
Salua d'un cœur vaillant chapeau claque et gants blancs
Salua dis-je le dis-je et la lune en mousseline
Salua bien des choses
Salua surtout le dis-je
Salua vraiment salua
Salua
Et comme j'ai l'honneur de le dire
La cataracte du Niagara ne tiendrait peut-être pas dans votre verre.
Peut-être pas Monsieur peut-être
Peut-être et comment va Madame peut-être
Madame peut-être s'ennuie
Madame peut-être a des vapeurs
Peut-être.

Quand il mit son doigt sur le plaid
Sur le plaid d'Égypte monsieur mais oui
Nous ne sommes pas tous comme ça dans la famille
C'est heureux pour mon père et ma mère
Et pourtant plus on est de fous…
Oui c'est heureux
Plus on rit
Oui.
J'ai écrit cette chanson qui en vaut bien d'autres
Un soir où je n'étais ni gai ni triste
Bien que de jour en jour je connaisse mieux les hommes
Ni gai ni triste
Un soir où je n'avais pas bu
Un soir où j'avais vu celle que j'aime

I'm not saying goodbye to you yet
I'll see you again
But I'm afraid of not having much time left to see you.

Bitter fate, to count the leaf and the white stone
Malice wandering the first day of May
Respects from a valiant heart opera hat and white gloves
Respects I say I tell her and the moon in muslin
Respects plenty of things
Respects mainly I tell her
Respects truly respects
Respects
And as I have the honour to tell her
Niagara Falls might not fit in your glass
Maybe not Sir maybe
Maybe and how is Madam maybe
Maybe Madam is bored
Maybe Madam has the vapours
Maybe

When he put his finger on the tartan rug
On the Egyptian rug sir oh yes
We aren't all like that in the family
It's lucky for my father and mother
Then again the crazier you are...
Yes it's lucky
The more you laugh
Yes.
I wrote this song worth plenty of others
One evening when I was not merry, not sad
Though as time goes on I understand people better
Not merry, not sad
An evening when I hadn't drunk
An evening when I hadn't seen my darling

J'ai écrit cette chanson qui en vaut bien d'autres
Pour amuser celle que j'aime.

Mais je connais une chanson bien plus belle
Celle d'une aube dans la rue ou parmi les champs prêts à la moisson ou sur un lit désert
On a brillé ce début de printemps les dernières bûches de l'hiver
De vieilles douleurs deviennent douces au souvenir
Des yeux plus jeunes s'ouvrent sur un univers lavé.
J'ai connu cette aube grâce à toi
Mais se lèvera-t-elle jamais
Sur les douleurs que tu provoques?

Tu sais de quelle apparition je parle
Et de quelle réincarnation
Coulez coulez larmes et fleuves
Et vins dans les verres.

Le temps n'est plus où nous riions
Quand nous étions ivres.

Elle est haut la sirène parmi les étoiles sœurs de la vaincue. Impératrices de peu de nuages, reines d'une heure de la nuit, planètes néfastes. Et voici que d'un seul bond, d'une seule chute, la sirène plonge dans la mer au milieu d'une gerbe d'écume qui fait pâlir la Voie Lactée.

L'épave est toujours à la même place enlisée dans le sable où ses armes rouillées ont des allures de poulpes.

Une huitre gigantesque bâille et montre sa gigantesque perle dans l'orient de laquelle le homard et le crabe écartent les algues comme une forêt vierge.

Il était une fois une algue errante
Il était une fois un rein et une reine

I wrote this song worth plenty of others
To amuse my darling.

But I know a much lovelier song
About a dawn in the road or among fields ripe for harvest or
on a deserted bed
When spring came they burnt the last winter logs
Old sorrows become sweet in the memory
Younger eyes open on a washed universe.
I knew this dawn thanks to you.
But will it ever rise
On the sorrows you provoke?

You know what apparition I'm talking about
What incarnation
Flow, flow, tears and streams
And wines in the glasses.

Those times are gone when we laughed
when we were drunk.

She's a long way up the mermaid among the stars whose sisters were crushed, empresses of not many clouds, queens of one hour of night, evil planets. And look, with one bound, one plunge, the mermaid dives into the sea amid a mass of foam that pales the Milky Way.

The flotsam is still there embedded in the sand, its rusty weapons alluring as an octopus.

A gigantic oyster yawns and shows its gigantic pearl in whose rising the lobster and the crab part the algae like a virgin forest.

Once upon a time there was a wandering alga.
Once upon a time there was a queen and a kidney

Dans des courants de tulle et de tussor
Une algue qui avait vu bien des choses, bien des actes répréhensibles
Et bien des couchers de soleil
Et bien des couchers de sirènes.
Elle voguait à l'aventure, rêvant aux résédas qui s'ennuient dans leur pot de terre, sur l'appui de la fenêtre des demoiselles vieillies par l'abstinence et le regret de leur jeunesse.
Une hélice après l'autre avait meurtri les branches et les graines magiques de cette algue qui se dissolvait lentement en pourriture dans l'eau salée.
Un poisson volant lui dit: Bonjour l'algue.
Car, si l'on peut donner la parole à un poisson volant, il n'est pas d'exemple qu'on puisse la donner à une algue perdue au large, détachée d'on ne sait quel haut-fond et travaillée par les phénomènes de la dissolution et de la germination.
La sirène, je la perds, je crois la perdre, mais je la retrouve toujours, la sirène nage vers la plage, pénètre dans la forêt du rosier mortel et, là, rencontre l'oiseau hideux, l'oiseau muet et, durant un jour ou mille ans, lui apprend à chanter et transfigure cette bête.
Les arbres se penchent longuement sur cette rencontre et des drapeaux inconnus fleurissent dans leur feuillage.
Fougères, rasoirs, baisers perdus, tout s'écroule et renaît par une belle matinée tandis que, par un sentier désert, délaissant sur l'herbe les cartes d'une réussite certaine, la sirène s'éloigne vers la plage d'où elle partit au début de cette histoire décousue.
Regagne la plage au pied du château fort
La mer a regagné son lit
L'étoile ne brille plus mais sa place décolorée comme une vieille robe luit sinistrement.
Regagne la plage.
Regagne la bouteille
S'y couche.
L'ivrogne remet le bouchon
Le ciel est calme.
Tout va s'endormir au bruit du flux blanchi d'écume.

in draughts of tulle and tussore,
An alga that had seen many things, many reprehensible deeds,
Many suns going down,
Many mermaids going down.
It roved for adventure, dreaming of resedas bored in their clay pot, on the windowsill of old maids wrinkled by abstinence and regretted youth.
Propellers had destroyed the branches and magic seeds of this alga which was slowly dissolving to rottenness in the salt water.
A flying fish spoke to it: "Good morning, alga."
Because you may have a flying fish speaking, but perhaps not an alga lost at large, detached from its unknown shallows, and subject to the phenomena of dissolution and germination.
The mermaid, I lose her, I think I do, but I always find her again, the mermaid swims towards the beach, enters the forest of the mortal rosebush and, there, she meets the hideous bird, the mute bird and, for a day or a thousand years, teaches it to sing, transfiguring the creature.
The trees lean tall over this encounter and unknown flags bloom in their foliage.
Ferns, razors, lost kisses, it all crumbles and is reborn on a lovely morning while, on a secluded path, leaving on the grass the charts of a certain success, the mermaid heads for the beach from which she started this disjointed tale.
Back to the beach at the foot of the castle
The sea is back in its bed
The star isn't shining now but its place, discoloured like an old frock, has a sinister glow.
Back to the beach
Back to the bottle
Resting there
The drunk puts back the cork
The sky is calm.
Everything will fall asleep to the sound of the foam-whitened ebb and flow.

Ô rien ne peut séparer la sirène de l'hippocampe!
Rien ne peut défaire cette union
Rien
C'est la nuit
Tout dort ou fait semblant de dormir
Dormons, dormons,
Ou faisons semblant de dormir.
Ne manie pas ce livre à la légère
À la légère à la légère à la légère à la légère.
Je sais ce qu'il veut dire mieux que personne.
Je sais où je vais,
Ce ne sera pas toujours gai.
Mais l'amour et moi
L'aurons voulu ainsi.

1934-37

LES QUATRE SANS COU

Ils étaient quatre qui n'avaient plus de tête,
Quatre à qui l'on avait coupé le cou,
On les appelait les quatre sans cou.

Quand ils buvaient un verre,
Au café de la place ou du boulevard,
Les garçons n'oubliaient pas d'apporter des entonnoirs.

Quand ils mangeaient, c'était sanglant,
Et tous quatre chantant et sanglotant,
Quand ils aimaient, c'était du sang.

O nothing can part the mermaid from the seahorse.
Nothing can undo this union
Nothing
It's night
All is asleep or else pretending.
Don't handle this book lightly
lightly lightly lightly lightly.
I know what it means better than anyone.
I know where I'm going,
It won't always be fun.
But love and I
will have wished it so.

1934-37

THE FOUR CUT NECKS

They were four without their heads,
Four who'd had their necks cut,
Known as the four cut necks.

When they took a drink
In the café on the square or the boulevard
The waiters remembered to bring funnels.

When they ate, it was bloody,
And all four singing and sobbing,
When they made love, it was blood.

Quand ils couraient, c'était du vent,
Quand ils pleuraient, c'était vivant,
Quand ils dormaient, c'était sans regret.

Quand ils travaillaient, c'était méchant,
Quand ils rôdaient, c'était effrayant,
Quand ils jouaient, c'était différent,

Quand ils jouaient, c'était comme tout le monde,
Comme vous et moi, vous et nous et tous les autres,
Quand ils jouaient, c'était étonnant.

Mais quand ils parlaient, c'était d'amour.
Ils auraient pour un baiser
Donné ce qui leur restait de sang.

Leurs mains avaient des lignes sans nombre
Qui se perdaient parmi les ombres
Comme des rails dans la forêt.

Quand ils s'asseyaient, c'était plus majestueux que des rois
Et les idoles se cachaient derrière leurs croix
Quand devant elles ils passaient droits.

On leur avait rapporté leur tête
Plus de vingt fois, plus de cent fois,
Les ayants retrouvés à la chasse ou dans les fêtes,

Mais jamais ils ne voulurent reprendre
Ces têtes où brillaient leurs yeux,
Où les souvenirs dormaient dans leur cervelle.

Cela ne faisait peut-être pas l'affaire
Des chapeliers et des dentistes.
La gaieté des uns rend les autres tristes.

When they ran, it was wind.
When they wept, it was alive.
When they slept, it was with no regrets.

When they worked, it was naughty.
When they prowled, it was scary.
When they played, it was extraordinary.

When they played, it was like everybody,
Like you and me, you and us and all the others,
When they played, it was uncanny.

But when they spoke, it was of love.
For a kiss they would have
Given away what blood they had left.

Lines on their hands most numerous
Ran into regions tenebrous
Like railway tracks in greenery.

They sat like kings, most royally
And idols cowered fearfully
Behind a cross, when they passed by.

A score of times, a hundred times,
People had brought them back their heads,
Found while out shooting, or at fêtes.

But they would never take them back,
Those heads from which their eyes shone out,
Those brains with memories asleep.

This hardly served the interests
Of dental specialists and hatters.
What's fun for some is sad for others.

Les quatre sans cou vivent encore, c'est certain.
J'en connais au moins un
Et peut-être aussi les trois autres.

Le premier, c'est Anatole,
Le second, c'est Croquignole,
Le troisième, c'est Barbemolle,
Le quatrième, c'est encore Anatole.

Je les vois de moins en moins,
Car c'est déprimant, à la fin,
La fréquentation des gens trop malins.

COMME

Come, dit l'Anglais à l'Anglais, et l'Anglais vient.
Côme, dit le chef de gare, et le voyageur qui vient dans cette ville descend du train, sa valise à la main.
Come, dit l'autre, et il mange.
Comme, je dis comme et tout se métamorphose, le marbre en eau, le ciel en orange, le vin en plaine, le fil en six, le cœur en peine, la peur en seine.
Mais si l'Anglais dit as, c'est à son tour de voir le monde changer de forme à sa convenance.
Et moi je ne vois plus qu'un signe unique sur une carte
L'as de cœur si c'est en février,
L'as de carreau et l'as de trèfle, misère en Flandre,
L'as de pique aux mains des aventuriers.
Et si cela me plait à moi de vous dire machin,

The four cut necks are still alive, for sure.
I know at least one,
Possibly the other three.

The first is Anatole.
The second is Cracknole.
The third is Baby-jowl.
The fourth is again Anatole.

I find I see them less and less.
People of too much artfulness,
In time, are certain to depress.

LIKE

Laïque says Frenchman to Frenchman civil as you like.
Lake? says Como stationmaster, and toting his bag, tripper trips up skipper's gangplank.
Leica tourist he's snap-happy he clicks away.
Lick, says someone, and he likes eating.
Like I say like and everything is metamorphosed. Marble into water, sky into sturmers, wines into bottlefields, liquors into slickers, heart into hurtbeat, fright into stageflight.
But when the Englishman says "as", it's his turn to watch the world change shape to his taste.
And me I see just one aspect one sign on a playing-card,
The ace of hearts assuming it's February,
The ace of diamonds and the ace of clubs in astounding 'Asselt, astringent Asturias,
The ace of spades assaulted by astronauts.
And what if I fancy saying "whatsit" to you,

Pot à eau, mousseline et potiron.
Que l'Anglais dise machin,
Que machin dise le chef de gare,
Machin dise l'autre,
Et moi aussi.
Machin.
Et même machin chose.
Il est vrai que vous vous en foutez
Que vous ne comprenez pas la raison de ce poème.
Moi non plus d'ailleurs.
Poème, je vous demande un peu?
Poème? je vous demande un peu de confiture,
Encore un peu de gigot,
Encore un petit verre de vin
Pour nous mettre en train…
Poème, je ne vous demande pas l'heure qu'il est,
Poème, je ne vous demande pas si votre beau-père est poilu
comme un sapeur.
Poème, je vous demande un peu…?

Poème, je ne vous demande pas l'aumône,
Je vous la fais.
Poème, je ne vous demande pas l'heure qu'il est,
Je vous la donne.
Poème, je ne vous demande pas si vous allez bien,
Cela se devine.
Poème, poème, je vous demande un peu…
Je vous demande un peu d'or pour être heureux avec celle
que j'aime.

Pitcher mashed potato pumpkin.
Let the Englishman say whatsit,
Say whatsit the stationmaster,
Say whatsit what's his name,
And me as well.
Whatsit.
And even whatsit thingummy.
Frankly you don't give a damn
You don't get the point of this poem.
Me neither as it goes.
Poem I'd like a bit?
Poem? I'd like a bit of jam,
A bit more lamb,
Another little glass of wine
To get us into the swing...
Poem I'm not asking you what the time is.
Poem I'm not asking if your good lady's daddy's as hairy as a
navvy's navel.
Poem I'd like a bit...?

Poem I'm not looking for charity,
I'm giving it.
Poem I'm not asking you what the time is,
I'm telling you.
Poem I'm not asking if you're well,
I can guess.
Poem poem I'd like a bit...
A bit of gold to make us happy, me and my love.

Adapted, with kind permission, from a translation by Martin Sorrell

COMPLAINTE DE FANTÔMAS

Écoutez,... Faites silence
La triste énumération
De tous les forfaits sans nom,
Des tortures, des violences
Toujours impunis, hélas!
Du criminel Fantômas.

Lady Beltham, sa maîtresse,
Le vit tuer son mari
Car il les avait surpris
Au milieu de leurs caresses.
Il coula le paquebot
Lancaster au fond des flots.

Cent personnes il assassine
Mais Juve aidé de Fandor
Va lui faire subir son sort
Enfin sur la guillotine...
Mais un acteur, très bien grimé,
À sa place est exécuté.

Un phare dans la tempête
Croule, et les pauvres bateaux
Font naufrage au fond de l'eau.
Mais surgissent quatre têtes:
Lady Beltham aux yeux d'or,
Fantômas, Juve et Fandor.

Le monstre avait une fille
Aussi jolie qu'une fleur.
La douce Hélène au grand cœur
Ne tenait pas de sa famille,

BALLAD OF FANTOMAS

Your attention, please! Pray silence
For the sad and sorry story,
All the grievous inventory,
Nameless acts of harm and violence,
Every one scot-free, alas!
Of the felon Fantomas.

First, his mistress, Lady Beltham,
Saw the day her husband caught them
Making flagrant love together:
On the spot the felon killed him.
Next he sank the good ship *Leopard,*
Sabotaged, submerged, and scuppered.

He commits his hundredth murder.
Juve and his assistant Fandor
Think to see this libertine
Punished by the guillotine.
But an actor's crayoned face
Fills the basket in his place.

Lighthouse shattered, just like glass.
Storm-tossed, luckless ships go down
To the lowest depths, and drown.
Four heads bobbing on the tide:
Lady Beltham, golden-eyed,
Fandor, Juve, and Fantomas.

Yet the monster's pretty daughter,
Helen, had a noble nature:
She was sweet, not taking after
Her appalling family,

Car elle sauva Fandor
Qu'était condamné à mort.

En consigne d'une gare
Un colis ensanglanté!
Un escroc est arrêté!
Qu'est devenu le cadavre?
Le cadavre est bien vivant
C'est Fantômas, mes enfants!

Prisonnier dans une cloche
Sonnant un enterrement
Ainsi mourut son lieutenant.
Le sang de sa pauv' caboche
Avec saphirs et diamants
Pleuvait sur les assistants.

Un beau jour des fontaines
Soudain chantèr'nt à Paris.
Le monde était surpris,
Ignorant que ces sirènes
De la Concorde enfermaient
Un roi captif qui pleurait.

Certain secret d'importance
Allait être dit au tzar.
Fantômas, lui, le reçut car
Ayant pris sa ressemblance
Il remplaçait l'empereur
Quand Juv' l'arrêta sans peur.

Il fit tuer par la Toulouche,
Vieillarde aux yeux dégoûtants,
Un Anglais à grands coups de dents
Et le sang remplit sa bouche.

For she rescued poor young Fandor,
Who had been condemned to die.

In the railway baggage-lockers
There's a gory parcel, bleeding.
They've detained some gangster cove.
What has happened to the carcass?
Why, the stiff's alive and breathing!
It is Fantomas, by Jove!

Bottled up inside a bell
Tolling for a funeral,
Death rubbed out his Number Two.
Blood cascaded from the skull,
Sapphires, diamonds as well,
On the gathering below.

Paris, one fine day in spring:
Suddenly, the fountains sing!
People listen in surprise.
Little do they realise
That the siren melodies
Cage a weeping captive king.

Vital military clues:
Secrets, destined for the Tsar.
Smartly turning similar,
Fantomas receives the news,
Personates the autocrat.
Juve arrests him, just like that.

He got La Toulouche to kill
An Englishman with monstrous bites.
She was a hag, a foul-eyed beast!
There was blood, he drank his fill,

Puis il cacha un trésor
Dans les entrailles du mort.

Cette grande catastrophe
De l'autobus qui rentra
Dans la banque qu'on pilla
Dont on éventra les coffres…
Vous vous souvenez de ça…
Ce fut lui qui l'agença.

La peste en épidémie
Ravage un grand paquebot
Tout seul au milieu des flots.
Quel spectacle de folie!
Agonies et morts hélas!
Qui a fait ça? Fantômas.

Il tua un cocher de fiacre.
Au siège il le ficela
Et roulant cahin-caha,
Malgré les clients qui sacrent,
Il ne s'arrêtait jamais
L' fiacre qu'un mort conduisait.

Méfiez-vous des roses noires,
Il en sort une langueur
Épuisante et l'on en meurt.
C'est une bien sombre histoire
Encore un triste forfait
De Fantômas en effet!

Il assassina la mère
De l'héroïque Fandor.
Quelle injustice du sort
Douleur poignante et amère…

Stashed his looted perquisites
In the guts of the deceased.

You recall that huge fracas –
Raiders took a motor-bus,
Rammed the bank, whose vaults they cleared,
Rifling safe and automat:
Terrible – I'm sure you heard...
He was at the back of that.

Epidemic of bubonic
Plague attacks an oceanic
Liner, caught far out at sea.
Horrid sights, what lunacy!
Agonies and deaths, alas!
Who's the culprit? Fantomas.

Killed: one cabman plying for hire,
Knotted neatly to his post:
Going like a house on fire!
Let the inmates curse and swear:
They cannot dispute the fare,
Driven by a lifeless ghost.

Be afraid of jet-black roses.
They exhale a languid breath,
Murky vapours, dismal gases,
Enervating, dealing death.
Lamentably, one more time,
Fantomas commits the crime!

Next he killed the aged mother
Of Fandor, the valiant sleuth.
Fate miscarried altogether,
Sorrow has a bitter tooth...

Il n'avait donc pas de cœur,
Cet infâme malfaiteur!

Du Dôme des Invalides
On volait l'or chaque nuit.
Qui c'était? mais c'était lui,
L'auteur de ce plan cupide.
User aussi mal son temps
Quand on est intelligent!

À la Reine de Hollande
Même, il osa s'attaquer.
Juve le fit prisonnier
Ainsi que toute sa bande.
Mais il échappa pourtant
À un juste châtiment.

Pour effacer sa trace
Il se fit tailler des gants
Dans la peau d'un trophée sanglant,
Dans d' la peau de mains d' cadavre
Et c'était ce mort qu'accusaient
Les empreintes qu'on trouvait.

À Valmondois un fantôme
Sur la rivière marchait.
En vain Juve le cherchait.
Effrayant vieillards et mômes,
C'était Fantômas qui fuyait
Après l' coup qu'il avait fait.

La police d'Angleterre
Par lui fut mystifiée.
Mais, à la fin, arrêté,
Fut pendu et mis en terre.

Sure, he had no heart at all,
This notorious criminal!

Golden-domed, the Invalides
Was despoiled by nightly theft.
Fantomas devised the deed,
Carried out the greedy crime.
Having such a mental gift,
What a way to use one's time!

He assailed – what insolence!
The Queen of the Netherlands.
Gallant Juve was quick to bang
Up the rogue, with all his gang.
Even so, in the event,
He evaded punishment.

Just in case his dabs betrayed,
Fantomas had gloves, well-made
From a bleeding trophy's skin,
Hands of one he'd just done in:
And the dead man was arraigned
By the thumb-prints they obtained.

On the waters of the Seine
There's a phantom takes a walk.
Juve's enquiries are in vain.
Scaring spooks and older folk,
Fantomas is making tracks,
After one of his attacks.

Scotland Yard: the CID
Could not solve the mystery,
Till an overdue arrest
Saw him hanged and laid to rest.

Devinez ce qui arriva:
Le bandit en réchappa.

Dans la nuit, sinistre et sombre
À travers la Tour Eiffel,
Juv' poursuit le criminel.
En vain guette-t-il son ombre.
Faisant un suprême effort
Fantômas échappe encor.

D'vant le casino d' Monte-Carlo
Un cuirassé évoluait.
Son commandant qui perdait
Voulait bombarder la rade.
Fantômas, c'est évident
Était donc ce commandant.

Dans la mer un bateau sombre
Avec Fantômas à bord,
Hélène Juve et Fandor
Et des passagers sans nombre.
On ne sait s'ils sont tous morts,
Nul n'a retrouvé leurs corps.

Ceux de sa bande, Beaumôme,
Bec de Gaz et le Bedeau,
Le rempart du Montparno,
Ont fait trembler Paris, Rome
Et Londres par leurs exploits.
Se sont-ils soumis aux lois?

Pour ceux du peuple et du monde,
J'ai écrit cette chanson
Sur Fantômas, dont le nom
Fait tout trembler à la ronde.

Guess what happened. Need I say?
Still the ruffian got away.

Up across the Eiffel Tower
In the eerie midnight hour
Juve pursues the criminal,
Trails the shadow. All in vain:
With fantastic strength and skill
Fantomas escapes again.

Monte Carlo. Rouge, pair, passe.
Armoured gunboat mounting guard.
Captain with gigantic loss
Gives the order to bombard.
Who's this captain mounting guard?
Clearly, it was Fantomas.

Out at sea a vessel founders.
Fantomas had been on board.
So were Helen, Juve and Fandor
And too many to record.
Since no bodies have been found,
No-one knows if they were drowned.

At the deeds of Fantomas
And his gang from Montparnasse,
(Pretty Boy Sarcophagus,
Bill the Beadle, Sniff the Gas),
Paris, Rome and London shook.
Were they ever brought to book?

For yourselves I wrote this song,
For the world, for everyone.
Everyone is tremulous
At the name of Fantomas.

Maintenant vivez longtemps
Je le souhaite en partant.

Final

Allongeant son ombre immense
Sur le monde et sur Paris,
Quel est ce spectre aux yeux gris
Qui surgit dans le silence?
Fantômas, serait-ce toi
Qui te dresses sur les toits?

May each one of you live long:
That's my wish, and I am gone.

FINALE

Spreading like a mighty pall
Over Paris, over all,
Who's the ghost with sombre eyes,
Silently observed to rise?
Fantomas – a wild surmise:
Is that you, against the skies?

TRANSLATOR'S NOTE

'Ballad' was published in *Fortunes*, 1942. A radio version by Desnos had been broadcast in 1933, in a 'superproduction'. All the stanzas were recited, many being amplified by sketches with several actors and elaborate sound-effects. Music was by Kurt Weill; radio production by Paul Deharme; Antonin Artaud directed, and took the title role. The original Fantomas books were by Pierre Souvestre and Marcel Allain, the silent films by Feuillade. Desnos was now the French poet with the biggest audience, and the literary director at the tiptop Foniric studios, doing a job he loved. His Cuban friend Alejo Carpentier was artistic director. Every day on Radio Paris he devoted half-an-hour of peak time to some notable birthday or anniversary, with wit and fun, dialogue and sound effects. The same skills went into a hundred commercials, many set to music by Charles Trenet. Meanwhile he denounced the Cuban dictator Machado in print. In 1936 he brilliantly presented Walt Whitman's poem 'Salut au Monde', and in 1938-9, in his famous Key of Dreams, he interpreted listeners' dreams, again on Poste-Parisien.

L'ÉVADÉ

Vieux cheval de retour remâchant son avoine,
Fourrage salé des «C'était à telle date»,
Aujourd'hui voyageur guetté à chaque douane,
Épuisé et vaincu, capot, échec et mat,

Il rêvait les yeux clos au coin de la portière,
Tandis qu'au long des rails se couchaient les forêts,
Tandis que les sillons tracés droits dans la terre,
Comme une roue immense rayonnaient.

Quand il ouvrit les yeux au sifflet déchirant,
Ni le ciel ni la plaine où naissaient des villages
Plus desséchés que la morue ou le hareng,
Par le feu du soleil marqués comme un pelage,

Salés, rôtis, flambés, assaillis de poussière,
Absorbés par le sol, rongés par les abcès
De la pierre et du chaume et les griffes du lierre,
Fantômes de maisons aux relents de décès,

Ni le ciel ni la plaine où naissaient des villages
Ne rappelaient ses souvenirs. Déjà ce ciel
N'était plus que le ciel à l'absurde visage,
Identique en tout lieu, ranci comme le miel.

Regarde! mais regarde! au coin de cette borne
La même capucine a fleuri ce matin.
Regarde la fermière en bonnet à deux cornes
Étendre sa lessive aux buissons du jardin.

from **SWING DOORS 1936-8**

THE ESCAPER

Old horse that chews its oats rehashed,
Soiled fodder past its sell-by date,
At every customs-post he's watched,
Worn out, a loser, dope, checkmate…

Propped on the carriage door he dozed
While forests slumbered by the rails,
Or furrows in the earth lay traced,
Straight as the spokes of mighty wheels.

The whistle sheared and he awoke.
Not sky, nor plain where hamlets bred
Like cod or herring dried in smoke,
Burnt by the sun to brindle-red,

Roast, salted, seared; soil's clammy touch,
Dust's onslaught; gnawed by rotting teeth
Of stone and straw and ivy's clutch,
Ghost-houses at the point of death;

Not sky, nor plain where hamlets bred,
Brought back his memories. The sky
By now looked silly overhead,
All honey-stale conformity.

But look! In this sequestered nook,
The same nasturtium blooms today.
Lace-capped, the farmer's-wife – just look! –
Spreads laundry on her shrubs to dry.

Regarde! mais regarde! et respire! L'odeur
Est la même qu'au soir d'un semblable voyage,
Aux vitres des wagons c'est la même vapeur
Et c'est dans le filet d'identiques bagages.

Mais, quoi, tu poursuivais ta route en sens contraire,
Suffit-il de si peu pour changer un pays?
Tu fuyais la prison aux geôles solitaires
Et les réveils, la nuit, de désirs assaillis,

Le pas des surveillants, les chansons dans la nuit
Que chantent les captifs écœurés de silence,
La cour de promenade où, main douce, la suie
Se posait sur la bouche ouverte aux confidences,

La gamelle et le pain, la cruche d'eau, la chiotte,
Nain roteur ouvrant l'œil humide, salement,
Et les livres souillés de réflexions idiotes,
Les graffiti gonflant les murs comme un ferment,

La rouille des verrous, les escaliers sonores,
Sentant l'eau de Javel, l'urine et le crésyl,
Le furtif balayage au long des corridors
Et les crachats mêlés de sanie et de bile…

Mais lui, loin des signaux fleuris le long des voies
Parcourait une plage où se brisait la mer:
C'était à l'aube de la vie et de la joie
Un orage, au lointain, astiquait ses éclairs.

Mais après l'aiguillage et la garde-barrière
Apparut la banlieue au pied de la colline,
Son gazon charbonneux mêlé de mâchefer
Et la prison bâtie derrière les usines.

But look! Just look! Breathe in! The smell
Is that of any evening train;
Same luggage in the rack as well,
Same misting on the window-pane.

You've reversed out, gone somewhere else.
Is the scene changed so readily?
You fled the jail of lonely cells,
The night-waked lusts of misery;

Nocturnal singing that resents
The silence and the warder's boot;
The yard where a mumbled confidence
Is choked by one deft glob of soot;

Tin mug, the bread, the jug, the bogs,
Books by an idiot's thoughts defaced,
Runt belching into bleary rags,
Wall swollen with graffiti's yeast,

The rusting bolts, the echoing stairs,
That smell of bleach and Jeyes and piss,
The furtive brooms in corridors,
The gobs of spit and bile and pus...

No tracks, no signals now. He ran
On the sand where the sea-wave splashes.
New life, new joy. The break of dawn!
A storm buffed up its lightning-flashes.

The points and level-crossing pass,
And little streets below the hill,
With slag and coal-dust on the grass;
Behind the factories, the jail.

Il se souvient: quand il passa, la porte close
Était baignée par le reflet du ciel dans le ruisseau,
Un molosse aboyait, et pour faire une pause
Dans l'ombre il s'appuya contre l'un des vantaux.

L'odeur de chèvrefeuille et de terre mouillée
Montait dans la nuit blanche et de grands papillons
Tournaient autour des réverbères surannés.
Son ventre palpitait au souffle des sillons.

Et les sillons qui rayonnaient autour du train
Avaient porté, blessure ouverte, leurs moissons,
Des robustes valets avaient battu le grain,
Les almanachs avaient usé trente saisons.

Mais ces wagons, filant au milieu des campagnes,
Que signale aux geôliers un panache éclatant,
Nul ne peut deviner qu'en rupture de bagne
Y rêve un évadé cherché depuis sept ans.

Tu revois la prison, c'est le château sans âge.
Ton voisin te regarde et ne soupçonne pas
Qu'en ton cœur est inscrit ce banal paysage
Exactement, comme à la règle et au compas.

Écoute la chanson qui naît dans ta mémoire.
Le soleil y rayonne et la rose y fleurit.
Tu es gai, tu souris, c'est une bonne histoire
Dont s'illumine la prison et ses murs gris.

Le train s'éloigne. Aux camarades prisonniers
Tu donnes un adieu et l'air que tu respires
Te gonfle les poumons d'un souffle ardent et ton empire
C'est la terre tout entière avec ses mers et ses palmiers,

Remember the escape: the gate
Was bathed in moonlight from the brook.
A mastiff barked. He leant his weight
On the dim door-flaps, for a break.

The fragrance of the pallid night
Was honeysuckle and moist earth.
Great moths flew round each faded light.
His gut throbbed to the furrows' breath.

The furrows, spokes around the train,
Had borne their open wound, their crop;
Strong farmer's-lads had threshed the grain
While Time used thirty seasons up.

Across the fields the coaches go.
Smoke-plumes alert the officers.
A man at large - who'd ever know? –
Dreams, on the run for seven years.

You see the prison, ageless fort.
Your glancing neighbour won't surmise
This dreary tract's carved on your heart,
Ruler and compass, so precise.

Enjoy that song your mind recalls:
Roses in bloom, sun shining bright.
Great story! You are wreathed in smiles,
The grey-walled prison basks in light.

Goodbye, my cellmates. Whistle blows:
And you inhale an ardent breath
That swells your lungs. Your empire is all those
Palm-trees and seas and forests, all the earth

Avec ses forêts et ses lacs et ses fleuves au cours pacifique
Et ses villes dressées malgré de nombreux avatars,
La guerre, l'incendie et les secousses sismiques,
Par les hommes, par les hommes et leur art.

Va, poursuis ton chemin, il n'est plus de frontières,
Plus de douanes, plus de gendarmes, plus de prisons.
Tu es libre et tu ris et tu parcours la terre
Et tu passes, devant les détectives, sans un frisson.

Liberté retrouvée, ah! joie! ah! rire aux anges
J'écoute la chanson des oiseaux, près du lac, dans la forêt,
Je sens mon sang,
Je devine tous les secrets,
J'affronte tous les baisers.

Saveur de l'air, saveur de mon sang dans mes veines,
Saveur de ma salive et de ma propre chair…
Les cailloux seront plus doux que la laine
Pour y dormir, tandis que l'étoile polaire

Montera sur l'horizon dans le bruit des échos
des villes, des campagnes et de toute la terre,
Dans le battement des ailes des oiseaux
Et celui des portes des maisons pénitentiaires.

Je vous offre camarades encore emprisonnés
Un peu de ma liberté et de ma force,
Le ciel s'éteint, les heures vont sonner…
L'itinéraire je le grave sur les arbres, dans l'écorce
En entailles profondes que le printemps fera saigner,

Afin que vous trouviez facilement le chemin
Qui ramène à la vie sans embûches,
Aux rivières fraîches pour le bain,
Aux jardins frémissant de fontaines et de ruches.

With its lakes and rivers in their peaceful course,
Cities of many avatars, rearing still
Through conflagrations, wars and seismic shocks,
The work of men, of men and human skill.

Go on your way! No boundary,
No jail, no checkpoint, no gendarme.
You roam the world, exulting, free,
You pass peeled eyes without a qualm.

Liberty regained, ah, joy! ah! laughter of angels!
I listen to birdsong by the lake, in the forest,
I sense my blood,
I guess all the secrets,
I take on all the kisses.

Taste of my spittle, of my blood in my veins,
The taste of my own flesh, the taste of air…
Softer than wool will be the pebble-stones
To sleep on, while the Pole-star and the Bear

Mount the horizon to the echoings
Of urban and bucolic harmonies
Of the whole earth; the flapping of birds' wings,
And of the gates of penitentiaries.

I offer you, comrades, serving out your time,
Some of my strength and my liberty: share them, please…
The sky is darkening, the hours will chime,
I am scoring the route for you on the bark of trees
With deep incisions. Spring will draw blood from these,

So that you easily may find the path
To free and unentangled lives,
Cool rivers perfect for a bath,
And gardens resonant with springs and hives.

10 JUIN 1936

Au détour du chemin,
Il entendit la main,
Devant le beau matin.

Le ciel était si clair
Que les nuages dans l'air
Ressemblaient à l'écume de la mer.

Et la fleur des pommiers
Blanchissait dans les près
Où séchait le linge lavé.

La source qui chantait,
Chantait la vie qui passait
Au long des prés, au long des haies

Et la forêt à l'horizon,
Où verdissait le gazon,
Comme une cloche était pleine de sons.

La vie était si belle,
Elle entrait si bien dans ses prunelles
Dans son cœur et dans ses oreilles,

Qu'il éclata de rire:
Il rit au monde et aux soupirs
Du vent dans les arbres en fleur.

Il rit à l'odeur de la terre,
Il rit au linge des lavandières,
Il rit aux nuages passant dans l'air.

Comme il riait en haut de la colline,
Parut la fille de belle mine
Qui venait de la maison voisine.

10 JUNE 1936

At the corner of the way
He spread his hand as if to say
isn't this a lovely day.

and the sky so clear that day
kept the clouds in airy play
light and loose as ocean spray.

Laundry hanging clean and bright
on the line a splendid sight
fields with apple-blossom white

Singing streamlet from the spring
sang that life was happening
hedgerows meadows burgeoning

And the distant scene all round,
forest-green and meadow-ground,
like a bell was full of sound.

Life was lovely, life was dear,
entering the deepest core
of his heart and eye and ear,

and he laughed and laughed, at ease
with the world and with the breeze
sighing in the flowery trees,

laughed at honest earthy smells,
laughed at freshly-laundered clothes,
laughed at all the passing clouds.

He was laughing on the hill.
As he laughed, the pretty girl
from next door turned up as well.

Et la fille rit aussi
Et quand son rire s'évanouit
Les oiseaux chantaient à nouveau.

Elle rit de le voir rire
Et les colombes qui se mirent
Dans le bassin aux calmes eaux
Écoutèrent son rire
Dans l'air s'évanouir.

Jamais plus ils ne se revirent.
Elle passa souvent sur le chemin
Où l'homme tendit la main
À la lumière du matin.

Maintes fois il se souvint d'elle
Et sa mémoire trop fidèle
Se reflétait dans ses prunelles.

Maintes fois elle se souvint de lui
Et dans l'eau profonde du puits
C'est son visage qu'elle revit.

Les ans passèrent un à un
En pâlissant comme au matin
Les cartes qu'un joueur tient dans sa main.

Tous deux pourrissent dans la terre,
Mordus par les vers sincères.
La terre emplit leur bouche pour les faire taire.

Peut-être s'appelleraient-ils dans la nuit,
Si la mort n'avait horreur du bruit:
Le chemin reste et le temps fuit.

And the girl was laughing too.
When her merriment was through,
all the wood-birds laughed anew.

She was laughing to have seen
how he laughed, till doves that preen
in calm waters of the mere
heard his laughter disappear,
slowly vanish in the air.

From that day they met no more.
Many times she walked that way
where he spread his hand to say
isn't this a lovely day.

She remained for long in his
thoughts, the doting memories
still reflected in his eyes.

He in hers for long did dwell:
in deep waters of a well,
hers the face he knew so well.

The years have passed, one by one,
gradually growing wan
like a hand of cards at dawn.

Both lie rotting in the ground.
Gagged by earth, they make no sound.
Worms, plain-speakers, bite and wound.

They might hear each other's cries:
sadly, though, death hates a noise.
Still the lane remains, time flies.

Mais chaque jour le beau matin
Comme un œuf tombe dans la main
Du passant sur le chemin.

Chaque jour le ciel est si clair
Que les nuages dans l'air
Sont comme l'écume sur la mer.

Morts! Épaves sombrées dans la terre,
Nous ignorons vos misères
Chantées par les solitaires.

Nous nageons, nous vivons,
Dans l'air pur de chaque saison.
La vie est belle et l'air est bon.

FUNÉRAILLES

«Ne poussez pas! ne poussez pas!
«Tas de salauds!
«Espèce de vache avec vos mamelles pendantes avez-vous fini de pousser!
«Du calme, il y en a pour tout le monde.
«Regardez-moi cette putain avec ses airs de marquise!
«Tu pues! tu pues!
«C'est criminel d'emmener des enfants dans cette foule!
«Si on les emmène c'est qu'on peut pas faire autrement.
«Ça va durer encore longtemps?
«Madame vous perdez votre culotte.
«Qu'est-ce que ça peut vous faire?
«Et puis d'abord je vous emmerde

Yet dawn daily lights the land,
shines on some itinerant,
nestling, egg-like, in his hand,

and the sky so clear each day
keeps the clouds in airy play
light and loose as ocean spray.

You, the dead, each foundered waif,
we know nothing of your grief,
sung by those of lonely life.

We are swimming, living – where?
In each season's good fresh air.
Life is sweet, the day is fair.

FUNERAL

'Don't push! Don't push!'
'Lot of bastards!'
'Finished pushing yet, you cow? Droopy tits!'
'Relax, there's room for all.'
'Look at that tart carrying on like a duchess!'
'You stink! You stink!'
'It's criminal to bring children into this crowd!'
'We bring them because we've no choice.'
'Is this going to take much longer?'
'You're losing your knickers, madam.'
'What's that to you?'
'I've got you going, anyway.'

– C'est un enterrement, un bel enterrement.
Tout le monde veut en être.
On se piétine pour entrer au cimetière,
Mais il y aura de la place pour tout le monde.

ÉROTISME DE LA MÉMOIRE

Cuisses de Diane
Ventre de Diane
Seins de Diane
Yeux de Diane

Le petit jour point dans la forêt où tout est orange!
Sauf le tronc marqué de craie des bouleaux.

C'est là près de cet arbre aux feuilles vieillissant avant la saison que j'ai rencontré Diane dans une attitude naturelle mais rarement décrite dans les poèmes.
Les fesses ovales se dessinaient entre le désordre du linge et le vert gris tendre de l'herbe
Dans un sentier voisin le pas d'un garde retentit
Il passa sans qu'on le vit.
Tandis que Diane se dissolvait dans le jour,
comme le croissant de la lune,
À cet endroit de la forêt il y a les débris d'une bouteille
Un vieux livre que les pluies et les rosées renvoient au terreau
Une plume d'oiseau
Un morceau de silex
Une empreinte de pas profondément marquée dans la terre
Et quelqu'un, peut-être, passera là au jour et à l'heure de ma mort
Ô vie, enivrante vie
Aveuglante et bienfaisante.

– It's a funeral, a lovely funeral.
Everyone wants to be there.
People are trampling each other to get into the cemetery.
But there'll be room for all.

EROTICS OF MEMORY

Diana's breasts
Diana's thighs
Diana's belly
Diana's eyes

Dawn breaks in the forest. All is orange!
Except the birch-trunks marked with chalk.

There, near that tree whose leaves grow old too early, I came across Diana in a natural posture not often described in poems.
Her oval buttocks were outlined between disarranged underwear and the soft green-grey of grass
On a nearby path echoed the step of a keeper
He went past unseen.
While Diana melted in daylight,
like the crescent moon.
At this spot in the forest there are fragments of a bottle
An old book that rain and dew are rotting down to mould
A bird's feather
A scrap of flint
A footprint deeply etched in the ground
And maybe someone will pass there, the day and hour that I die.
O life, heady life
Blinding and bountiful.

CHANSON DE MONSIEUR DE CHARETTE

Monsieur de Charette a dit
À ceux de Charenton et de Vincennes
C'est aujourd'hui Dimanche, hier était Samedi,
La fuite des jours me fait de la peine.

Monsieur de Charette a dit
J'ai un nom à coucher dehors
Et puis toujours derrière les fesses des chevaux
Ça n'est pas propre, ça n'est pas beau.

Monsieur de Charette a dit
J'en ai assez de rouler dans le crottin,
Moi qui appartiens au gratin
Avec mes deux brancards et ma manivelle.

Monsieur de Charette a dit
Je suis d'un autre âge
Comme les poètes Voiture et Ménage
Qui sont maintenant au paradis.

L'automobile m'a fait beaucoup de tort,
Tous ces chauffeurs sont des butors
Où est-il le temps des cochers?
Il est tard, allons nous coucher.

SONG OF MR CART

Said Mr Cart
To all at Carterton and at Crewe
Incarcerated in fort or zoo
Saturday yesterday Sunday today
I hate the way days flitter away

Said Mr Cart
I'm noted for sleeping out of doors
And being behind the back end of a horse
Not clean not smart
Said Mr Cart

Said Mr Cart
I'm tired of trundling in horse-manure
With a pair of shafts and a handlebar
I'm one of the smart set, someone apart
Said Mr Cart

Said Mr Cart
I come from another age, I'm sure
Like the poet Ménage and the poet Voiture
Who went to heaven because of their art
Said Mr Cart

The horseless carriage has done me down
Show me a chauffeur I'll show you a clown
When will the carter be cock of the town?
It's late he said
It's time for bed.

APRÈS MOI

D'une pluie une goutte,
D'une goutte une poussière.
De poussière en poussières
Un grain de sable.
D'un grain de sable un caillou.
D'un caillou un coup de pied.
Le coup de pied d'un voyageur
Sur la route entre les montagnes.
L'empreinte du pied s'efface dans la poussière.
L'écho se perd de la chanson qu'il chantait.

Un voyageur de moins sur la terre
Toujours semblable à elle-même
Ou si peu s'en faut!

BONSOIR TOUT LE MONDE

– Couché dans ton lit
Entre tes draps,
Comme une lettre dans son enveloppe,
Tu t'imagines que tu pars
Pour un long voyage.

– Mais non, je n'imagine rien.
Je suis pas né d'hier
Je connais le sommeil et ses mystères
Je connais la nuit et ses ténèbres
Et je dors comme je vis.

AFTER ME

Drop of rain,
Speck of a drop.
Specks of dust
Sandgrain.
Sandgrain a pebble.
Pebble a kick.
Kick of a wayfarer
On the mountain pass.
Footprint erased in the dust.
Fading echo of song he sang.

One wayfarer the less on this earth
Which stays just the same
Or near enough!

GOODNIGHT EVERYONE

'Lying in bed
Between your sheets,
Like a letter in its envelope,
You imagine you're off
On a long journey.'

'No, I don't imagine anything.
I wasn't born yesterday.
I know sleep and its mysteries
I know night and its shadows
And I sleep as I live.'

L'HOMME QUI A PERDU SON OMBRE

– Où l'ai-je laissée dans quelle cave? dans quel puits?
À quel carrefour du jour et de la nuit?
Dans quelle caverne dans quelle cheminée de fumée et de suie?

– Tu marchais peut-être dans les marais
Au crépuscule ou bien parmi tes effets
Défroque, uniforme aux galons défaits,
(Quel souvenir de jugement et de dégradation!)
Tu l'accrochas par distraction.

– Mais pourquoi cela le gêne-t-il?
L'ombre me paraît tellement inutile
Il n'y a pas de quoi se faire de bile.

– J'essaie de me souvenir
Mais je n'en ai ni la puissance ni peut-être le désir.

– Cherche au fond des rivières
Où tu mirais encore hier
Ton visage qui est ce que tu possèdes de plus cher.

– Quoi? Ni cœur ni sexe ni diamant
Ni l'ivresse du vin et celle des amants
Ne lui paraissent plus précieux et plus charmants.

– Non ce qui m'est le plus cher c'est mon ombre
Qui m'accompagnait sans encombre
Dans les rues bien pavées et les décombres.

THE MAN WHO LOST HIS SHADOW

"Where have I
laid it by?
Down what well or
in what cellar?
Was it where the nights and days
cross their ways?
In what cavern have I put it?
In what fireplace, smoked and sooted?"

"Walking in the twilit marsh,
or among your own effects,
unfrocked, stripped of epaulettes,
(verdict and disgrace – what scars!)
you with *maladresse* mistook,
must have stuck it on a hook."

Surely, though, a shadow's rather
non-essential? What's the bother?
Why get into such a lather?

"Can't remember – cannot figure.
No desire, and still less vigour."

"Search and drag the rivers where
yesterday I saw you stare
at your dear face, mirrored there."

What? Not heart nor sex nor sapphires,
drunkenness of wine and lovers,
seem more precious, charm him better.

"More than all I loved my shadow,
staunch companion, faithful Fido,
on the pavement, in the gutter."

– Comme un chien tenu en laisse
Ton ombre pleine de paresse
Était lourde sans qu'il y paraisse.

– Mon ombre était la caverne
Où comme un œil dans son cerne
Taureau de feu vendangeur sanglant hydre de Lerne
Guettaient les rêves taciturnes araignées des citernes.

– Eh bien? Si tu perdis la tienne
Envolée par la fente des persiennes
Sur un chemin de poussières aériennes
Prends-en une autre sans honte ni gêne.

– Voilà qu'il sort son couteau
Et qu'il coupe comme un gâteau
L'ombre immense d'un château.

– De ton ombre s'envolent des ombres
Et ton corps lui-même sombre
Ombre parmi les ombres nombre parmi les nombres.

– Je traîne après moi maintes forteresses
Maints paysages de détresses
Et le regret de ma jeunesse.

– Il abomine le soleil et la lune
Et il recherche sa fortune
Dans l'eau putride des lagunes.

– Voila qu'il jette aux orties
Lundi mardi mercredi jeudi
Vendredi samedi.

"What a weight, your shiftless shade!
Like a dog that tugs a lead:
quite deceptive, what it weighed!"

"No, my shadow was the cavern.
Eyeball-orb in orbit-haven,
stubble-bull and bleeding Hydra,
silent dreams, that spied a spider."

"Very well, if yours got lost,
flitted through a slatted blind
on a path of airy dust –
take another, never mind!"

This is when he takes his dirk,
cuts the shadow, like a cake,
from a castle, vast and dark.

"From your shadow shadows gambol,
and your frame itself shall stumble,
just one number, one penumbra."

"Dragged behind me, fortresses,
countrysides of miseries,
sorrows of my tender years."

He detests the sun and moon,
searches, hoping for a boon,
each malodorous lagoon.

In the nettles he has thrown
all six weekdays one by one.
Now it's Sunday and the sun

– Aujourd'hui c'est Dimanche
C'est le soleil perçant les branches
C'est le muguet c'est la pervenche.

C'est l'oubli des vieux chagrins
Au chapelet le dernier grain
C'est le cheval sans mors ni frein.

Ainsi que sur une image
Mon corps se dresse sur les nuages
Sans ombre et sans âge.

Le vieux tombeau de nos ancêtres
La flamme aux lueurs de salpêtre
Autour de mes membres s'enchevêtre.

Le vieux tombeau de mes pères
Le vieux tombeau c'est la terre
C'est la mer et c'est l'air.

– Ton ombre tombe en ruine
Et tout ton corps se déracine
À l'envers et tombe dans les mines.

– Qu'il disparaisse à jamais
Celui que nulle ombre ne suivait
Celui qui fut l'homme imparfait

Car il faut à l'homme son ombre
Au comptable il faut le nombre
Au château les décombres.

– Je renais baigné de lumière
Je renais vivant sur la terre
Plus féconde et plus prospère

shines on periwinkle alley,
parts the foliage, O sole
mio, *lily-of-the-valley.*

"It is old regrets forgot,
bead of penance ultimate,
horse with neither rein nor bit.

Like an image my corsage
rises up on a mirage,
has no shadow, has no age.

At our old ancestral tomb
the saltpetre-tinted flame
tangles closely with my frame.

All my forebears, buried there!
It is earth, that sepulchre,
it is sea and it is air."

"Ruined shadow falling prone,
all your body is undone,
tumbling down a mineshaft, gone."

Let him disappear for good,
person by no shade pursued,
lacking proper plenitude.

Man must have his shadow-nimbus
as accountants need their numbers,
stately homes their lumber-chambers.

"I'm reborn in shining light,
living on this earth that's yet
More fecund, more fortunate.

Mon ombre n'appartient pas au soleil
Et la nuit pendant mon sommeil
Mon ombre est là sur moi qui veille

Lasse de suivre les contours
De mon corps pendant le jour
Et de traîner sur terre toujours

Mon ombre enfin sort des limites
Mon ombre enfin sort de son gîte
Et va où son désir l'invite

Mon ombre se confond avec la nuit
Avec le charbon et la suie
Et fume parce que je vis

Mon ombre envahit la moitié du monde
Et flotte avec les vents et les ondes
Avec les fleuves et la mer qui gronde.

– Son ombre est-elle douée de parole?
Elle l'injurie et le console
Et joue pour lui les plus beaux rôles.

– Ton ombre elle est galonnée
Mais elle a mis un faux nez
Et chante un refrain suranné.

– À la croisée des chemins
Ton ombre t'a fait de la main
Un adieu jusqu'à demain.

– Jusqu'à toujours elle est partie
Pour fonder parmi les orties
Dans tes rêves une dynastie.

Sunlight cannot hold my shade:
When at night I rest my head,
still my shadow guards my bed.

Tired of always trailing round
with my body's daily round,
always dragging on the ground,

now my shade goes everywhere,
stirs at long last from its lair,
heeds the promptings of desire.

My shade merges with the night,
mixes in with coal and soot,
smokes, because I live in light.

It's invaded half the world,
with the waves and winds is whirled,
with the streams, the seas that scold."

Is it skilled in vocables?
It insults him and consoles,
plays for him the finest roles.

"Though your shadow's pips impress,
that's a false nose on its face,
and its song is out to grass."

"At the corner of the way,
shadow waved to you to say:
we shall meet in just a day.

Gone for ever, frisking free
through the nettle-beds! there'll be,
in your dreams, a dynasty."

– Il la retrouvera quand l'heure
Sonnera où sans couleur
Le corps qui meurt perd sa chaleur.

– Mon ombre elle est là dans ma tête
Bien enfoncée dans sa cachette
Mon ombre est sourde aveugle et muette.

– Je suis ton ombre du matin
Celle du jour à son déclin
Et de midi sur les jardins.

– Elle est aussi l'ombre de nuit
C'est elle qui tourne et le suit
Quand le réverbère s'allume et luit.

– Je suis environné d'ombres
Car il est l'ombre de son ombre
Un nombre parmi les nombres.

– Le sang circule dans mes veines
Je m'incarne et pleins d'oxygène
Mes poumons respirent sans peine

Je m'en vais parmi les vivants
Je marche vers la lumière
Et mon ombre n'est pas derrière:
Comme il se doit elle est devant

– J'entendais jadis une voix
Elle se tait et dans les bois
L'écho lui-même se tient coi

– Tu te dissous et moi aussi
Et notre mort sans autopsie
Ne laissera pas trace ici

He shall find it when the hour
strikes, when body's laid on bier:
body-heat shall disappear.

"No, my shadow's billeted
in its hide-out, in my head:
speech, sight, hearing, all are dead."

"I'm your shadow of the dawn
and your garden-shade of noon
and your shade when day is done,

your tenebral acolyte
turning, following at night
in the artificial light."

I am hedged with shadow sombre:
he is umbrage and penumbra,
nothing but a numbered number.

"Flows my blood from vein to vein,
lungs are breathing oxygen:
man of flesh, I feel no pain.

To the living, not the dead,
to the light and not the shade,
see, my shadow strides ahead,
leading, as a shadow should."

"In the woods a song was sung
long ago, when I was young:
now the echo's lost its tongue."

"You dissolve and so do I,
dying with no autopsy:
not one vestige, by and by."

– J'entends l'orchestre de la fête
Les chants et les cris du travail
Aucun obstacle ne m'arrête
Libre et vivant dans ma conquête

Car les muses sont illusoires
Dont le cœur reste silencieux
Ce n'est pas dans les ciboires
Que le vin se boit le mieux

La vie est au cœur de la vie
Le sang qui chante sous la chair
Dessine la géographie
Du corps, du monde et du mystère

Rapport de l'astre et de la terre
Rassurant témoignage, aimable compagnon
Ombre flexible et jamais solitaire
C'est dans tes plis que nous dormirons.

BACCHUS ET APOLLON

Marchant ensemble, en compagnons
Voici Bacchus et Apollon
Le temps est court, l'espace est long.

Frères ennemis,
Qu'il fasse jour, qu'il fasse nuit,
Une seule ombre vous précède et vous suit.

"I can hear the flag-day band,
songs and shouts of those who toil.
Nothing in my way can stand,
free and living I prevail

Muses disappoint and fail us
if their heart is mute and void.
Not from reverential chalice
is the vintage best enjoyed.

At the heart of life is life.
Singing in the flesh, the blood
sketches out the geography:
body, world and mystery,

earth and star in harmony,
friend, sustaining story told,
pliant never-lonely shade,
we shall sleep where you enfold."

BACCHUS AND APOLLO

Bacchus and Apollo stride
here together side by side.
Time is narrow, space is wide.

Night and day, fraternal foes,
jointly-owned, your shadow grows
from your ankles, or your toes.

Pivot d'une horloge indéchiffrable
Votre couple marche sur le sable:
Beaux enfants de la Fable.

Je vous suis à travers les forêts,
Je vous suis à travers les marais
À travers tout ce qui est.

Je vous suis jusqu'à la clairière
Où jaillit l'eau dans la lumière…
Nécessaires à la terre.

Alors vous avez lutté
Et vous voilà ensanglantés,
Le ventre ouvert, les yeux crevés.

Bataille semblable à l'amour
Étreinte féconde du jour
Avec la nuit qui revient toujours.

Que s'enfle votre ventre
De larves et de vers qui entrent
Vers votre cœur et votre centre.

Mettez bas comme des femelles
Après votre lutte fraternelle.
La mort vous donnera des ailes.

Bacchus et Apollon,
Sales geôliers de nos prisons,
Cadavres dont nous périssons,

Couple infâme et semblable à l'homme
Qui n'a jamais connu, en somme,
Qu'un seul aspect des choses qu'il nomme.

Treading sand, your pretty couple
powers an indecipherable
timepiece, like twin babes of fable.

I shall track you through the trees,
through the marshy moistnesses,
track you through whatever is.

I shall track you to the glen
where the stream leaps in the sun:
earth has need of them, each one.

There you fought as enemies,
Now you bleed from injuries,
bellies slit and blinded eyes.

Battle like an act of love,
day's prolific squeezing of
night, who takes no evenings off.

May your swollen belly rot,
worms and grubs invertebrate
breach your centre and your heart.

Sheathe your blades, be womanly,
you whose fight was brotherly,
death shall give you wings to fly.

Vile Apollo, dirty Bacchus,
in their prison-house they lock us,
we the victims, they the carcass:

evil couple, just like man,
never knowing more than one
side of what he comments on.

Ah! voir se dérouler ensemble
La nuit calme et le jour qui tremble,
Le crépuscule et l'aube et minuit et midi.

Qui sortira de vos entrailles
Sera le bâtard de vos funérailles,
De vos mensonges et de vos épousailles.

Ce sera de nouveau la sirène
Avec son diadème de reine
Et ses chants doux comme la laine.

Chaque matin le soleil se lève
L'ombre se dissout dans l'ombre
L'homme réfléchit l'homme.

Simultaneous, what a sight,
trembling day and tranquil night,
dusk, dawn, midnight, noonday light.

Soon she'll issue from your bowels,
bastard of your funerals,
marriages, and false avowals:

she the siren comes again,
sparkling circlet of a queen,
songs as soft as lambs-wool skein.

Shadow at the dawn of day
into shadow fades away.
But a man reflects a man.

RESISTANT

Translator's Note

All the following poems are from the period of the Nazi Occupation. They reflect that Occupation, and the French Resistance to it in which Desnos took an active part. He was in two networks, Agir and Combat. Agir told the British where V-1 rocket sites were being built, among them the 'Watten Bunker' (Blockhaus d'Éperlecques): the Allies bombed it and it could never fire.

État de Veille (State of Alert) was published in April 1943, though the first few poems had been written in peacetime. In the same month, he entrusted to publishers two of his three great Occupation sequences, *Contrée* and *Le Bain avec Andromède*, as well as *Chantefables* (for children: it is now available in bilingual text, with English). In 1944 France was liberated and these works were published, but by then, he had been arrested and deported, never to return: he never saw them in print. *Calixto* only appeared many years later. The nymph Calixto represents Liberation, as does the she-bear in the earlier poem.

There is a legend of Desnos' captivity: that he managed to save the lives of a few prisoners who were about to be executed, by reading their palms and predicting in detail their lives after the war: and that the guards, confused, returned these victims to the barracks. It is only half true. Desnos on arriving at the charnel-house of Auschwitz in spring 1944 moved among the other exhausted, starving victims, reading their palms and confidently making detailed predictions. He was able to comfort these few unfortunates: to distract them, but not to save them, from their imminent doom. It was the inspired act of a poet, a man of the greatest humanity and compassion. Desnos died at Terezin in June 1945.

HISTOIRE D'UN CHAMEAU

Le chameau qui n'a plus de dents,
Ce soir, n'est pas content.
Il est allé chez le dentiste,
Un homme noir et triste,
Et le dentiste lui a dit
Que ses soins n'étaient pas pour lui.
Tas de salauds, qu'il dit le chameau,
Vous êtes venus parmi mes sables
Avec des airs peu aimables,
Des airs de désert, bien sûr,
Aussi sûrs que les pommes sures.
Vous m'avez mis une selle,
Vous m'avez chevauché surmontés d'une ombrelle,
Et va te faire foutre,
Si j'ai mal aux dents...
Mais puisque tu n'as pas de dents!
Précisément, j'ai mal aux dents de n'en plus avoir.
Alors tu désires un râtelier?
Je voudrais bien voir un chameau porter râtelier!
Un râtelier manger au râtelier!
Le chameau qui n'a plus de dents,
On l'abandonne dans le désert.
Alors il pisse lentement dans le sable qui se creuse en entonnoir
Tandis que la caravane s'éloigne, à travers les dunes creusées en
entonnoirs,
À travers les dunes,
Elles-mêmes creusées en entonnoirs.

TALE OF A CAMEL

The camel with toothless gums
tonight has a fit of the glums
He's been and seen
the ungentle dental practitioner's room
full of doom and gloom
and the dentist hissed
'I cannot assist'.
The camel says You're a heap of creeps
you assailed my seas
like a hostile breeze
a breeze of the desert for sure, onshore,
whose fiery power makes apples go sour.
You had me saddled
sunshaded and straddled,
so go to hell!
I've a pain in the teeth…
But you've lost your teeth!
Exactly, so I've a pain in the teeth, from having no teeth.
So do you want dentures?
I'd like to see a camel with dentures!
Dentures for munchers in mangers!
The toothless camel
turned loose in the desert
slowly widdles into the sand that hollows into a crater
the caravan vanishes over the dunes hollowed out into craters,
over the dunes,
themselves hollowed out into craters.

HISTOIRE D'UNE OURSE

Une ourse fit son entrée dans la ville.
Elle marchait pesamment
Et des gouttes d'eau brillaient dans son pelage
Comme des diamants.

Elle marcha méconnue,
Elle marcha par les rues
Dans son manteau poilu.

La foule passait,
Nul ne la regardait
Et même on la bousculait.

Enfin la nuit tomba à genoux
Laissant ruisseler ses cheveux roux
Dans les ruisseaux pleins de boue,

Dans la mer en mal de marée,
Sur les prairies, sur les forêts
Et sur les villes illuminées.

L'ourse disparut aspirée par les nombres
Avec la foule, avec les ombres
Confondues dans les décombres.

Seuls quelques astronomes,
Embusqués sous des dômes,
Virent passer son fantôme.

Qu'on te nomme Grande Ourse
Tandis que tu poursuis ta course
Vers la lumière et vers ses sources,

TALE OF A BEAR

A bear entered the city.
She trod heavily
And drops of water shone in her pelt
Like diamonds.

She walked unrecognised
She walked through the streets
In her pelt of fur.

The crowd passed by.
No-one gave her a glance.
She was even jostled.

Night had fallen on its knees,
Let its auburn tresses ease
Into streams of muddy ooze,

In the heaving sea-sick sea,
Rolling plain and field and tree,
Cities of electricity.

The bear vanished in the sombre
Crowd, absorbed into the number,
Just another lump of lumber.

Some astronomers, at most,
In their dome and at their post,
Traced and tracked her passing ghost.

You deserve your name, because,
Great She-Bear, you set your course
To the bright light's radiant source.

Que l'on te pare d'étoiles
Et que du fond de leur geôle
Les prisonniers te voient passer devant le soupirail,

Ourse qu'importe, ourse de plume,
Ourse rugissante et bavant l'écume,
Plus étincelante qu'un marteau frappant l'enclume,

Ourse qu'importe la fable
Et ta piste sur le sable
S'effilochant comme un vieux câble.

J'entends des pas lourds dans la nuit,
J'entends des chants, j'entends des cris,
Les cris, les chants de mes amis.

Leurs pas sont lourds
Mais quand naîtra le jour
Naîtra la liberté et l'amour.

Qu'il naisse demain ou dans cent ans
Il sera fait de lumière et de sang
Et renouvellera les quatre éléments.

Plus lourdes que l'ourse dans la cité
Par le monde je sens monter
La grande invasion, la grande marée.

Grande Ourse au ciel tu resplendis
Tandis que j'écoute dans la nuit
Les cris, les chants de mes amis.

Stars should deck you out like jewels,
Prisoners in deepest jails
See you pass their breathing-holes.

Don't-care, she-bear, penman's plume,
Bear that roars and slavers spume,
Hammer-spark in forging-room.

Don't-care, she-bear of the fable,
Footprints in the sand, unstable,
Fraying like a worn-out cable.

I hear heavy tread go by,
I hear shouts and revelry,
Hear my friends who sing and cry.

Heavy though the tread may be,
Yet the new-born day shall see
Birth of love and liberty.

Born at once or ages hence,
Blood and light, deliverance
Freshening four elements.

Bear and city, small beside
Heavy swell I feel world-wide,
Great invasion, great flood-tide.

Great Bear shining in the sky!
Wide awake, alert I lie,
Hear my friends who sing and cry.

HISTOIRE D'UNE ABEILLE

Abeille bruissante des matins d'été,
Abeille qui bourdonnes dans la tasse,
Abeille où es-tu allée?
Abeille bruissante et jamais lasse.

J'ai construit ma ruche
Dans la cervelle d'un enfant
Mais tant va l'abeille à la cruche
Que la fleur fleurit dedans.

Ce furent d'abord les yeux étonnés
Et le miel, et la cire bien construite,
Le sourire et le rire et le mot chantonné
Et la question jamais détruite.

Tant qu'à force de bourdonner
Dans la cervelle de l'enfant
Il finit par s'en étonner
Et par inquiéter ses parents.

Quand il fut approvisionné
De miel et de cire bien mûrs
Alors je l'ai abandonné
Dans le baiser d'une piqûre.

Mais nul jamais ne fera sortir de sa mémoire
Mon bourdonnement a moi, l'abeille,

Et jamais il ne voudra croire
Aux mots pourris qu'on glisse dans l'oreille,

Qu'on glisse sournoisement
Dans l'oreille des enfants,
Avec la complicité des parents.

TALE OF A BEE

Buzzing bee on summer morn,
Bee that buzzes in the cup:
Buzzing bee, where have you gone?
Buzzing, never letting up.

I built my hive
In a little one's brain,
For my bud to thrive
Came again and again.

First, the eyes' astonishment:
Honey's waxen bastion.
Smiles and laughs and babblement,
One persistent question.

So much did I hum
In the little one's head,
The child was struck dumb,
The parents dismayed.

When the child was well supplied,
Comb of honey mellowing,
Then it was I left its side,
With a kiss that was a sting.

Child for ever after hears
Buzz of busy hive,
Disregards
Rotten words
Slyly slipped in little ears,
Parents that connive.

TERRE

Un jour après un jour,
Une vague après une vague.
Où vas-tu? Où allez-vous?
Terre meurtrie par tant d'hommes errants!
Terre enrichie par les cadavres de tant d'hommes.
Mais la terre c'est nous,
Nous ne sommes pas sur elle
Mais en elle depuis toujours.

RÊVES

Poser sa tête sur un oreiller
Et sur cet oreiller dormir
Et dormant rêver
À des choses curieuses ou d'avenir

Rêvant croire à ce qu'on rêve
Et rêvant garder la notion
De la vie qui passe sans trêve
Du soir à l'aube sans rémission.

Ceci est presque normal,
Ceci est presque délicieux
Mais je plains ceux
Qui dorment vite et mal,

Et, mal éveillés, rêvent en marchant.

Ainsi j'ai marché autrefois,
J'ai marché, agi en rêvant,
Prenant les rues pour les allées d'un bois.

EARTH

A day, another day,
A wave, another wave.
Where are you going? One and all?
Earth bruised by so many wanderers!
Earth enriched by so many of our corpses.
But the earth is ourselves,
We are not on it,
But in it, and always have been.

DREAMS

To put your head on a pillow
On a pillow to sleep and dream
To dream of the unusual,
Perhaps of things to come,

To dream a dream and believe it
Keeping this notion in sight
With nothing to halt or reprieve it
Life runs to the dawn, all night

And this is almost normal
It's almost a tasty treat
I'm sorry for those people
Who sleep très mal and trop vite

They wake up all wrong, walk dreaming

Time was when I walked just so
I walked and I acted dreaming
Thought the streets were a woodland stroll.

Une place pour les rêves
Mais les rêves à leur place.

ALORS LA TROMPETTE

Alors la trompette retentira à toutes les portes de la ville
Et des oiseaux s'envoleront au bruit des fanfares.
Ils voleront longtemps au-dessus de la ville
Et, quand ils se posent,
Déjà nous reposerons
Heureux, joyeux, le cœur contenté.
Dormant dans la nuit qui précédera le premier lever de soleil du bonheur retrouvé.

À CINQ HEURES

À cinq heures du matin dans une rue neuve et vide j'entends le bruit d'une voiture qui s'éloigne.
Un avertisseur d'incendie a sa glace brisée et les debris de verre resplendissent dans le ruisseau.

Sur le pavé il y a une flaque de sang et un peu de fumée se dissout dans l'air.
Ohé! Ohé! racontez-moi ce qui s'est passé.
Éveillez-vous! Je veux savoir ce qui s'est passé.
Racontez-moi les aventures des hommes.

A place for dreams
But dreams in their place.

THEN THE TRUMPET

Then the trumpet shall sound at all the gates of the city
And birds take flight at the noise of the fanfares.
They shall fly for a long time above the city
And when they settle
We shall already be at rest
Happy, joyful, the heart contented,
Sleeping in the night before the first sunrise of happiness
regained.

AT FIVE O'CLOCK

At five o'clock in the morning in a new, empty street I hear
the noise of a car driving away.
A fire alarm has had its glass broken and the fragments are
sparkling in the gutter.

On the cobbles there is a small pool of blood and there is
smoke dissolving in the air.
Hey! Hey! Tell me what's happened.
Wake up! I want to know what's happened.
Tell me the adventures of men.

AUJOURD'HUI JE ME SUIS PROMENÉ...

Aujourd'hui je me suis promené avec mon camarade,
Même s'il est mort,
Je me suis promené avec mon camarade.

Qu'ils étaient beaux les arbres en fleurs,
Les marronniers qui neigeaient le jour de sa mort.
Avec mon camarade je me suis promené.

Jadis mes parents
Allaient seuls aux enterrements
Et je me sentais petit enfant.

Maintenant je connais pas mal de morts,
J'ai vu beaucoup de croque-morts
Mais je n'approche pas de leur bord.

C'est pourquoi tout aujourd'hui
Je me suis promené avec mon ami.
Il m'a trouve un peu vieilli,

Un peu vieilli, mais il m'a dit
Toi aussi tu viendras où je suis,
Un Dimanche ou un Samedi,

Moi, je regardais les arbres en fleurs,
La rivière passer sous le pont
Et soudain j'ai vu que j'étais seul.

Alors je suis rentré parmi les hommes.

TODAY I WENT FOR A WALK...

Today I went for a walk with my friend,
Even if he is dead,
I went for a walk with my friend.

The trees in flower were so beautiful,
The chestnut-trees, that were snowing the day he died.
With my friend I went for a walk.

Years ago my parents
Would go to funerals without me
And I knew I was a small child.

Now I know plenty of dead people,
I've seen plenty of undertakers' mutes
But I steer clear of them.

That's why only today
I went for a walk with my friend.
He found me a bit older,

A bit older, but he told me:
You'll come where I am,
One Sunday or Saturday.

I looked at the trees in flower,
The river going under the bridge
And suddenly saw I was alone.

So I went back to the world of men.

COUPLET DES PORTES SAINT-MARTIN ET SAINT-DENIS

Porte Saint-Martin, Porte Saint-Denis,
Voir briller la lune à travers la voûte,
Porte Saint-Martin, Porte Saint-Denis,
Du nord vers le sud s'allonge la route,
Porte Saint-Denis, Porte Saint-Martin,
Au nord ou au sud suivre son chemin,
Porte Saint-Denis, Porte Saint-Martin,
Passer sous la voûte au petit matin,
Porte Saint-Martin, Porte Saint-Denis,
Boire un café noir avec des amis,
Porte Saint-Martin, Porte Saint-Denis,
Quand le ciel blanchit au petit matin,
Porte Saint-Denis, Porte Saint-Martin,
Dans l'aube noyer les anciens chagrins,
Partir en chantant vers un but lointain,
Avec nos copains, avec nos amis,
Porte Saint-Denis, Porte Saint-Martin
Par un beau soleil, par un beau matin.

COUPLETS DE LA RUE SAINT-MARTIN

Je n'aime plus la rue Saint-Martin
Depuis qu'André Platard l'a quittée.
Je n'aime plus la rue Saint-Martin,
Je n'aime rien, pas même le vin.

Je n'aime plus la rue Saint-Martin
Depuis qu'André Platard l'a quittée.
C'est mon ami, c'est mon copain.
Nous partagions la chambre et le pain.
Je n'aime plus la rue Saint-Martin.

SONG OF THE ST MARTIN AND ST DENIS GATES

St Martin Gate, St Denis Gate,
See the moon shining through the arch.
St Martin Gate, St Denis Gate,
From north to south the road runs on,
St Martin Gate, St Denis Gate,
Northward or southward on the march,
St Martin Gate, St Denis Gate,
Pass at first light beneath the arch,
St Martin Gate, St Denis Gate,
With friends to drink black coffee down,
St Martin Gate, St Denis Gate,
When at first light the sky is white,
St Martin Gate, St Denis Gate,
Drowning old sorrows in the dawn,
Start a long journey with a song,
Our friends and mates all come along,
St Martin Gate, St Denis Gate
On a fine morning, in the sun.

SONG OF THE RUE ST-MARTIN

St Martin Street's no good at all
Now Andrew Platt's not there at all.
St Martin Street's no good at all,
Nor's wine, nor's anything at all.

St Martin Street's no good at all
Now Andrew Platt's not there at all.
He is my friend, he is my pal.
We shared our room, our bread and all.
St Martin Street's no good at all.

C'est mon ami, c'est mon copain.
Il a disparu un matin,
Ils l'ont emmené, on ne sait plus rien.
On ne l'a plus revu dans la rue Saint-Martin.

Pas la peine d'implorer les saints,
Saints Merri, Jacques, Gervais et Martin,
Pas même Valérien qui se cache sur la colline.
Le temps passe, on ne sait rien.
André Platard a quitté la rue Saint-Martin.

COUPLETS DE LA RUE DE BAGNOLET

Le soleil de la rue de Bagnolet
N'est pas un soleil comme les autres.
Il se baigne dans le ruisseau
Il se coiffe avec un seau,
Tout comme les autres.
Mais quand il caresse mes épaules,
C'est bien lui et pas un autre,
Le soleil de la rue de Bagnolet
Qui conduit son cabriolet,
Ailleurs qu'aux portes des palais,
Soleil, soleil ni beau ni laid,
Soleil tout drôle et tout content,
Soleil de la rue de Bagnolet,
Soleil d'hiver et de printemps,
Soleil de la rue de Bagnolet,
Pas comme les autres.

He is my friend, he is my pal.
One morning he was gone, that's all.
We know they've taken him, that's all.
He's not been seen again at all.

Prayers to saints won't help at all,
Saints Martin, Merry, James and all,
Nor shy Valerian up the hill.
Time passes and we know dam-all.
Now Andrew Platt's not there, that's all.

SONG OF THE RUE DE BAGNOLET

The sun in rue de Bagnolet
Is not a sun like any sun.
Swims in brook and trims his nut
With a pudding-basin cut,
Just like any other sun.
When he strokes my shoulders, though,
I just know it's him, I know,
Sun in rue de Bagnolet
Geeing-up his cabriolet,
Not to palace gates he'll get
But to quite another place,
Sun, not fair nor foul of face,
Happy sun, sun of fun,
Sun in rue de Bagnolet,
Winter sun, spring sun,
Sun in rue de Bagnolet,
Not a sun like any sun.

COUPLET DU TROTTOIR D'ÉTÉ

Couchons-nous sur le pavé
Par le soleil chauffé, par le soleil lavé,
Dans la bonne odeur de poussière
De la journée achevée
Avant la nuit levée
Avant la première lumière
Et nous guetterons dans le ruisseau
Les reflets des nuages en assaut,
Le coup de sang de l'horizon
Et la première étoile au-dessus des maisons.

COUPLET DU VERRE DE VIN

Quand le train partira n'agite pas la main,
Ni ton mouchoir, ni ton ombrelle,
Mais emplis un verre de vin
Et lance vers le train dont chantent les ridelles
La longue flamme du vin,
La sanglante flamme du vin pareille a ta langue
Et partageant avec elle
Le palais et la couche
De tes lèvres et de ta bouche.

COUPLET DU BOUCHER

La belle, si tu veux, je ferai ton lit
Dans le décor sanglant de ma boutique.

SONG OF THE SUMMER PAVEMENT

On the cobbles let us rest,
That are warmed and washed by sun,
In the pleasant smell of dust,
When the day is done,
Before the night,
Before first light.
We shall watch the streams' reflection,
See the clouds go into action,
Stroke of blood on the horizon,
That first star above the houses rising.

SONG OF THE GLASS OF WINE

When the train goes don't wave your hand,
Your handkerchief, your parasol,
But fill a glass with wine,
And throw, towards the train whose grab-rails are singing,
The wine's long flame,
The wine's bloody flame that is like your tongue,
And shares with it
The palate and the couch
Of your lips and your mouth.

SONG OF THE BUTCHER

If you like, my beauty, I'll make your bed
In my shop's interior, bloody-red.

Mes couteaux seront les miroirs magiques
Où le jour se lève, éclate et pâlit.
Je ferai ton lit creux et chaud
Dans le ventre ouvert d'une génisse
Et, quand tu dormiras, pour qu'il te rajeunisse
Je veillerai sur lui comme un bourreau sur l'échafaud.

FANTÔME

Arrête-toi! Je suis ici, mais tant de nuit
Nous sépare qu'en vain tu fatigues ta vue:
Tu te tais car l'espace, où se dissout la rue,
Nous-mêmes nous dissout et nous saoule de bruit.

C'est l'heure où, panaché de fumée et de suie
Le toit comme une plage offre au fantôme nu
Son ardoise où mirer le visage inconnu
De son double vivant dans un miroir de pluie.

Fantôme, laisse-nous rire de ta sottise.
Tu habites les bois, les châteaux, les églises
Mais tu es le valet de tout homme vivant.

Aussi n'as-tu jamais fait de mal à ces êtres
Tant, s'ils ouvraient un soir la porte et les fenêtres
Te dissoudrait la nuit dans le bruit et le vent.

My knives shall be the magic mirrors
Where the daylight rises, flares and flickers.
I'll make your bed hollow and hot
In a heifer's slitted gut
To restore your youth. While you sleep I'll watch it
Like an executioner wielding his hatchet.

PHANTOM

Don't move! I'm here, but save your straining eyes:
Thick night divides us: they are mis-employed.
You're quiet, for where the road dissolves, the void
Dissolves us too, and fuddles us with noise.

A plume of smoke and soot. This is the hour
The roof becomes a beach: the slate has shown
A face, the living face of your unknown
Double, mere phantom! in its rainy mirror.

Phantom, you're just a fool we can deride.
You lurk in castles, churches, woods; but all
The living have you at their beck and call.

You couldn't harm them with your evil mind:
The night they fling the doors and windows wide,
You'll be dissolved by dark and noise and wind.

AU TEMPS DES DONJONS

As-tu déjà perdu le mot de passe?

Le château se ferme et devient prison,
La belle aux créneaux chante sa chanson
Et le prisonnier gémit dans l'*In Pace.*
Retrouveras-tu le chemin, la plaine,
La source et l'asile au cœur des forêts
Le détour du fleuve ou l'aube apparaît,
L'étoile du soir et la lune pleine?
Un serpent darde vers l'homme s'élance,
L'enlace, l'étreint entre ses anneaux,
La belle soupire au bord des créneaux,
Le soleil couchant brille sur les lances,
L'âge sans retour vers l'homme jaillit,
L'enlace, l'étreint entre ses années.
Amours! Ô saisons! Ô belles fanées!
Serpents lovés à l'ombre des taillis.

DEMAIN

Agé de cent mille ans, j'aurais encor la force
De t'attendre, ô demain pressenti par l'espoir.
Le temps, vieillard souffrant de multiples entorses,
Peut gémir: Le matin est neuf, neuf est le soir.

Mais depuis trop de mois nous vivons à la veille,
Nous veillons, nous gardons la lumière et le feu,
Nous parlons à voix basse et nous tendons l'oreille
À maint bruit vite éteint et perdu comme au jeu.

IN THE TIME OF EVIL STRONGHOLDS

Password slipped your memory?

Castle's closed, become a cage,
Maiden sings on ramparts high,
Prisoner descries *In Pace,*
Groans to hear God's lullaby.
Will you find the streams again,
Forest refuge, path, and plain,
River-bed where dawn appears,
Great big moon and evening stars?
Poison-fanged, a serpent springs,
Crushes man with coiling rings.
Maiden sighs amid the towers,
Setting sun lights up the spears,
Age of no return appears,
Leaps at man and overpowers,
Crushes him with coiling years.
Loves and seasons, charms of yore!
Snakes coil close on forest floor.

TOMORROW

I'd live a hundred thousand years, and still
Be staunch in hope's foreknowledge of the dawn.
Old Father Time, whom sprains and shocks make ill,
Protests, but dusk and daybreak are reborn.

Too many months by now we've been on guard.
Alert, we've kept our firelight and our flame,
Talked low and pricked our ears at noises heard
That soon fell silent, lost, as in a game.

Or, du fond de la nuit, nous témoignons encore
De la splendeur du jour et de tous ses présents.
Si nous ne dormons pas c'est pour guetter l'aurore
Qui prouvera qu'enfin nous vivons au présent.

SAISONS

Le jour est à sa place et coule au fond de temps,
À moins que l'être monte à travers des espaces
Superposés dans la mémoire et délestant
La cervelle et le cœur de souvenirs tenaces.

Étés, puissants étés, votre nom même passe,
Être et avoir été, passe-temps et printemps,
Il passe, il est passé comme une eau jamais lasse,
Sans cicatrices, sans témoins et sans étangs.

Saisons, vous chérissez du moins le grain de blé
Qui doit germer aux jours de dégel et la clé
Pour ouvrir aux départs les portes charretières.

Les astres dans le ciel par vous sont rassemblés,
L'an va bientôt finir et des pas accablés
Traînent sur les chemins ramenant aux frontières.

Now from night's fastness we attest again
The splendour that accompanies the day.
Unsleeping, we are watchers for the dawn,
Proof that, at last, we are alive today.

SEASONS

Day is in place, runs down as time expires,
Unless one soars through the successive layers
Of a recall that disencumbers, clears
The heart and brain of clinging souvenirs.

Great summers, étés, even your name goes past,
Now is, now has-been, pastimes, primes of years,
Tireless as water it goes past, has passed,
Leaving no pools, no witnesses, no scars.

Seasons, at least you nurse the corn, the grain
That burgeons in the thaw, you have the key
That opens gates for wagonloads to leave.

You bring the stars together in the sky.
The year will soon be done: tired footsteps heave
Down trails that lead to frontiers, back again.

CRÉPUSCULE D'ÉTÉ

Crépuscule d'été baigné de brouillard rose
Déchiré par le bleu des ardoises des toits,
Le bleu du ciel, le bleu de l'asphalte et, parfois
Saignant sur une vitre où des reflets s'opposent

Reflet de la rivière en le feuillage enclose
Reflet du son, reflet du lit en désarroi,
Vibrations des carreaux au fracas des convois,
Tout ici se rencontre et se métamorphose.

Le soleil lourdement roule sur les maisons,
Dans la rumeur du soir et l'écho des chansons:
La nuit effacera cet univers fragile,

Le fantôme du lit quitté par les amants
Et le défaut du verre imitant le diamant.
Mais la vitre longtemps vibrera sur la ville.

L'ÉTOILE DU MATIN

C'est l'appel du village aux paresseux bergers
Qui chante ce matin dans mon cœur, et j'aspire,
Tous les verres vidés, à dormir aux vergers
Où chantent les oiseaux, où les abeilles girent.

Face au ciel, et cherchant dans les nuages en marche
Des géants abrutis par le froid et la nuit,
Je verrais se creuser des tunnels et des arches
Et des arbres de lueurs porter des lueurs de fruits.

SUMMER TWILIGHT

Bathed in pink fog the long day's end
Snagged by the rooftops' quarried blue,
Blue sky, blue asphalt, sometimes too
Bleeding on glass where ghosts contend,

Image of river framed in leaves,
Image of sound, and bedclothes' tumble,
Panes shaking at the convoys' rumble,
Meetings and metamorphoses;

Trundling on housetops treads the sun,
Echoing songs, day's noises done:
Frail universe to darkness gone,

Ghost of the lovers' empty bed,
Not diamond, only glass instead.
Above the town the panes shake on.

MORNING STAR

The call to lazy shepherds from the spire
Sings in my heart this morning. I desire,
When we have drunk, to sleep by apple-trees,
Orchards of singing birds and circling bees.

I'd search the sky, where clouds are on their marches,
For giants stupid with the cold of night;
See tunnels hollowed out, and lines of arches,
And lights of fruit that grow on trees of light.

Tout au fond d'un cratère écrasant de vertiges
Apparaîtrait l'étoile aux pointes de cristal,
La rose du matin détachée de sa tige,
La belle promeneuse au regard sans rival

Robe de velours noir et diadème éclatant
De la boue de comète à la soie du corsage,
Collier brisé laissant tomber tant de diamants
Que l'herbe autour de moi pleure comme un visage

Je t'enferme en mes yeux clos sur ta belle image
Aux ténébreux jardins roués par les éclairs
Que ta robe et tes pieds laissent sur leur passage
Quand tu sors de la mer tumultueuse de l'air.

Mais je voudrais savoir où tu passas la nuit.
Ainsi que moi, tu dors aux heures de lumière
Indifférente aux cris, aux chants, au jour, aux bruits
Ainsi que moi, tu dors et rêves la dernière.

Et je souhaite de dormir sous tes réseaux
De te voir apparaître au-dessus des campagnes
Dans un verger bruyant d'abeilles et d'oiseaux
À l'ombre du plus grand des châteaux en Espagne

Et je me dissoudrais dans un sommeil profond
Comme le café noir et comme la migraine
Ou la sonorité du bronze des bourdons
Et la monotonie du feu et des fontaines.

Tandis que toi, pâlie à l'écume du jour,
Disparaîtrais du ciel comme un reste de poudre
Sur un visage en proie aux charmes de l'amour
Qui flambe et monte avec le fracas de la foudre.

Out of a dizzy crater would advance
The star with crystal-pointed diadem,
The fair proud walker of the matchless glance,
Rose of the morning, severed from its stem.

Jewels resplendent on black velvet gown
On silk corsage, a comet's muddy trace:
The necklace breaks, the diamonds shower down,
The grass around me weeps like someone's face.

I close my eyes and hold your beauty there
In twilit gardens lightning beats them down
You rise tumultuous from the sea of air
Spark lightning from your feet and from your gown

I'd like to know just where you spent the night.
Heedless of day of songs of noise of cries,
Like me you sleep through all the hours of light,
You're last to dream, you're last to close your eyes.

I'd wish to sleep beneath your nets, I'd see
You soar through countrysides, appear again,
In orchards resonant with birds and bees,
And castle-shade, the mightiest in Spain.

And I'd dissolve myself in sleep profound,
Deep as a migraine and as café noir,
As droning bumble-bees' bronze humming-sound,
The monotone of fountains and of fire

While you grown pallid in the foam of day
Would quit the sky like some last scrap of powder
When love's bewitched a face to be its prey,
And flames and climbs with flash and crash of thunder.

TRANSLATOR'S NOTE*

Against the Grain (Contrée) which follows is a sequence of poems published in 1944. Some of the poems had been published or quoted as early as 1942. 'It's an odd experience for me,' Desnos wrote to Paul Éluard that year. 'I'm feeling my way forward, but the images, words and rhymes come to me like the details of a key to open a lock. Everything must be useful and essential for the poem to work, everything must be there to finish it and nothing else. I wonder why they come out so easily as sonnets. I believe more and more that automatic writing and speech are only the elementary stages of poetic initiation... I dream of poems which could not be other than they are: for which a different outcome could not be imagined. Something as implacable as the resolution of an equation.'

The title *Contrée* denotes both the various places visited in each poem (because it can mean something like Back Country) and the effect of 'countering', more or less by stealth, an enemy whose defeat is proclaimed: 'I have wished your death and there is nothing that can delay it.' The allusions multiply. Here is denunciation: 'on a yellow poster the word in black letters, plague;' the voice declaring 'the beautiful season is near;' and the poet's anticipatory epitaph, his refusal to give in: 'I lived intact, but I was prey.' Classic in form, and drawing on mythology, the poems were able to pass the censor; and their philosophy of human destiny puts into a wider context various topical allusions which those in the know could understand.

Contrée is full of highly-charged references, obscure enough to pass the censor. 'The Vintage' finds a great classical civilisation in collapse and invokes the transforming power of wine. 'The Equinox' builds on this, bringing in the cockerel of France and the beheaded patron saint. Barbarians triumph, shrines fall apart, but in all the murk there is a glimmer of hope.

Desnos is a master of rhyme and metre (though he does not limit himself) and therefore is under-translated. The translator attempting some formal mode will work to less restrictive patterns. In 'The Equinox', my rhyme-scheme begins *abba abba*, which is frequent in original sonnets, but very rare in my translated versions. The last six lines rhyme in a dim and dull way, resembling the text, and putting just enough final stress on the word 'fire'. By contrast, in 'The

Vintage' the pattern of rhyme at the end is complicated and lyrical. Such effects (if they are real) are unconscious, and only perceived after the event.

Comparisons will be made between *Contrée*, written while at large but in deadly and increasing danger, and the *33 Sonnets of the Resistance* of the imprisoned Jean Cassou, who survived, and who had 'only the night for his ink, only memory for his paper'.

'Le Paysage' was the first Desnos poem I discovered and translated: it was in the *Penguin Book of French Verse*. Much of his poetry is in paperbacks from Gallimard (whose copyright is acknowledged); but *Contrée* could be found only in a library, before Desnos' *Œuvres* (Works) appeared. I knew his surrealist super-spoonerisms, inspired by Duchamp's altera ego, Rrose Sélavy, and was curious to know how he matured, as the times changed.

* This note draws on the learned work of Mme. Marie-Claire Dumas and Dr. Katharine Conley, to both of whom I am very grateful.

CONTRÉE

LA CASCADE

Quelle flèche a percé le ciel et le rocher?
Elle vibre. Elle étale, ainsi qu'un paon, sa queue
Ou, comme la comète à minuit vient nicher,
Le brouillard de sa tige et ses pennes sans nœuds.

Que surgisse le sang de la chair entr'ouverte,
Lèvres taisant déjà le murmure et le cri,
Un doigt posé suspend le temps et déconcerte
Le témoin dans les yeux duquel le fait s'inscrit.

Silence? nous savons pourtant les mots de passe,
Sentinelles perdues loin des feux de bivouac
Nous sentirons monter dans les ténèbres basses
L'odeur du chèvrefeuille et celle du ressac.

Qu'enfin l'aube jaillisse à travers tes abîmes,
Distance, et qu'un rayon dessine sur les eaux,
Présage du retour de l'archer et des hymnes,
Un arc-en-ciel et son carquois plein de roseaux.

LA RIVIÈRE

D'un bord à l'autre bord j'ai passé la rivière,
Suivant à pied le pont qui la franchit d'un jet
Et mêle dans les eaux son ombre et son reflet
Au fil bleui par le savon des lavandières.

THE WATERFALL

What arrow split the sky and pierced the rock?
Vibrant, it spreads its peacock tail and flaunts
Its blurry shaft and sleek unblemished flights,
The way the midnight comet finds its mark.

The flesh is opened. For the blood to rise,
While lips suppress the murmurs and the cries,
A finger bids time stop, pre-occupies
The witness who records it with his eyes.

Silence? And yet we know the passwords well.
We strayed from our camp-fires, we sentinels:
Drifting from shady corners we can smell
Salt surf aromas, honeysuckle smells.

Dawn bursts on far-off depths; a sunbeam limns
Upon the waves, at last, a sketch that leads
Back the returning archer and his hymns:
A rainbow, with its quiver full of reeds.

THE RIVER

I walked to where the river can be crossed –
A jutting point: from bank to bank I passed.
Its shadow and reflection merge their hue;
Laundresses turn the stream a soapy blue.

J'ai marché dans le gué qui chante à sa manière.
Étoiles et cailloux sous mes pas le jonchaient.
J'allais vers le gazon, j'allais vers la forêt
Où le vent frissonnait dans sa robe légère.

J'ai nagé. J'ai passé, mieux vêtu par cette eau
Que par ma propre chair et par ma propre peau.
C'était hier. Déjà l'aube et le ciel s'épousent.

Et voici que mes yeux et mon corps sont pesants,
Il fait clair et j'ai soif et je cherche à présent
La fontaine qui chante au cœur d'une pelouse.

LE COTEAU

Derrière ce coteau la vallée est dans l'ombre,
L'odeur du bois qui flambe et de l'herbe parvient
Jusqu'au désert présent, lueurs et rocs sans nombre,
Avec des cris d'enfant et des abois de chien.

Les cris sont déchirants de l'enfant qu'on égorge.
Le chien appelle en vain. Un sort est sur ces lieux.
Rien n'est réel ici que cette odeur de forge
Qui nous berce et nous saoule et nous rougit les yeux.

L'aube peut revenir et le soleil nous prendre.
En vain: les aboiements et les cris perceront
L'épaisseur de la nuit, l'épaisseur de la cendre
Qui remplissent nos cœurs, qui brûlent sous nos fronts.

I trudged the ford, that sings to suit its mood,
Strewn underfoot with stars and bits of rock.
I headed for the greensward and the wood
Where the wind shivered in its flimsy frock.

I swam, I got across, clothed better in
That water than in my own flesh and skin.
A night has passed. Now, sky has married dawn.

And see, my eyes and limbs are faltering,
It's bright, I'm thirsty, looking for the spring
Whose song regales the middle of a lawn.

THE SLOPE

Behind this slope the valley is in shade.
Odours of burning wood and grass pervade
The bare expanse, crag after fire-flecked crag;
The loud voice of a child, a barking dog.

The child is being murdered. Rending cries;
Barking, no use. A doom is on this dell.
Nothing is real but this hot iron smell
That lulls us, gets us drunk, and reds our eyes.

Dawn may return and sunlight may refresh;
But all in vain: the barking and the yells
Pierce the thick night, the cinders and the ash
That fill our hearts and burn inside our skulls.

LA ROUTE

Une route est près d'ici,
J'entends le bruit des voitures,
Le vent, les pas indécis
D'une lourde créature
Qui va, qui vient, qui soupire,
Trébuche sur les cailloux,
Implore, mendie, expire.
Est-ce un dieu? Est-ce un voyou?

Lourdement sa main se dresse
Sur la prairie des cheveux.
Elle esquisse une caresse
Et crispe ses doigts nerveux.
Enfin le restant du corps
Surgit droit jusqu'aux nuages
Et le soleil couvre d'or
Le géant des marécages.

Est-ce Hercule? Ou est-ce Atlas?
Il marche à travers la plaine.
De son long sans un hélas
Il tombe et perd son haleine.
Il recouvre de sa masse
Le paysage en entier
Et puis plus rien, plus de trace,
Ni colline, ni sentier.

Moins réel que les mirages
Ainsi disparaît celui
Qui voulait dicter aux âges,
Aux vents, aux jours et aux nuits.

THE ROAD

Hereabouts there is a road
Where I hear the cars go by,
The wind, and the uncertain plod
Of a heavy entity,
Coming, going, with a sigh,
Stumbling on the stones, and I
Hear it beg and plead and die.
Is it guttersnipe or god?

Heavily one hand he raises
To the meadow of his hair,
He delineates caresses,
Clamps the nervous fingers there.
Then his other parts all rush
Helter-skelter to the moon
And the sun gilds with its brush
The big beast of the lagoon.

Is it Hercules? Or Atlas?
Striding on across the plain
Falls full-length, no cry of pain,
Winded in the solar plexus.
Blotting out the countryside
He obliterates the place,
Not a single mountainside,
Not a pathway, not a trace.

Less real than mirror-images
The man who would be disappears,
Dictator of the centuries,
The winds, the nights, the days, the years.

LE CIMETIÈRE

Ici sera ma tombe, et pas ailleurs, sous ces trois arbres.
J'en cueille les premières feuilles du printemps
Entre un socle de granit et une colonne de marbre.

J'en cueille les premières feuilles du printemps,
Mais d'autres feuilles se nourriront de l'heureuse pourriture
De ce corps qui vivra, s'il le peut, cent mille ans.

Mais d'autres feuilles se nourriront de l'heureuse pourriture,
Mais d'autres feuilles se noirciront
Sous la plume de ceux qui content leurs aventures.

Mais d'autres feuilles se noirciront
D'une encre plus liquide que le sang et l'eau des fontaines :
Testaments non observés, paroles perdues au-delà des monts.

D'une encre plus liquide que le sang et l'eau des fontaines
Puis-je défendre ma mémoire contre l'oubli
Comme une seiche qui s'enfuit à perdre sang, à perdre haleine?

Puis-je défendre ma mémoire contre l'oubli?

LA CLAIRIÈRE

Le socle sans statue, à l'ombre de ces arbres
S'enfonce dans le sol un peu plus chaque jour
Sous l'invisible poids d'un fantôme de marbre
Qui le piétine et le talonne et se fait lourd.

À moins qu'en s'en allant vers un fatal banquet
Le commandeur ne l'ait renvoyé au naufrage.

THE CEMETERY

Under these three trees, nowhere else, is my burial-place.
I pluck from them spring's first and earliest leaves
Between a marble column and a granite base.

I pluck from them spring's first and earliest leaves,
But other leaves shall grow thick on the fortunate rotting
Of this corpse that may have ten thousand years to live.

But other leaves shall grow thick on the fortunate rotting
But other leaves shall grow black
From the pens of those with adventures to tell in writing.

But other leaves shall grow black
With an ink more liquid than blood and the water of fountains:
Neglected testaments, words lost across the mountains.

With an ink more liquid than blood and the water of fountains
Can I protect my memory from forgetting
As a cuttlefish spends its blood and breath, retreating?

Can I protect my memory from forgetting?

THE CLEARING

This empty plinth with tall trees shaded round
Bears the unseen load of a marble ghost
That tramples, kicks, exerts a downward thrust,
Driving it daily deeper in the ground.

Or else, on leaving for a fatal feast,
One who Commands consigned it to be wrecked,

Comme un caillou qu'on jette à l'eau, du bord des plages,
Il fait mouche à sa cible et rejoint son reflet.

Mais je devrais entendre, au moins, près de l'étang
La fanfare sonnée par Don Juan qui l'invite…
La voici, les échos la portent, je l'entends.
Je sens sous mes deux pieds la terre qui palpite.

LA CAVERNE

Voici dans les rochers l'accès du corridor,
Il descend, dans la nuit, au cœur de la planète.
Le bruit du monde ici se dissout et s'endort.
À son seuil le soleil et la lune s'arrêtent.

Eurydice est passée par là, voici son pied
Dans la terre marqué mais la piste se brise,
La phrase s'interrompt, le serment est délié,
Le cavalier se cabre et se fixe à la frise.

Ces autres pas qui vont ailleurs sont ceux d'Orphée,
L'éclipse est terminée et le ciel resplendit
En nous rendant notre ombre et sa maison hantée.

Loin, derrière un fourré d'épines et de roses
La ménade s'endort dans le bois interdit.
Un nuage est au ciel comme une fleur éclose.

As a small stone, across the tide-line tossed,
Meets its own bull's-eye that the waves reflect.

But I should hear, beside the pond, at least,
The fanfare Don Giovanni blows, inviting…
Yes, now I hear it, on the echoes riding.
Beneath my feet I sense the earth's heart racing.

THE CAVE

Here is the entrance in the rock, the start:
Here, the world's tumult sleeps and comes apart.
Beyond this point, the sun and moon depart:
Dark downward passage to the planet's heart.

Eurydice walked here, you see her trail,
These are her footprints, but the traces fail,
The phrase breaks off, the vow achieves release,
The horseman jibs at the cheval-de-frise.

These other steps diverge, which Orpheus made,
It's bright, and the eclipse has had its hour,
Giving us back our haunted house of shade.

Where thorns and roses weave a bramble-bower,
The mænad sleeps in the forbidden glade.
A cloud above is like an open flower.

LE SOUVENIR

M'étant par bonheur attardé,
En flânant dans les avenues,
À votre fenêtre accoudée
Je vous ai bien surprise nue,
Mais mon cœur était accordé.

Mais mon cœur était accordé
À des voix de très loin venues.
Le noir de l'ombre avait fardé
Les grands yeux blancs de la statue
Du carrefour où j'ai rôdé.

Venant d'Arcueil ou de Passy
Un vent frais soufflait dans la rue:
Je suis passé, c'était ici
Et je vous ai surprise nue
Tachant de blanc la molle nuit.

Feuille morte des temps passés,
Fantôme une nuit apparue,
Beaux drapeaux au matin hissés,
Qu'êtes-vous belle devenue,
Dans Paris la ville pressée?

Pressée de vivre et de flamber,
Impassible et bien vite émue,
De tant de nuits vite tombées,
Telle celle où vous étiez nue
À votre fenêtre accoudée.

THE MEMORY

Lucky to be overdue,
Strolling down each avenue,
At your window I saw you,
Caught you wearing rien du tout;
To another I was true.

Yes, my heart already loved
Voices very far removed.
Shadows of black night had daubed
The big statue's pale eyes, carved
At the crossroads where I roved.

In the street the breeze blew fair
From Passy or Pépinière:
I was passing, I know where,
And I chanced to find you bare,
Blot of white on soft night air.

Fallen leaf of seasons past,
Phantom and nocturnal ghost,
Pennants proud for daybreak hoist,
With what future were you faced,
In our capital hard-pressed?

Paris, pressed to live and flame,
Stolid, fired up all the same
By the nights that quickly came,
Like the night you had no shame,
Propping up your window-frame.

LA PROPHÉTIE

D'une place de Paris jaillira une si claire fontaine
Que le sang des vierges et les ruisseaux des glaciers
Près d'elle paraîtront opaques.
Les étoiles sortiront en essaim de leurs ruches lointaines
Et s'aggloméreront pour se mirer dans ses eaux près de la
Tour Saint-Jacques.

D'une place de Paris jaillira une si claire fontaine
Qu'on viendra s'y baigner, en cachette, dès l'aurore.
Sainte Opportune et ses lavandières seront ses marraines
Et ses eaux couleront vers le sud venant du nord.

Un grand marronnier rouge fleurit à la place
Où coulera la fontaine future,
Peut-être dans mon grand âge
Entendrai-je son murmure;

Or le chant est si doux de la claire fontaine
Qu'il baigne déjà mes yeux et mon cœur.
Ce sera le plus bel affluent de la Seine,
Le gage le plus sûr des printemps à venir, de leurs oiseaux et
de leurs fleurs.

LE SORT

J'ai souhaité ta mort et rien ne peut l'empêcher de venir
prématurément
Je t'ai vu couvert de sueur et de sanies
À l'instant même de ton agonie
Et tout en toi était cruel et dément.

THE PROPHECY

From a Paris square a fountain so clear shall spring
That virgins' blood and glacier streams
Beside it shall seem opaque.
The stars shall emerge in a swarm from their distant hives
And mass to admire themselves in its waters near the Tour
St-Jacques.

From a Paris square a fountain so clear shall spring
That from daybreak onward the bathers will tiptoe forth.
St Opportune and her laundresses will be godmothers
And its waters shall run south, coming out of the north.

A great red chestnut-tree is in bloom in the square
Where the fountain will run, in the future.
Perhaps in my later years
I shall hear its murmur;

So sweet is this clear fountain's melody
That already it bathes my eyes and heart with its waters.
It will be the Seine's most beautiful tributary,
The surest token of spring-times to come, their birds and
their flowers.

THE DESTINY

I have wished your death and there is nothing that can
delay it.
At the very moment of your greatest pain
I have seen you covered in pus and sweat
And everything in you was cruel and insane.

Écoute. Ce jour-là un gros nuage s'élevait des collines de Bicêtre
Et montait derrière le Dôme du Val-de-Grâce.
Un enfant criait qui venait de naître,
Rue Saint-Jacques, dans une maison basse.

Rien ne peut désormais te sauver de la honte et de la douleur
Car mon souhait avait la saveur des choses qui se réalisent.
Déjà d'imperceptibles signes physiques, dans ton esprit et dans ton cœur,
T'avertissent qu'il est temps et adieu la valise.

Rien ne te servirait de pleurer et te repentir,
Rien ne te servirait d'avoir une attitude noble,
Car le néant est ton seul devenir
Et ton nom ne survivra pas dans les proverbes du peuple.

Le nuage noir a débordé le Val-de-Grâce et Saint-Sulpice,
Il s'est longuement reflété dans la Seine avant de se résoudre en orage.
Moi je le regardais du haut d'une blanche bâtisse
Et son tonnerre a libéré de grands oiseaux de leur cage.

LA MOISSON

Incroyable est de se croire
Vivant, réel, existant.
Incroyable est de se croire
Mort, feu, défunt, hors du temps.
Incroyable est de se croire
Et plus incroyable encore
De se croire, pour mémoire,
Un rêve, une âme sans corps.

Listen. That day from the hills of Bicêtre a great big cloud
Climbed up behind the Val-de-Grâce and its Dome.
A child had just been born and it cried aloud,
In the Rue Saint-Jacques, in a low-built home.

From now on nothing can save you from shame and pain
For my wish had the taste of things that materialise.
Already imperceptible physical signs, in your heart and
    your brain,
Warn you it's time you were saying your goodbyes.

It would be pointless for you to weep in repentance
Pointless to have an attitude fine and noble,
Because your only future is non-existence
And your name will not live in the sayings of the people.

The cloud passed the Val-de-Grâce and Saint-Sulpice,
Was reflected for long in the Seine before resolving
Into a storm. I watched from a tall white building,
There were great caged birds, its thunder was their release.

THE HARVEST

It's incredible to credit
One's alive, existing, real.
It's incredible to credit
One's the late, defunct and dead. It
Is incredible to credit
And least credible of all
Is to credit, you'll recall,
One is dream, unbodied soul.

Belles roses du passé,
Roses, odorantes roses,
Qui dès l'aube frémissez,
À la nuit déjà décloses,
Votre sort rapide et long
Est égal à nos années
Même si, dans le salon,
On vous apporte fanées.

Nos dieux étaient trop fragiles,
C'étaient de petites gens,
Dans un petit domicile,
Vivant de fort peu d'argent.
Plus grande est notre fortune
Et plus sombre est notre sort.
Nous ne voulons pas la lune.
Nous ne craignons pas la mort.

Par nos cinq sens ligoté
Notre univers rapetisse.
Adieu rêve, adieu beauté!
De vous je fais sacrifice
Au monde trop limité.

LA SIESTE

Cent mille années dans mon sommeil d'après-midi
Ont duré moins longtemps qu'une exacte seconde.
Je reparais du fond d'un rêve incontredit
Dans la réalité de ma chair et du monde.

Lovely roses passed away,
Lovely roses, scented flowers,
Trembling since the break of day,
Now disclosed to midnight hours,
Your prolonged and rapid doom
Measures up to our decades
Though you reach the sitting-room
Even as your colour fades.

They were frail, our deities,
They were little nobodies,
Living in a little street,
Managing to make ends meet.
Greater is our own fortune,
Darker is our destiny.
We do not desire the moon,
We are not afraid to die.

Trussed by our five senses, this
Universe is shrunk in size.
Goodbye, dream and loveliness!
You shall be my sacrifice
To a world not limitless.

THE SIESTA

Ten thousand decades of my noonday sleep
Endure a second's-breadth or even less.
I rise from dreams unquestioned and most deep
To my reality of world and flesh.

Je retrouve en ma bouche une ancienne saveur
Et des noms de jadis et des baisers si tendres
Que je ne sais plus qui je suis ni si mon cœur
Bat dans le sûr présent ou le passé de cendres.

Éclatez! Ô volcans! du fond des souvenirs,
Noyez sous votre lave un esprit qui se lasse,
Brûlez les vieux billets et puissiez-vous ternir
À jamais le miroir dont le tain mord la glace.

LA VILLE

Se heurter à la foule et courir par les rues,
Saisi en plein soleil par l'angoisse et la peur,
Pressentir le danger, la mort et le malheur,
Brouiller sa piste et fuir une ombre inaperçue,

C'est le sort de celui qui, rêvant en chemin,
S'égare dans son rêve et se mêle aux fantômes,
Se glisse en leur manteau, prend leur place au royaume
Où la matière cède aux caresses des mains.

Tout ce monde est sorti du creux de sa cervelle.
Il l'entoure, il le masque, il le trompe, il l'étreint,
Il lui faut s'arrêter, laisser passer le train
Des créatures nées dans un corps qui chancelle.

Nausée de souvenirs, regrets des soleils veufs,
Résurgence de source, écho d'un chant de brume,
Vous n'êtes que scories et vous n'êtes qu'écume.
Je voudrais naître chaque jour sous un ciel neuf.

Here in my mouth again I find that taste,
Long-vanished names, kisses of tender greeting:
Don't know my name, or if my heart is beating
In the sure present or the ashen past.

Volcanoes, burst from memory's depths, and boil!
Drown me in lava, for my mind is slack.
Burn the old screeds, turn permanently black
The mirror that is bitten by the foil.

THE CITY

Jostling the crowds and running down the roads,
Gripped in full sun, he's suffering, afraid;
It's danger, death, disaster he forebodes,
Twisting his tracks to flee an unknown shade,

The fate of one who drifts and dreams along,
Strays in his dream and joins the phantom throng,
Purloins their coat, supplanting them in lands
Where matter yields to warm caressing hands.

This whole world issues from his bony crown.
He coops it, cloaks it, tricks it and constrains,
He has to halt, give way to passing trains
Of creatures born in bodies tumbling down.

Suns mourning, yearning; nauseous memory;
Wellsprings resurgent, echoing fogs' refrain:
You are mere scum and scouring. I would fain
Be born each day beneath a brand-new sky.

LA MAISON

Trois fois le vent, plus libre et plus furieux qu'un ange,
À soufflé dans son cor auprès de la maison.
Qu'un ange? C'est un ange évadé de prison
Qui descend l'escalier mais que l'ombre dérange,

L'ombre qui le repousse et dont la toile étrange
Accroche des soleils aux fils de l'horizon
Et plus de vers luisants qu'il n'en est au gazon
Ou dans l'obscurité protectrice des granges.

Il descend et son pas tinte dans l'escalier
Comme un pot de cristal sur le sol du cellier.
Il descend, il atteint déjà le vestibule.

Le porche s'ouvre en grand sur l'entonnoir des nuits.
J'écoute et l'imagine. Il marche, il sort, il fuit,
Il vole dans un ciel crevé de péninsules.

LE PAYSAGE

J'avais rêvé d'aimer. J'aime encor mais l'amour
Ce n'est plus ce bouquet de lilas et de roses
Chargeant de leurs parfums la forêt où repose
Une flamme à l'issue de sentiers sans détour.

J'avais rêvé d'aimer. J'aime encor mais l'amour
Ce n'est plus cet orage où l'éclair superpose
Ses bûchers aux châteaux, déroute, décompose,
Illumine en fuyant l'adieu du carrefour.

THE HOUSE

Freer and fiercer than an angel, wind
Has blown around the house its triple horn.
An angel? One from prison, on the run,
Coming downstairs, though shadows tease its mind,

Driving it back, their curious canvases
Hanging the far horizon's wires with suns,
More glow-worms too than gather on the lawn,
Or in the sheltering darkness of the barn.

As it comes down, its foot chinks on the stair
Like crystal glassware on the cellar floor.
It's near the hallway, it will soon be there.

Night's funnel is beyond the open door.
Listening, I sense it walk, and leave, and fly
Into peninsulas of broken sky.

THE COUNTRYSIDE

I dreamed of loving. Still I love, but now
Love is no more that rose and lilac spray
Whose perfume filled the woods where each pathway
Led on directly to the blazing glow

I dreamed of loving. Still I love, but now
Love's not that storm whose lightning kindled high
Towers, unhorsed, unhinged, and fleetingly
Would set the parting of the ways aglow.

C'est le silex en feu sous mon pas dans la nuit,
Le mot qu'aucun lexique au monde n'a traduit
L'écume sur la mer, dans le ciel ce nuage.

À vieillir tout devient rigide et lumineux,
Des boulevards sans noms et des cordes sans nœuds.
Je me sens me roidir avec le paysage.

LA NUIT D'ÉTÉ

Aux rosiers remontants ta robe déchirée
Accroche des lambeaux, les vapeurs du matin.
Tu mêles en marchant les lilas et le thym
Aux fleurs d'autres saisons et d'une autre contrée.

Tu te diriges vers le bois, là où l'orée
Ouvre un chemin retentissant de cris lointains.
Le feu de la Saint-Jean dans le vallon s'éteint.
La nuit, la courte nuit, déjà s'est égarée.

Jeune fille aux beaux seins, au regard sans lumière,
J'ai déjà vu tes sœurs. Tu n'es pas la première
À te perdre en courant les jardins et les champs.

Quand, à travers la haie, tu te fis un passage
La ronce t'a griffé la cuisse et le visage
Et le ciel a pâli au bruit de nouveaux chants.

Love is the flint my footstep sparks at night,
The word no lexicon can render right,
Foam of the sea, the cloud across the sky.

Old age makes all things fixed and luminous:
Knots are unravelled, streets anonymous;
Set in our ways, the countryside and I.

THE SUMMER NIGHT

Roses go rambling up. Your dress is torn,
Snagging the bush with scraps of misty morn.
Perfumes from other days, another clime,
Blend, as you walk, with lilac and with thyme.

You move towards the wood, whose boundaries
Open a path that's loud with distant cries.
Fires of midsummer in the vale die back;
The night, so short, has soon strayed off the track.

Fine-bosomed girl, no light shines in your gaze.
I've seen your sisters. You are not the first
To run through fields and gardens and be lost.

You scrambled through the hedge and, as you passed,
The bramble-bushes scratched your thigh and face;
New songs were heard; the sky turned pale at last.

LA PESTE

Dans la rue un pas retentit. La cloche n'a qu'un seul battant. Où va-t-il le promeneur qui se rapproche lentement et s'arrête par instant? Le voici devant la maison. J'entends son souffle derrière la porte.

Je vois le ciel à travers la vitre. Je vois le ciel où les astres roulent sur l'arête des toits. C'est la grande Ourse ou Bételgeuse, c'est Vénus au ventre blanc, c'est Diane qui dégrafe sa tunique près d'une fontaine de lumière.

Jamais lunes ni soleils ne roulèrent si loin de la terre, jamais l'air de nuit ne fut si opaque et si lourd. Je pèse sur ma porte qui résiste…

Elle s'ouvre enfin, son battant claque contre le mur. Et tandis que le pas s'éloigne je déchiffre sur une affiche jaune les lettres noires du mot «Peste».

LA NYMPHE ALCESTE

Tu es née, à minuit, du baiser de deux sources,
Alceste, et l'univers ne t'offre que reflets,
Lueurs, lampe allumée au lointain, feux follets
Et dans le ciel les sept flambeaux de la Grande Ourse.

Il fait noir et, partant au signal de la course,
Tu ne soupçonnes pas que la nuit se soumet
Et se dissout quand le soleil, sur les sommets,
Par le chant des oiseaux répand l'or de sa bourse.

Je sais que reviendront l'aurore et le matin.
Je les ai vus, tu les verras, j'en suis certain.
Déjà mon cœur se gonfle au rythme de leur danse.

Mais saurai-je à ta sœur qui doit naître en plein jour,
Nymphe Alceste, annoncer, dès midi, le retour
Du crépuscule, de la nuit et du silence?

LA VOIX

Une voix, une voix qui vient de si loin
Qu'elle ne fait plus tinter les oreilles,
Une voix, comme un tambour, voilée
Parvient pourtant, distinctement, jusqu'à nous.
Bien qu'elle semble sortir d'un tombeau
Elle ne parle que d'été et de printemps,
Elle emplit le corps de joie,
Elle allume aux lèvres le sourire.

Je l'écoute. Ce n'est qu'une voix humaine
Qui traverse les fracas de la vie et des batailles,
L'écroulement du tonnerre et le murmure des bavardages.

Et vous? ne l'entendez-vous pas?
Elle dit «La peine sera de peu de durée»
Elle dit «La belle saison est proche».

Ne l'entendez-vous pas?

I know that dawn and morning will resume.
I've seen them, you will see them, I know well:
Their rhythmic dance excites my heart to swell.

But, nymph, your sister's born in noonday light:
How shall I tell her of the coming gloom,
Return of dusk, of silence, and of night?

THE VOICE

A voice, a voice coming from so far away
That it no longer rings in the ears,
A voice, like a drumbeat, muffled
Reaches us even so, distinctly.
Though it seems to issue from a tomb
It speaks only of summer and spring,
It fills the body with joy,
It kindles a smile on the lips.

I'm listening. It's only a human voice
Coming across the din of life and of battles,
The crash of thunder and the babble of talk.

What about you? Don't you hear it?
It says "The pain will be short-lived"
It says "The beautiful season is near".

Don't you hear it?

LA VENDANGE

Les fauves sont partis, soumis au vendangeur
Tandis qu'en la cité, construite à son de flûte,
Au cirque, le laurier se fane après la lutte,
Que le nom des champions s'efface au mur d'honneur.

Le cortège s'éloigne. Il passe les hauteurs,
Des tas de soldats tués pourrissent sous les buttes,
La terre, ivre de sang, transpire, écume, jute
Et d'un fumier puissant submerge les vainqueurs.

Toi seul restes toi-même, ô Vin, dans tes barriques,
Tu teindras notre bouche à tes couleurs magiques,
Puis nous irons rejoindre en terre les palais

Dont la cloche rythmant la chanson des cigales,
Se tait, comme autrefois la flûte et les cymbales.
Le vent même s'est tu. Le tonnerre se tait.

L'ÉQUINOXE

Un coq à d'autres coqs répond. Le temps est gris,
L'équinoxe roulant ses tonneaux à grand-peine
Depuis la mer du Nord jusqu'aux bords de la Seine
À travers les odeurs, les éclairs et les cris.

Le corps décapité de l'évêque Denis
Saigne avec les raisins d'Argenteuil et Suresnes.
On enchaîne à des chars des héros et des reines.
Les temples, un à un, croulent sur les parvis

THE VINTAGE

The fallow deer are gone, culled in the fall,
While in the city that the flute-song made
The games are finished and the laurels fade,
And names of champions rub off the wall.

The escort climbs the street of sepulture.
Below the bluffs, the soldiers rot in heaps;
The earth, blood-sodden, sweats and froths and weeps,
Drowning the victors in a rich manure.

Wine, in your casks, unscathed! Your colours will
Transmute our lips until we lie at last
Beneath the earth, at one with palace bells

That chimed with the cicada's canticles,
Stilled now, like flutes and cymbals long since past.
Today the thunder and the wind are still.

THE EQUINOX

Cocks crow repeatedly. Beneath grey skies
The equinox rolls out its barrel-train
And trundles from the North Sea to the Seine
Through all the smells, the lightning and the cries.

The martyred corpse of Bishop Denis lies
Bleeding with grapes of Argenteuil, Suresnes.
Chariots haul queens and heroes on a chain.
Each temple crumbles to its roots and dies,

Mais, tout à l'heure encore, un arc-en-ciel de nuit
Enjambait la vallée et la lune vers lui
Roulait. Le jour parut et tout ne fut que brume.

Mérite-t-il vraiment le nom de jour, ce jour
Dont s'encrasse la ville et la vie et l'amour?
Oui, car la flamme enfin, dans le brouillard s'allume.

LA PLAGE

Sur la plage où blanchit la mer dans les ténèbres,
Où le figuier frémit sous le poids des oiseaux,
Un homme, à demi-voix, n'a prononcé qu'un mot:
Celui qui l'a reçu s'éloigne sous les cèdres.

Il est l'heure. Bacchus entreprend sa conquête.
Un rendez-vous l'accable et, comme un ruisseau sourd,
L'espace le pénètre. Il fit nuit. Fait-il jour?
Qu'importe, dispersez les foyers de la fête.

Dans un pays de bois et de fraîches rivières
Un homme sent couler, dans ses veines, son sang.
Il connaît ce pays, ces hommes, leur accent.
Déjà l'odeur du sol lui était familière.

Sur la plage celui qui livra le secret
Gît avec un poignard entre les deux épaules,
Mais sa voix flotte encor sur l'eau, le long du môle
Et répète le mot d'où naquit son regret.

Sans cesse elle redit ces syllabes: Corinthe,
Et la terre gémit de langueur et de crainte.

And yet just now a midnight rainbow shone,
Spanning the valley, to entice the moon.
Day broke; thick vapours hid the world away.

Can it be truly called a day, this day
That drags love, life and Paris in the mire?
Yes: in the fog, a spark flares into fire.

THE BEACH

On the beach, the sea whitens in the shadows.
A fig-tree quivers with the weight of birds.
A certain man has breathed one word of words;
His hearer moves away among the cedars.

It's time to go and conquer. Bacchus girds
for the grim tryst; the void, like muffled waters,
Creeps into him. Night's over. Is it day?
Put out the party bonfires, anyway.

A country of fresh streams and trackless wood
Lets a man feel his veins, his coursing blood.
He knows this land and people, knows their sound,
Well-versed in the aromas of the ground.

On the beach, he who gave the secret sign
Lies with a dagger sticking in his spine.
Along the mole his voice, still waterborne,
Repeats the word from which his grief was born.

That word is Corinth, copiously said,
And the earth groans with lassitude and dread.

L'ASILE

Celui-là que trahit les rages de son ventre
Et que tel pâle éclair de ses nuits a, souvent,
Humilié, s'humilie. Il se soumet, il entre
À l'asile de fous comme on entre au couvent.

Puissé-je rester libre et garder ma raison
Comme un sextant précis à travers les tempêtes,
Lieux d'asile mon cœur, ma tête et ma maison
Et le droit de fixer en face hommes et bêtes.

Vertu tu n'es qu'un mot, mais le seul mot de passe
Qui m'ouvre l'horizon, déchire le décor
Et soumet à mes vœux l'espéré Val-de-Grâce

Où le sage s'éveille, où le héros s'endort.
Que le rêve de l'un et la réalité
De l'autre soient présents bientôt dans la cité.

LE RÉVEIL

Entendez-vous le bruit des roues sur le pavé?
Il est tard. Levez-vous. Midi à son de trompe
Réclame le passage à l'écluse et, rêvé,
Le monde enfin s'incarne et déroule ses pompes.

Il est tard. Levez-vous. L'eau coule en la baignoire.
Il faut laver ce corps que la nuit a souillé.
Il faut nourrir ce corps affamé de victoire.
Il faut vêtir ce corps après l'avoir mouillé.

Après avoir frotté les mains que tachait l'encre,
Après avoir brossé les dents où pourrissaient

THE ASYLUM

The one whom his own belly's rage betrays,
Many times humbled when his nights glow pale,
Humbles himself, submits, and joins the strays
In the asylum, as one takes the veil.

May I stay free and healthy in my thinking
Like an unfailing sextant in a storm,
Take refuge in my heart, my head, my home,
And gaze on man and beast with eye unblinking.

Virtue, mere word, you've set me free to pass:
You've opened up the view, torn down the drapes,
Bent to my prayers the hoped-for Val-de-Grâce,

Where the sage wakens and the hero sleeps.
Grant that the city soon enjoys their presence:
The wise man's dream, the warrior's vital essence.

THE AWAKENING

Listen: the noise of wheels on cobbled streets.
It's late. Get up. Noon blasts its foghorn trump,
Keen to go through the lock-gates. Sleep recedes:
The world of dreams takes flesh and flaunts its pomp.

It's late. Get up. The bath-tap's on, and splashing.
This body that the night has soiled needs washing.
This body, starved of victory, needs feeding.
This body needs a thorough soak, then clothing.

When we have scrubbed these hands of inky stains,
When we have brushed these teeth that hold decaying

Tant de mots retenus comme bateaux à l'ancre,
Tant de chansons, de vérités et de secrets.

Il est tard. Levez-vous. Dans la rue un refrain
Vous appelle et vous dit «Voici la vie réelle».
On a mis le couvert. Mangez à votre faim
Puis remettez le mors au cheval qu'on attelle.

Pourtant pensez à ceux qui sont muets et sourds
Car ils sont morts, assassinés, au petit jour.

L'ÉPITAPHE

J'ai vécu dans ces temps et depuis mille années
Je suis mort. Je vivais, non déchu mais traqué.
Toute noblesse humaine étant emprisonnée
J'étais libre parmi les esclaves masqués.

J'ai vécu dans ces temps et pourtant j'étais libre.
Je regardais le fleuve et la terre et le ciel
Tourner autour de moi, garder leur équilibre
Et les saisons fournir leurs oiseaux et leur miel.

Vous qui vivez qu'avez-vous fait de ces fortunes?
Regrettez-vous les temps où je me débattais?
Avez-vous cultivé pour des moissons communes?
Avez-vous enrichi la ville où j'habitais?

Vivants, ne craignez rien de moi, car je suis mort.
Rien ne survit de mon esprit ni de mon corps.

Words, like boats rotting on their anchor-chains,
Words of a song, a true or secret saying.

It's late. Get up. The clarion in the street
Summons you. "This is real life. This is it."
The table's laid, and you are hungry: eat.
The horse is being bridled: fix the bit.

Think, though, of those who neither speak nor hear,
Having been murdered as the day dawned clear.

THE EPITAPH

I've lived today, and since antiquity
Been dead. I lived intact, but I was prey.
Man's nobler side was jailed and put away;
Among the slaves in face-masks, I was free.

I've lived today, and nonetheless been free.
I watched the river and the earth and sky
Turn round me, and they kept their harmony;
Honey and birds, a seasonal supply.

How did you use these gifts, you there alive?
Did you misuse the days I spent in toil?
Did you make common cause and till the soil
To harvest? Did you make my city thrive?

Don't fear me, you who live: I'm dead and gone:
Not soul nor body, nothing lingers on.

BATHING WITH ANDROMEDA

A sequence from 1944.
In the classical myth, Andromeda is chained
to a rock to be the prey of a sea-monster,
but is rescued by Perseus. At the same time,
this is about France and the invader.

Introductory Note by Marie-Claire Dumas

'Bathing with Andromeda' comprises nine poems, which were illustrated in colour by Felix Labisse. His images, classically drawn, their themes strangely erotic, make an effective counterpoint to the sensuality of the poems. These form a coherent set proceeding by scenes or episodes, a 'morality' whose characters all have an allegorical dimension. Labisse had worked on the images of Andromeda and the monster since the 1930's. In the ancient myth, Andromeda's parents deliver her to the monster threatening the city; Perseus, on the winged horse Pegasus, rescues the girl and marries her. Between the myth and Desnos' version stands 'Perseus and Andromeda, or the Happiest of the Three', from the 'Legendary Moralities' of Jules Laforgue, where, as in 'Beauty and the Beast', an idyll is proposed between captor and prisoner. The myth, then, illustrated by Labisse and altered by Laforgue, is re-focused by Desnos on Andromeda and her fancies: a virgin on the edge of reality, dreaming of rape, intensely corporeal and projected on a void symbolic of the world. Hence the erotic violence of some scenes and 'the rescue of Andromeda', on her own: 'Andromeda travels [...] The monster has fled. It's too much for high heaven.' No raising-up of the heroine to be a constellation, in this version: she vanishes, giving way to 'the handsome young man's return' – the day, that lights up the earth: 'The day's to be lived and the hour's to be savoured'. In these nine poems, their lines rhyming regularly and mostly ordered in stanzas, Desnos evidently wanted to build a formal structure with symbolic import: time is announced by the return of verses of fifty-two lines, as many as weeks in the year; the banquet of twelve young persons - the twelve months; the nine poems – nine months of gestation. Andromeda and her three companions symbolise seasons, elements, the compass: she is summer, water, east; Hippolyte is autumn, earth, west; Sabina winter, north, fire; Rose spring, south, air. The whole poem runs from one dawn to the next, a complete day, the banquet in the middle under the noon sun: 'It's the noon [...] Time to panic.' Desnos has multiplied the formal and thematic links so that the poem celebrates the great global mechanism in which man exists, the

complexity of the human spirit, shared by the imaginary and the real, and the pleasure of living, in full acceptance of this situation.

Finally the monster can also be the occupier, and the last *carpe diem* a salute to the coming day of victory over the oppressor.

LA BAIGNADE

Andromède, au matin, sur la plage, a donné
Rendez-vous à tous ceux qui veulent se baigner
Dans la mer fraîche éclose, enceinte de lumière.
L'étoile brille encor, qu'arrive, la première,
Rosemonde aux beaux seins qui, seule, se devêt
Et livre son corps nu, que roussit le duvet,
Aux dernières lueurs de la nuit, aux prémices
De l'aube qui se dresse au fond des précipices.
Sabine la rejoint, tige en fleur qui jaillit
D'un flot de linge, par le vent frais assailli.
Une neige d'écume éclabousse leurs cuisses
Et la première vague attache, par malice,
Une ceinture d'algue à ces corps qu'embellit
Le reflet d'une étoile et la langueur du lit.
Les astres dans le ciel grandissent et déclinent,
La neige sur les monts, à la fois, s'illumine
Des feux, naissants, du jour et, mourants, de la nuit.
Dans le sentier, bordé de genêt et de buis,
Hyppolite paraît qui, tandis qu'elle avance,
Se déshabille et jette, en figures de danse,
La robe et la chemise et le court pantalon.
Ils flottent, un instant, au-dessus des buissons,
Dans le vent, puis, soudain, s'accrochent et fleurissent,
Fleurs d'étoffe, bouquets qui, vers la donatrice,
Exhalent des parfums de chair dans ceux du sol.
Ainsi, durant le jour, tourne le tournesol
Vers l'astre dont il est le sujet et l'image.
Hyppolite, à son tour, dans la mer plonge et nage
Et l'on connaît, enfin, la présence du jour
À la blancheur du linge, aux chants des basses-cours,
À l'envol des oiseaux, à l'eclat des nuages,
Au divorce de l'eau, du ciel et du rivage.

Par quel chemin vint-elle? Andromède, soudain,
Est présente et se livre à la douceur du bain.

THE BATHING

Morning: the beach. Andromeda's invited
All those who wish to bathe in the fresh-spread sea,
Pregnant with light. A star's still bright when, first,
Fair-breasted Rosamund arrives, strips off, alone,
Surrenders her bare body's russet down
To the last glow of night and to the traces
Of dawn, resurgent in deep precipices.
Sabina's next, a flowering stem that rises
From a froth of linen, assaulted by the breezes.
A snow of spray foams up around their thighs
And the first wave maliciously attaches
A belt of seaweed to these bodies, lovely
From starlight's lustre and the languid bed.
The stars above grow bigger and sink lower;
The mountain snows illuminate two fires:
Fires of the day at birth, the night at death.
On the path, edged with broom and box, appears
Hippolytê, who, even as she comes,
Disrobes, and dances as she throws aside
Her gown, chemise, and little pantaloons.
A moment first they float above the shrubs;
Then suddenly they're caught, and start to flower,
Bouquets of fabric-flowers that exhale,
To the donor, flesh-notes mixed with scent of earth.
Just so the sunflower turns towards the bright
Day-star, being both its subject and its image.
In turn Hippolytê dives in and swims.
At length the presence of the day is known
By the white linen and the farmyard songs,
The flight of birds, the brilliance of clouds,
The separateness of water, shore, and sky.

Which way did she come? Andromeda appears
Suddenly, yielding to the bath's caress.

Elle nage. On peut suivre, encore, son sillage
Entre son corps doré et le bord de la plage.
Et ce sont des envols de bras, par-dessus l'eau,
Des battements de pieds et des éclairs de peau,
Des rires, des appels dans les éclaboussures,
Des cuisses se fermant et s'ouvrant, en mesure,
Ou, parfois, la baigneuse étendue, sur le dos,
Et se cambrant, plus souple et plus léger fardeau,
Un triangle mouillé, brillant et symétrique
À celui d'un oiseau qui vole sur la crique.
Une croupe à méplats s'illumine et surgit
Quand la baigneuse plonge et cherche, en leur logis,
L'étoile ou le galet, l'algue ou le coquillage.
L'étoile? Mais le ciel est clair! Quelque mirage
Métamorphose en flamme un vol de goélands,
En saveur de baisers l'air et ses parfums lents.

Qu'un pied se marque, ici dans l'épaisseur du sable,
Le soleil séchera cette empreinte et sa fable.

DÉCOUVERTE DU TRÉSOR

Est-il poitrine, où batte un cœur de chair et flamme,
Qu'une lame, ou la griffe, aille ouvrir et piller,
Est-il océan, lac ou fleuve que la rame,
Ou l'hélice, aille en flots, sans trace, éparpiller,

Est-il poitrine ou fleuve ou lac ou océan
Ou terre, aussi fendue à renfort de charrues,
Qui ne puissent livrer des moissons et, béants,
Le noyé, le poisson, l'épave disparue?

She swims. Her wake is traceable between
Her golden body and the beach's rim.
Arm-strokes above the water, beating feet,
The flashing skin, the merry laughing cries,
Splish-splash, the thighs that close and open up
In rhythm, or at times, the bather stretched
Belly-up, a lighter, smoothly curving load,
Shining wet triangle, symmetrical
With those of birds that fly about the cove.
A rump catches the light, protruded when
A swimmer dives, pursuing in their lair
Starfish or seaweed, stone or cockleshell.
What star? The sky is bright. By some mirage,
A flight of gulls is magicked into flame,
And into kisses the slow-perfumed air.

Seeing a foot imprinted here in sand,
The sun shall dry the mark, the tale shall stand.

FINDING THE TREASURE

Is there a breast where beats a heart of flesh and of blazing
  That knife or claw may open up and raid,
Is there an ocean, lake, or river, which the blade
  Of oar or screw may spread on the waves beyond tracing,

Is there a breast or ocean, lake, river, or even
  Earth itself, cloven by the main force of ploughs,
That cannot yield a crop, and belch from gaping jaws
  The fish, the man who drowned, the disappeared orphan?

Mieux, le trésor caché, le bijou, l'or, la gemme,
Plutôt que le cadavre et le vide tombeau
Et, plutôt que l'épi, né du grain que l'on sème,
Le métal par la rouille échappant au corbeau.

Quel poignard fouillera votre ventre et vos seins,
Rosemonde, Sabine, Hyppolite, Andromède?
Quel chercheur d'or, quel outlaw, quel assassin
En vous dépossédant dira qui vous possède?

Qu'il illumine les ténèbres des cavernes,
Qu'il jaillisse du flanc d'une épave, à vau-l'eau,
Ou qu'une source apporte, aux lumières modernes,
L'éclat des vieux soleils serti dans un joyau,

Que le profil d'un roi, sans regard, sans odeur
S'y multiplie en vain contre la pourriture,
Ou que l'heure s'y lise, à des cadrans a fleurs,
Mais arrêtée au seuil d'une longue aventure,

Qu'importe, jaillissant des conques et des cornes,
Il recèlera plus de chair que de métaux,
Une chair odorante, aux corridors sans bornes
Vers une aube brillant comme un fil de couteau.

L'homme, au moment qu'il sent la saveur des cailloux
Dans sa bouche, habituée a la saveur des lèvres,
Arrête le voyage, au rythme de son pouls
Commencé dès les jours de jeunesse et de fièvres.

Il se sent désormais soudé à sa monture,
Centaure poursuivant un gibier reconnu
Insaisissable. Il le poursuit, dans ses pâtures,
Non plus par besoin, mais par désir, d'inconnu.

Better the hidden treasure, gem or gold or jewel,
Than the grave untenanted, better than the cadaver.
Better too, than the corn which is sown, is what for ever
Rusts to escape the jackdaws, namely metal.

What dagger shall ransack your belly and breasts, Hippolytê,
Sabina, Rosamund, even yours, Andromeda?
What gold-digger, what desperado, what murderer
Shall dispossess you, name your possessor-to-be?

If it illuminates the shadows in cavernous dens,
Or spurts from the flank of a lost child, floating away,
Or if clear streams to our modern lights convey,
Inset in a gem, the brightness of ancient suns,

If a royal profile that neither sees nor smells
Is replicated in vain against perdition,
Or if the time is told there on flowery dials,
Though stopped on the brink of a lengthy expedition,

What matter, for surging from every conch and horn
It shall be a receiver of flesh, more than of metals,
A fragrant flesh, through passages limitless
Wafting towards a glittering knife-sharp dawn!

A man, at the moment he senses in his mouth
The taste of stones, not the lips it's his habit to taste,
Breaks off the journey that follows the beat in his wrist
That has pulsed ever since his feverish days of youth.

From now, as he rides, he feels as if welded on,
A centaur pursuing a quarry he understands
Can't be caught. He chases it through its pasturelands,
Not needing now, but desiring, the object unknown.

Ivresse! Le courant, le cortège, les jours
Le font participer au mouvement du monde.
Au-delà de la joie, au-delà du retour
La vie et le destin le portent sur leurs ondes.

Mais vous, où courez-vous, femmes en proie a l'âge,
Quelle image de vous guettez-vous aux miroirs
Chaque jour plus profonds, encombrés de naufrages,
Quel trésor cherchez-vous pour payer votre espoir?

Le carnaval s'approche avec ses cheveux blancs
Et le trésor, cherche à travers les années,
Ce sont des grelots creux et des masques branlants
Qui vous cachent le sol sur quoi vous êtes nées.

NAISSANCE DU MONSTRE

Le paysage était fourrure,
Pelage de fleurs et moissons,
Brume vibrante, échos, frissons:
Le voici prêt à la morsure,
Il s'incarne et devient ce fauve
Qui, tour à tour, séduit, repousse
Et fait surgir, à la rescousse,
Un rêve de viols et d'alcôves.

Sabine, Hyppolite, Andromède
Et Rosemonde et leurs compagnes,
Un tel délire les possède,
Dansent de fureur et s'enfuient,
Aux quatre coins d'une campagne,

Mad-drunkenness! The procession, the stream, the days
   Cause him to share in the movement of all creation.
Out beyond joy, beyond the point of retracing,
   Life and destiny bear him along on their waves.

But you women, where are you heading, a prey to age?
   What images do you watch in your mirrors? For they
Are fraught with shipwreck, deeper every day.
   Do you search for treasure to pay your hopes a wage?

White-headed, now it approaches, the carnival,
   Bringing the treasure you hunted through the years.
For these are sounding masks, these are hollow tears
   That won't allow you to see your native soil.

BIRTH OF THE MONSTER

The landscape was fur,
Pelt of harvests and flowers,
Scary echoes, fog-blur.
He's here with his jaws,
Incarnate wild beast,
Repels and seduces
To rouse dreams of rescues,
Of rapes and recesses.

Driven wild by desire
All the bevy of girls
Madly dance and retire
To the distant four corners
To woods without wells

Vers des forêts, sans lacs ni puits,
Dont l'ombre, masquant les figures,
Adoptera leur chevelure.

Ronronnant, au creux du fauteuil,
Le monstre surveille la proie
Qui s'agite au fond de son œil.
II baille de faim et de joie,
Révélant la langue gourmande,
Le palais rose et les crocs blancs
Et l'haleine, à odeur de viande,
Qui d'abord soulève son flanc.

Enfant de quel tragique amour,
Hors de quel ventre ténébreux,
Vagissant, jaillit-il au jour?
Du haut des montagnes? Du creux
Où, bue, aux cris des tragédies,
Par un roi de flamme et de vent,
La lave craque et incendie,
Au soir, d'insolites levants.

Ventre palpitant de désirs,
À tous baisers la gorge offerte,
Prêt à pâmer, prêt à gésir,
Le monstre excite et déconcerte
Un appetit d'ombre et de sang,
De chair ouverte sous les griffes
Et, sous les poils qui s'ébouriffent,
D'un souffle bientôt rugissant.

Velours, satins, sang et baisers,
Tout est luxe, tout est horreur
Dans les corps, d'amour embrasés,
Dans les cœurs, sujets a l'erreur,

Or pools, where the shadow
Disguises their faces
Adopting their hairdo.

From a big chair he purrs,
Sees the scurrying prey
In the depth of his eye.
Joy and hunger! He yawns,
And shows his tongue, greedy,
Pink palate, white teeth,
Meat-stink of his breath,
Up-thrusting his haunch.

By what tragic love, run
Through what murky belly,
Did he cry out and spawn?
From hills? From the hollow,
Drunk down by some sovereign
Of flame-wind and wailing,
The lava creaked, kindled
At dusk the strange dawn.

Cupidinous belly
A throat for all kisses
Quick-swooning, quick-bedding,
He stirs and he baffles
A craving for shadow,
For blood, for fur ruffled,
Flesh opened by talons,
Breath presently roaring.

Kisses, blood, velvet, satins,
Luxurious horror
Of bodies impassioned,
Hearts tending to error:

Et quelque terrible mystère
De la matière même, à terre,
Réunira, dans une étreinte,
Les chairs aspirant à la plainte.

Oui, bien sûr, la nuit est propice
Aux plongeons dans les précipices.
Quant au soleil, qu'il s'abolisse
À l'instant de ces exercices.

BANQUET

La cote se découpe en golfes ou l'echo
Sonne, comme une trompe, aux murs de Jéricho,
Un Jéricho de brume et flexible comme elle,
La mer y gonfle en vain ses chants et ses querelles.
Dans un de ces abris est servi le banquet
Pour douze garçons nus qui n'ont d'autre projet
Que de boire les vins au goulot des bouteilles,
Mordre aux quartiers de viande et vider les corbeilles
Faire sécher leur corps au soleil de midi,
Chanter et puis dormir sur le sable tiédi.
Le sable, que le vent soulève et qu'il égraine,
Fait murmurer parfois les plats de porcelaine
Et le cristal où tremble une goutte de vin
Qui reflète le ciel et les doigts de la main.
Mais le sang apparaît aux bords d'une blessure
Lorsque le maladroit, d'une lame peu sûre,
Se coupe en entamant le jambon. Un rideau
Rouge flotte soudain, claquant comme un drapeau.
Il vacille et ses plis balaient le paysage.

O earth! Obscure terror
Inherent in matter!
Deep-moaning, the fleshes
Combine their embraces.

Yes, the night is most propitious
For a plunge down precipices;
And the sun should minimise his
Presence at such exercises.

BANQUET

The coast is cut up into gulfs where the echo
Sounds forth, like a trump at the old walls of Jericho,
Walled city of vapour and equally ductile.
The sea's swollen singing and sulking are futile.
In one of these havens they've served up the banquet
For twelve naked boys who have no other project
Than drinking the wines from the neck of the bottles,
And biting roast haunches and emptying baskets
And drying their bodies in noonday sun, and
Singing, then sleeping, on well-warmed sand.
The sand, which the wind likes to lift as it sifts,
Sometimes causes the porcelain dishes to murmur,
And the crystalline glass where a drop of wine shivers,
Reflecting the sky and a set of five fingers.
But there's blood to be seen at the edge of a wound
When the clumsy buffoon who's attacking the gammon
Cuts himself on the erring blade. All of a sudden
A red curtain waves, flaps and snaps like a flag,
Back and forth, and the landscape is swept in its pleats;

La mer, qui le répète agite son image
Et celle d'un bateau, toutes voiles dehors,
Qui figure une rose en un coin du décor.
Il aimerait, dit-il, que des lèvres plus tendres
Cicatrisent la plaie et, quitte pour répandre
Plus longuement son sang, à rendre ce baiser
Au monstre imaginaire en son cœur précisé.
N'entend-il pas des cris du haut de la falaise?
Son sang n'explique pas l'insolite malaise
Qui transforme la terre et lui fait souhaiter
Le silence et la nuit et la mort de l'été.
Il se lève et, fuyant ses onze camarades,
Disparaît au tournant des rochers de la rade.
Onze verres, levés au ciel par onze mains,
D'une combe identique ont renversé le vin
Dans des gorges, au chant prêtes, mais, vers la route
Indiquée, un regard s'alanguit et, sans doute,
Un convive bientôt quittera le banquet.
Il est une prairie où cueillir des bouquets,
Il est une forêt, derrière le rivage,
Et des sources d'eau fraîche où baigner les visages
Et le monde habité, ses villes, ses appels.
Qu'ils boivent! Le temps passe et dépose son sel
Sur les jours, sur les cœurs, les lèvres et les rêves.
Pourtant la vie est là, pourtant la vie est brève,
Qu'ils boivent! L'horizon se dénoue à l'entour,
L'heure vient, pour chacun, à partir à son tour.
C'est midi, tout sanglant, gisant dans sa tunique,
Sur le bûcher qu'il alluma. Heure panique,
Il faut choisir, il faut, vers le soir progresser
Ou vieillir en tentant d'évoquer le passé.
C'est midi. Dans le ciel claque une draperie
Rouge et le monde est plein d'amour et de féerie.

The sea takes its image and shakes and repeats
And adds in a boat with its sails to the wide
That sports a fine rose tucked away on its side.
He'd be happy, he says, for lips rather more yielding
To stitch up his wound; in return, too, for spreading
His blood rather far, he's a kiss to impart
To the monster, imagined, described in his heart.
Can't he hear any cries from the top of the bluff?
There's an awkward unease, not explained by his blood,
That has caused him to wish (for it's altered the earth)
For night and for silence and summertime's death.
On his feet to escape his eleven companions,
He's gone round the rocks by the roadstead. Eleven
Hands raise the same number of glasses to heaven.
One identical tilt and the wine is poured down
Into throats set to sing; but a slow glance is thrown
At the route aforementioned; quite shortly, it's clear,
One friend at the feast will no longer be here.
There's a field to pick flowers, a wood near the place
Of safe mooring, fresh water for washing your face,
And the world full of people, its cities and cries.
Let them drink! For time passes, its salts crystallise
On days and on hearts and on lips and desires.
Nonetheless there is life, nonetheless life expires.
Let them drink! The horizon unfolds all about,
And the time will arrive for each one to set out.
It's the noon that is bleeding, laid out in its tunic
On the pyre it has kindled. What's this! Time to panic.
Time to choose, to move on towards evening at last,
Or grow older from trying to call up the past.
It is noon. In the sky, flap and snap of red drapery.
The world's fully laden with love and with faërie.

ANDROMÈDE EN PROIE AU MONSTRE

Quel sera, monstre, mon supplice?
Déjà, dérisoire, ton nom
Devient mot d'amour et complice
De ma honte et de notre union.
J'adopterai, d'abord, la pose
Propice à ma métamorphose.
En t'épousant, que je m'endorme,
Par volupté, je prends ta forme.

Car au-delà de la nausée,
Je découvre, en moi, des domaines
Qui sont la dot à l'épousée:
J'y trouverai la clef des chaînes
Et l'endroit de ta sépulture
Quand, monstre, il te faudra mourir
À la fin de notre luxure,
De la mort de notre désir.

Car tout est nôtre, désormais,
Je suis ton monstre et ta réplique,
Je suis la porte du palais,
Je suis l'image symétrique
Qui surgit, lorsque tu parais,
Je suis ta rivale lubrique
Et mon désir se faisait fuite
Pour sentir ton souffle à ma suite.

Le monstre dit: «Pas tant d'histoires
Pas tant de cris et de paroles.
Je suis le maître et mon vouloir
Ne s'embarrasse ni d'un viol
Ni d'accordailles, ni de noces.
Ta voix me brise le tympan.
Je vais mon train, selon l'élan
Qui m'entraîne et me rend féroce.»

ANDROMEDA, THE MONSTER'S PREY

Monster, what's my punishment?
Now a mockery, your name
Has connived as blandishment
In our union and my shame.
There's a posture I'll assume,
Firstly, to transmute my form.
We shall marry, I must sleep:
Rapt with joy, I take your shape.

For, beyond disgust, inside
Myself I unearth domains
That are the dowry of the bride:
Find the key to free my chains,
And the place to lay you by,
Monster, when you have to die,
When our orgy shall expire
Of the death of our desire.

From this moment, all is ours:
I'm your monstrous duplicate,
I am the palatial doors,
When your lifelike form appears
I rise up in symmetry,
Rival of your lechery.
Quickly my desire took flight,
Felt your breath in hot pursuit.

Says the monster: 'Stop your cries,
Sobs and stories and alarms.
I am the master, and my will
Does not jib at marriages,
Rapes, or contracts, has no qualms.
Spare my eardrum with your voice!
I am fierce, I run my course,
Charging where my urges pull.'

Andromède, étant tout enfant
Chérissait un parc solitaire
Où, chaque soir, un éléphant
Se promenait en grand mystère.
Un éléphant? Est-ce bien vrai?
Ce n'est, peut-être, qu'un vieux rêve,
Mais elle y pense et jurerait
Qu'il la piétine et la soulève.

Andromède étant tout enfant
Andromède que fait la bête?
Andromède qui te défend?
Quelle tempête, dans ta tête,
Au réel mélange un vieux rêve?
Mais la chanson que tu répètes
Nul ne sait comme elle s'achève.
Andromède étant tout enfant…

Le monstre dit: «Je suis la bête
Mais, dans le ciel, tout comme toi,
Enrichi d'étoiles en fête
J'aurai ma place et mon emploi.»

MEURTRE

Andromède se tait au fond des bois,
Les guêpes, les abeilles et les mouches
En culbutant, dans l'air, font des tournois
Et le ciel est ouvert comme une bouche.

When Andromeda was small
She held dear a lonely park
Where a mystery elephant
Sauntered in the looming dark.
Could it be? A pachyderm?
Probably a childish dream,
But she dwells on it, would swear
She is trampled, swung in air.

When Andromeda was small...
Andromède, beware the beast!
Who will save you, Andromède?
What's the brainstorm in your head
Mixes fact with daydreams past?
Though the lines you sing are sweet,
None of us may know the last.
When Andromeda was small...

Says the monster: 'I'm the beast:
Yet like you, in skies above
Rich with stars that flaunt and feast,
I shall belong and I shall serve.'

MURDER

Andromède is in the forest,
Silent; bee and wasp and fly
Somersault in airy joust.
Open like a mouth, the sky.

Mais du ciel béant ne sort aucun cri,
L'heure est stupide, immense et solennelle,
La lumière est un fleuve tari
Surveillé par d'inertes sentinelles.

Pour animer ce pays suspendu,
Il faudrait l'appel d'un nageur qui coule
Ou, faisant danser le corps d'un pendu,
L'ouragan frémissant comme une foule.

Pourtant le meurtre, attendu par la terre
Pour s'imbiber de salive et de sang,
A lieu, sans qu'aucun geste altère
L'immobilité de l'instant présent.

Trésor sans gardien, banquet sans convives,
Femmes trépignant au seuil des saisons,
Cadavre étendu auprès de la rive
D'où la piste part jusqu'à l'horizon...

Retrouverez-vous, joyeux compagnons,
Les chants que l'on chante aux instants d'ivresse?
Retrouverez-vous au vin des flacons
La même saveur, la même sagesse?

N'est-ce pas pour vous, qu'au bois, Andromède
Charme un monstre né de ses cauchemars?
N'est-ce pas pour vous qu'elle appelle à l'aide
En feignant la peur jusqu'en son regard?

N'êtes-vous pas victime et meurtrier,
Abandonnant votre propre dépouille
Et le couteau que masquera de rouille
Le proche hiver à l'ombre du laurier?

From this yawning mouth, no cry.
The hour's stupid, solemn, vast,
And the light's a stream run dry,
Watched by dull guards at their post.

What can rouse this land from trance?
Drowning swimmer bawling loud,
Or, to make the hanged man dance,
Whirlwind roaring like a crowd.

Yet the crime that earth awaits
(Blood and spittle, tasty ferment)
Happens: no gesture moderates,
Alters the frozen present moment.

Guardless treasure, guestless feast,
Women's heels drum in the season.
On the shore lies one deceased,
Pathway makes for the horizon...

Happy band, will you recover
Songs that chime with drunkenness?
In the wine-jugs, find that flavour
And that same clear-headedness?

It's for you that Andromède
Charms the beast her nightmares rear;
It's from you she summons aid:
Even her eyes are faking fear.

Aren't you the killer and the killed,
Sloughing off your own apparel,
With the knife, by rust concealed,
Come the frosts, beneath the laurel?

Un passant, plus tard, passera sans doute
Et dira qu'un autre a tracé sa route,
Qu'ils ont accompli le rite tous deux
À la même époque et au même lieu,

Le parfum qui flotte est toujours le même,
L'homme a d'autres noms et d'autres grimaces,
Mais tout est semblable et le grain qu'on sème
Brisera toujours la même surface.

Un cadavre gît pourtant en ce lieu,
Il gît, il pourrit, il se désagrège,
Il est invisible et crève les yeux,
Il est invisible et pris à son piège.
Un arbre au cœur a planté ses racines.
Qu'il fructifie et qu'il porte ses fleurs,
Baisers perdus, aveux sous les glycines,
Chansons d'amour et chansons de haleurs.

Son double est mort, il poursuit son chemin
À travers les forêts, les cimetières,
Sous des nuages pareils à des mains
Montrant, au flanc des monts, une carrière.

DANSES

Vous avez faim, vous avez soif,
Rosemonde, c'est le vent d'est
    Qui vous décoiffe.
Que ce vent emporte la peste
Au fond du ciel et qu'elle y reste.

Someone's sure to say some other
Person trod the scene of crime,
That they did the deed together,
At that place and at that time.

Fixed is the wafting scent of flowers.
We may change a face, a name;
All's alike, though: ask the sowers:
Sow as they will, the field's the same.

Yet a corpse lies in this place.
Lies and rots and falls apart.
Invisible and in your face,
Invisible and neatly caught.
A tree has rooted in its heart.
Let it bear its fruit and flowers.
Lost kisses, vows under wistarias,
Songs of love, hauling-songs of rivers.

His double's dead. Through forest-lands
And cemetery-plots he strides.
The clouds above him look like hands
That trace a course on mountainsides.

DANCES

Hungry, thirsty Rosamund,
Tousled by the harsh east wind
   Is your hair.
Take the murrain anywhere
In the sky, wind! –
   Leave it there.

Hyppolite, l'oiseau du nord
    Qui passe sur la plaine
L'oiseau qui chante, rêve et mord,
    L'avez-vous vu à la fontaine?
Il chante, il rêve, il mord,
    Il dort.

Andromède, face à l'ouest,
    Figure de proue,
Pas un sourire, pas un geste,
L'écume jaillit sur vos joues
Et rouille le fer qui vous cloue.

Un géant viendra du sud
Sabine as-tu donné ton cœur
Porteur de fruits et de liqueurs,
    Sonneur de la solitude.

Rosemonde, aimez-vous l'été?
    Bagatelle, bagatelle,
J'aime mieux l'hiver, dit-elle,
    Et les rosiers désenchantés.

Andromède, aimez-vous l'automne?
    Il vente, il pleut, il tonne,
J'aime l'automne et le printemps
    Et la fleur de mes jeunes ans.

Hyppolite, aimez-vous l'hiver?
    Je ne sais pas, dit-elle,
Le seul été, j'ai découvert,
Mon esprit suit les hirondelles.

From the north, Hippolytê,
Sharp-beaked bird to dream and cheep,
Flew across the plains to be
At the well-spring, did you see?
Sharp-beaked bird to dream and cheep:
    Now asleep.

Facing westward, Andromède,
    Figurehead,
Stilled, unsmiling, hand and head.
Surging at your cheeks, the spray
Rusts your metal nails away.

Bearing fruits, a behemoth
(Is Sabina fancy-free?)
Comes with liquors from the south,
    Ringing bells of hermitry.

Rosamund, do you find
    Summer kind?
    – Fol-di-dee,
I love winter more, says she,
Roses shorn of wizardry.

Yours, Andromeda, the fall?
Love of thunder, gales, and showers?
– I love spring no less than fall,
I adore my girlhood's flowers.

Winter-time, Hippolytê:
Do you love it? – Don't ask me.
Summer's when my spirit follows,
As I've learnt, the wheeling swallows.

Sabine, aimez-vous le printemps?
J'aimais le printemps, je le pleure,
J'aime, je pleure avec le temps
    Je ris avec les heures.

Je danse, je ris dans le feu,
Je flambe, je suis Andromède,
Je me consume et c'est un jeu
Qui me délivre et qui m'obsède.

Rosemonde, écoutez la terre
    Qui peine sur son chemin.
Je l'entends, mais il faut se taire,
    Nous chanterons demain.

Hyppolite, fille de l'air
Parcourt à cheval le désert,
Cheval de nuage et de vent,
Air de jadis et d'à present.

Au point du jour et au point d'eau,
    Sabine se désaltère
Avec les lions et les panthères.
La nuit dépose son fardeau.

DÉLIVRANCE D'ANDROMÈDE

L'eau ne vêtirait plus ce corps à sa mesure.
La clairière l'absorbe autant que le miroir
Mais des griffes ont fait, au ventre, une blessure
Qui tache de son sang le tissu d'un mouchoir.

Does Sabina love the spring?
– Yes, I loved, I sorrow after:
Love, and mourn time's vanishing,
Sharing with the hours my laughter.

Dancing, laughing in the blaze,
I am Andromède, in flame:
I'm consumed, obsessed, released,
Burnt to ashes by the game.

Do you hear it, Rosamund?
Earth goes toiling on its way.
– Yes, but we must make no sound:
We shall sing another day.

Child of air, Hippolytê
Rides her horse across the plain:
Horse of cloud and wind was he,
Air of once and once again.

Edge of water, edge of dawn,
It's Sabina who unwinds
With the panthers and the lions.
Darkness lays its burden down.

ANDROMEDA SAVED

The water can tailor this body no more.
As much as the mirror, the glade in the wood
Drinks it in. But the belly's been gouged by a claw
And the weave of a hanky is spotted with blood.

De la main relevant, sur son front, une mèche,
Andromède s'éloigne et franchit les taillis
Comme un fauve portant, dans sa chair, une flèche
Qui lui dicte sa route à travers les pays.

La sueur et la salive ont souillé son visage
Mais la joie envahit ses sens et son esprit.
Jamais plus, de la nuit descendant les étages,
Des spectres ne viendront l'épouser dans son lit.

Adieu Sabine, adieu Rosemonde, Hyppolite,
Vers des lieux différents le soir vous précipite.

Andromède, livrée à sa propre fureur,
En elle apaise enfin sa soif et sa fatigue.
L'espace grand ouvert accueille, sans erreur
Et sans retour, pour cette fois, l'enfant prodigue.

Andromède s'en va et joint au crépuscule
Qui soulève, dans l'ouest, un funèbre océan,
Le sang de sa blessure ou son ombre bascule
Proie offerte aux baisers des nains et des géants.

Andromède s'en va. L'endroit qu'elle abandonne,
Endroit ou son destin s'efface et fut tracé,
Est marqué par le jet d'une blanche colonne.

Plus loin le monstre fuit.
Le ciel est dépassé.

Holding back her stray locks, an enveloping mesh,
Andromeda runs through the brush and the brakes
Like a creature that carries a dart in its flesh
Dictating the cross-country path that it takes.

Her face is all filthy with spittle and sweat
But joy has invaded her senses and spirit.
Nevermore dropping down through the night will she get
Ghosts filling her bed on a nuptial visit.

Adieu, Sabina, Rosamund, Hippolytê: adieu.
The twilight moves you on, has other places planned for you.

Andromeda yields to her innermost rage
In which her exhaustion and thirst are annealed;
There's a welcome, this time, from the wide open space,
No mistake, no return, for the prodigal child.

She goes, and she adds to the sun's dying blaze,
And the funeral ocean it props in the west,
The blood of her wound where her own shadow sways,
Prey offered to giants and dwarves to be kissed.

Andromeda travels. The place she has gone from,
The place where her fate that is cancelled was given,
Is marked by the jet of a snowy-white column.

The monster has fled.
It's too much for high heaven.

AUBE

La nuit grasse, penchée au bord de ses abîmes,
Contemple les jardins du jour qui disparaît.
Moins longtemps que l'éclair, sur le couteau du crime,
Ils ont fleuri. Déjà s'efface le portrait
D'un monde que la mort harcèle et précipite.
Que jaillissent les feux des phares, des bûchers,
Que les soleils lointains, les comètes prescrites
S'allument! Ce ne sont, près du mourant couché,
Que veilleuses, tremblant au courant d'air des portes
Ouvertes sur la terre et sur l'immensité.
Tout est nuit, tout est mort, tout est seul, mais qu'importe
Si l'on eut un instant, sous le soleil d'été,
L'illusion de l'amour et de la plénitude.
Viens donc, nuit incomprise et trompeuse et dis-nous
Que les baisers fiévreux, que les creuses études
Sont plus sages ici que, dites à genoux,
La prière du lâche et celle du débile.

La nuit grasse est tombée en des gouffres connus
Où le jour la suivra d'une chute docile
Car il dressa déjà sur les monts son corps nu.
Il se baigne à la source, il franchit la vallée,
Il pénètre la mer de son reflet puissant.
Le cortège des bruits va prendre sa volée
Pour chanter le retour du bel adolescent.

Éteignez tous les feux et dispersez la cendre,
Le jour est bon à vivre et l'heure est bonne à prendre.

DAWN

Fat night leans over the edge of the void
Watching the gardens of vanishing day.
Brief as the flash on the criminal blade
They flowered. The portrait is now in decay
Of a world that mortality hurries and harries.
Light up, destined comets and far-off suns,
Flare up, you beacons and warning fires,
Mere mourners who watch at the deathbed of day
And shiver in draughts from the open doors
That give on to earth and infinite sky!
All's night and death and alone, but who cares,
If just for a moment in midsummer sun
We had the illusion of fullness and love!
Tell us, night, deceitful and misconstrued,
That the feverish kiss and the tenuous zeal
Are wiser here than the kneeling prayer,
The kneeling prayer of the weak and the coward!

Fat night has plunged into gulfs she knows,
To be followed by day with a docile fall.
Day's reared its bare body on mountains tall,
It bathes in the spring, it crosses the vale,
Its potent reflection pervades the sea.
The concert of noises will take to the air,
Give song for the handsome young man's return.

Put out all the fires, let the cinders be scattered,
The day's to be lived and the hour to be savoured.

CALIXTO

A S'ENDORMIR À LA LÉGÈRE,
AU BRUIT DES SOURCES, SOUS LE CIEL,
RÊVANT AU RYTHME PLANÉTAIRE,
ON PLONGE, GISANT, DANS LA TERRE
ET SI JAMAIS RÊVE AU RÉEL
RÉVÉLA SECRET OU MYSTÈRE
C'EST EN DORMANT AU BRUIT DES EAUX
ET DU VENT FERMANT SES CISEAUX.

A S'ENDORMIR À LA LÉGÈRE,
SUR LA TERRE, DANS QUEL FOUILLIS,
TERRIENS, SOMBREZ-VOUS? LA FOUGÈRE
S'ÉCROULE EN PANIERS DE LINGÈRE
DANS UNE ARMOIRE DE TAILLIS
BRODÉS DE SOIE OÙ S'EXAGÈRE
LA LUMIÈRE, HORS DU MANTEAU,
DE TA CHAIR, NYMPHE CALIXTO.

Hors du manteau, la lumière
De ta chair, nymphe Calixto,
En pleine étoile se libère
Du clair de jour et nous éclaire
Tard ou, suivant la saison, tôt.
Mais qu'importe si l'on préfère,
Jailli du manteau de ta chair,
Ton cœur lui-même sombre et clair.

Que l'éclair sombre sur les rives
Où ta chair décline un couchant
Érotique au ciel où s'inscrivent
Nord, Sud, Est, Ouest et leurs dérives
Et les ourses qui dans ce champ
Vont brouter des herbes cursives,
Aurores, nuages, lueurs
Et boire aux rêves les sueurs.

CALIXTO

DRIFTING IN FREE AND EASY SLEEP
BENEATH THE SKY, TO SOUNDS OF STREAMS,
THE PLANETS' RHYTHM IN OUR DREAMS,
WE'RE PLUNGED IN EARTH AND LIE DOWN DEEP...
IF SECRET OR IF MYSTERY
IS EVER BROUGHT TO LIGHT BY DREAMS,
IT IS IN SLEEP BY SOUNDING STREAMS,
WHEN THE WIND'S BLADES GO SNIPPING BY.

DRIFTING IN FREE AND EASY SLEEP
ON BED OF EARTH, HOW DEEP, HOW DEEP,
YOU EARTHLINGS PLUNGE IN ROTTING MESS!
FERNS CRUMBLE IN THE LAUNDRY-PRESS
INSIDE A SILK-EDGED BRUSHWOOD CHEST,
WHERE, NYMPH CALIXTO, NOW UNDRESSED,
LIGHT OF YOUR FLESH ACHIEVES EXCESS.

Calixto, nymph! Your flesh unveiled,
Set free from day, becomes a star:
Its light illuminates us here,
Early or late, as ebbs the year.
What matter, though, if we prefer,
Sprung from your flesh and unconcealed,
Your heart itself, both dark and clear.

Let lightning's flash submerge on shores
Where your flesh wanes in sensual shift
Across the sky where someone scores
North east south west and points adrift
And cursive herbs are browsed by bears,
She-bears of clouds and dawns and gleams,
Who drink the sweat-drops out of dreams.

C'est l'heure où les robes s'écroulent,
Où les cuisses, le ventre rond,
Un sourire sous la cagoule,
Les hanches, la croupe qui roule
Vigne promise au vigneron,
Au bain de la nuit qui s'écoule
S'abandonnent dans les baisers
Et s'irritent pour s'apaiser.

Avec des femmes que j'ignore,
Ô mes amis d'Outre-Océan,
Sous un plafond de météores
Vous déterrez la mandragore.
Je suis toujours du même clan,
Je guette au même sémaphore,
Nymphe prétexte, Calixto,
Le prochain signal de morte-eau.

Que ton chariot, avec ses roues,
Ne puisse franchir l'horizon,
Ou qu'Artémis, le vent en proue,
Te rencontre en ourse garoue
Et t'ajoute à ses venaisons,
Que ton sang colore la boue
Avec celui, ô libation,
Du fruit de ta parturition

Au ciel des couches solitaires
Enfantant des rêves de feu
Ou de glace ou sentant la terre.
Sur les étreintes adultères,
Sur l'équivoque et sur le jeu
Dessinant ton quadrilatère,
Tu es froide comme le Nord,
Nymphe en peine, vaisseau sans port.

This is when dresses flake and fall,
When thighs and bellies, firm and full,
A smile concealed in a cagoule,
When rumps and haunches start to roll,
The viner takes the vine that's his,
And, in the night's clear waterfall,
All give themselves to kiss on kiss,
And irritate their way to bliss.

You friends on Ocean's distant shores
Whose womenfolk I never knew:
Under a roof of shooting-stars
You disinter mandragoras.
I am your distant cousin too:
I watch the selfsame semaphores,
praetexta nympha, Calixto:
Signs that neap-tides are overdue.

Your trundling chariot cannot cross
The far horizon: Artemis,
Wind on her prow, discovers there
A surly monster mother-bear.
That huntress adds you to her prey,
Your offspring too, and stains the mud
With a libation of your blood.

Single-bed sky: you've dreams for cubs,
Of ice and fire and smells of earth.
On grapplings of illicit loves,
On games of dice and doubt and dare,
You sketch your figure not foursquare,
A nymph in travail, cold as North,
A deep-sea ship that has no berth.

Depuis longtemps tu fais la bête
Mais la belle est sous le manteau,
Ainsi dans le poisson l'arête,
Ainsi sous ta chair le squelette
Sur quoi se brise le couteau,
Ainsi la pensée en ta tête,
Le souvenir, le vœu, l'espoir,
La lumière pour mieux voir.

Et de même sous le langage
Se dissimulent maints secrets.
La toute belle en ses bagages
Cache l'étoile aux bons présages
Et le prisonnier aux aguets,
Rêve de belle et de voyages
Comme aux jours de la nef Argo
Dont les marins parlaient argot.

Au rif d'abord, sans qui les châsses
N'auraient plus que dalle à bigler
Et seraient creuses comme un glasse
Lorsque le siffleur en a clâsse,
Au rif d'abord, la bonne clé
Ouvrant les lourdes pour la câsse,
Au rif d'abord, donnons condé
Pour cronir ceux qui sont ladé.

À la tardé, dans le silence,
Amis, c'est pallas d'esgourder
À la source, bonir la lance.
À la tardé, pourtant méfiance
Car elle peut tout inonder
Tout estourbir dans sa violence.
Ah! Que la lance à la tardé
Maccabe ceux qui sont ladé.

For quite some time you've played the beast
But beauty is beneath the cloak
As is the backbone in the fish,
The skeleton beneath your flesh
On which the knife-blade barked and broke:
As thoughts inside your head encased,
Memory, prayer, and hope, the light
Conducive to the sense of sight.

On language too, one lifts the lid
To find a store of secrets hid.
In her valise the queen of women
Conceals the star of friendly omen:
The prisoner whose eyes are peeled
Dreams of the fair, the far afield,
As in the days when Argonauts
Used argot to express their thoughts.

Start with the heat. Or else there'd be
Nix for the goggle-balls to shoof:
A noggin's blank transparency
After the lush has necked enough.
Start with the heat, the master-key
That cracks the crib for villainy:
The heat can take a liberty
And, by our leave, rub out the staff.

Twilight and silence. What a thrill
To cop an earful of a spring,
The pure and simple murmuring!
Twilight and silence. Right, but still,
Don't get caught out: a mighty whoosh
Can sweep away the whole kaboosh.
I only hope the twilit spring
Drowns the unlovely gathering.

Pour escoffier ces yeux de bronze,
Que l'air se frime en pur cambouis
Avant qu'ils prennent le train onze.
Et qu'il les sale et les déronce,
Les entubant jusqu'aux ripouis,
Jusqu'au battant, jusqu'aux engonces!
Qu'il soit bléchard et débridé
Pour pourrir ceux qui sont ladé.

Quant au bouzin, quant à la crotte
Qui pavoise et fait son persil,
Lorsque la moulana bagotte
À fond de baba sur les mottes,
Que son bide en soit bien farci,
Et que jamais ils n'en déhottent.
Qu'elle soit un Bagneux fadé
Pour saper ceux qui sont ladé!

La grande borgne est loucedoque!
C'est encor marre pour leur blot
Lorsque, mettant les loucepoques,
Ils chialeront la lousseroque
De les assister au pajot
Tant ils auront la loussefroque
De voir les largues en pétard
À labactem les passer dar.

Notre sorgue à nous sera douce,
Toute au béguin, toute aux bécots.
Sans gaffer rien, même la rousse,
Nous pioncerons jusqu'à plus pouce.
Même n'ayant qu'un monaco
Nous le piccolerons sans frousse
Tandis que les vers de sapin
Leur boufferont châsses et tarin.

To snuff those bronze-brown eyes to hell
The air should turn to axle-grease
Before their legs rise parallel.
I hope it gives them a disease
And runs them through from soles to cockles,
From clavicles to metacarpals.
I hope it's soiled and spavined too,
To rot the whole revolting crew.

As for the cathouse and the tart
Who struts and takes, hand over fist,
When the sun's up and pushing hard
Like an express across the clart,
I hope her belly's truly stuffed,
And every one of them stuck fast.
She'll make a first-rate Grove of Rest
For all who ride, a clinging shift.

Oft in the stilly blooming night,
Still early for their little shtick,
They'll up and take to blooming flight,
And squeal and whimper to the bill
To see them up the wooden hill.
What's given them a blooming fright?
The mares in heat, with appetite
To tan their cruppers double quick.

We'll have our night of saccharine,
The mouth-to-mouth, the big beguine.
No cops to dodge, no fear! We'll kip,
Mitts tightly clenched and thumb on lip:
Lay our last nickel on the bar,
Knock it back, cocky as we are,
While worms in softwood coffins chew
Their goggle-eyes and honkers too.

Mais plus vif que rif, air, bouzin, lance
Feront les pognes des butteurs
Pour liquider la connivence
Et le sapement en instance.
C'est le boniment des lutteurs
Le cri des piafs, le jour de danse
Le coup de bambou au château,
C'est du billard, c'est du gâteau.

Mais toi Calixto la grande ourse
N'aurais-tu pas largué ton bled?
Icicaille à tes grandes ourses,
Le raisiné cascade à sources
Rien n'est plus droit, tout est en Z.
Comme des faisans à la Bourse,
Les demi-sels se croient des mecs.
Mektoub! un jour ils l'auront sec.

Car le trèpe est toujours le trèpe,
Il la boucle et prend ses biftons
Pour régler leur compte à ces crèpes,
Visant leur mesure de crêpe
Pour le jour de la Saint-Bâton.
Elle n'est pas folle la guêpe
Qui, dans la noye, ô Calixto
Entrave ce jour pour bientôt.

Les clignotantes dans la sorgue
En attendant font leur tapin,
Le bourguignon fait ronfler l'orgue
Pendant que se bourre la morgue,
Le piaf des bois goualе aux lapins
Et le piscaille à pleines forgues
Ripe en fusant dans les coinstos
Où le flot frise et fait château.

But more than earth, air, water, fire,
The hitmen's mitts will liquidate
Conniving scabs, demob the dire
Snap-judgments of the lawless State.
Here is the fighting men's reward,
The castle toppled at a stroke,
The dancing day, the singing bird:
A doddle and a piece of cake.

But you, Calixto, great she-bear,
Haven't you beetled off your patch?
The claret is cascading where
Your excellency shirked the watch:
None of the good old rules are there.
Small fry who stag and shift a share
Think they are sharks: but there's a catch:
The stars decree they'll meet their match.

The people are the people still.
With buttoned lip they keep their place
To settle scores with fools who will
Shortly be stiffs, the cretinous:
Big Stick Day! Time to cut their crêpe.
No fools the wasps who understand,
Calixto, while we seem to sleep,
The day is very close at hand.

The twinklers winking in the sky
Entice the john who passes by,
The big red ball gets men to snore
While morgues are busied more and more,
The bunnies hear the birdy tweet,
The fish has stuffed himself replete,
Cruises the crannies, voids his vent.
The water curls for ornament.

DANS L'ALLÉE où la nuit s'épaissit sous les chênes
Le pas lent d'un cheval retentit et, parfois
S'attarde. Un son de cor s'efface dans la plaine
Et les arbres jumeaux grincent de tous leur bois

Comme le brodequin qu'aux mises en géhenne
On serrait sur le pied d'un captif aux abois.
Chambre ardente, réveils quand les hommes de peine
Chargent douze fusils pour outrager les lois.

Dans l'allée, à travers les feuilles de Septembre,
Je vois briller des nœuds d'étoiles à tes membres
Comme des feux de quart sur le pont des bateaux.

J'entends chanter un chant de meurtre et de torture
Par la coque et la barre et le bruit des mâtures
Imite un brodequin faisant craquer des os.

PAR LES ARBRES brisée en ténébreuse écume
La nuit connaît une agonie et sa fureur
Se transforme en cyclone où la flamme s'allume,
D'où le vent est absent, où le calme est terreur.

Tout est silence alors. La nébuleuse fume
Au trépied d'un destin convoité par la peur,
Le feu danse et, déjà, le marteau sur l'enclume
Attend le forgeron pour le dernier labeur.

Un milliard d'êtres souhaitaient voir ce spectacle
Et voici qu'en la nuit, où les constellations
Se rangent sans erreur en forme de pentacles,

In the oak-avenue where night is thick,
A horse's slow step echoes, now and then
Slows down. A horn-blast fades across the plain.
Twin lines of trees in all their branches creak,

As once in torture-cells the creaking boot
Clamped tight on some despairing captive's foot.
Hot room, in which at dawn the men of pain
Load their twelve guns: unlawful, flagrant breach.

Through autumn leaves in the oak-avenue
I see the knots of stars that shine on you
Like quarter-lights that light some skipper's deck.

I hear a song of murder and the rack
From helm and timbers, and the mainmast's groans
Sound like that torture-boot that cracks the bones.

Broken by trees into a murky foam,
The night knows agony, transforms its ire
Into a cyclone that ignites the flame:
The wind goes missing, and the calm is fear.

Silence is total, as the turgid air
Smokes on the trivet; terror craves its fate.
Flames leap. The hammer's on the anvil for
The blacksmith who shall make the work complete.

Myriads desired to see this spectacle;
And now by night, as constellations shape
Themselves each to a perfect pentacle,

Tout s'accomplit tandis que tout dort, homme ou femme;
Ah! que le jour se lève à la fin de l'action
Et je leur montrerai les vestiges du drame.

L'AUBE À LA FIN S'ENFUIT d'une cruche brisée
Quand tu trébuches, Calixto, et ta lanterne
Change et le paysage, avec lui-même, alterne
Révélant des tessons sur la terre baisée.

Tes baisers Calixto dans la vague alizée
Sont roulés et polis et tes yeux dans leur cerne
Sombrent à fond de larme et ton regard en berne
N'atteint plus ton reflet sur la mer apaisée.

Ourse, rejoins, c'est l'heure, une tanière obscure
À force de soleil et, courbant l'encolure,
Continue, invisible, à marcher par les airs.

On entendra pourtant tes râles et tes plaintes
Dans la vie où s'embrouille un fil de labyrinthe:
Écoutez Calixto rugir dans son désert.

QUE FUREUR soit ton cri! Les laves et les neiges
Se mêlent dans ce cœur vomissant les rayons,
Les dents mordant la langue et tranchant le bâillon
Plus dures qu'à ta chair les mâchoires du piège.

Et tournant et ruant autour de ton manège,
Soleil d'algèbre et son moyeu de tourbillons
Et tire et brise et scelle un à un les maillons
D'une chaîne enserrant les membres du cortège.

All is fulfilled while men and women sleep.
Roll on the daybreak, when the play is done:
I'll show them all the signs of what went on.

DAWN AT LAST EXITS from a jar that breaks,
Calixto, when you stumble: moments pass,
Your light is changed. The landscape flickers, shakes:
The earth is kissed by little bits of glass.

Your kisses, rolled and buffed by gentle waves,
Calixto, and your deep-ringed eyes succumb,
Drowning in tears, and your lacklustre gaze
Can't meet your image on the sea's flat calm.

She-bear, it's time. Back to your shady lair:
It's sunrise. Slink away, with lowered head:
Invisible, walk on, across the air.

We'll hear you railing and complaining yet,
Where life embroils a labyrinthine thread;
Calixto's in her home, and roaring there.

CRY FURY! Snows and lavas mix and swirl
Inside this heart that vomits up the sun
Teeth slice the muzzle through and bite the tongue,
Hurt, like your flesh when steel trap-jaws are sprung.

Turning and rushing round your carousel
With whirlwind hub the algebraic sun
Pulls, breaks, and welds together one by one
Links of the shackles of the shuffling gang.

THE PLAGUE

In the road a footstep echoes. The bell has only one
clapper. Where's he going, the walker, coming
slowly nearer and briefly stopping? Now he's outside
the house. I hear him breathing behind the door.

I see the sky through the glass. I see the sky where the
stars run on the rooftops. It's the great
Bear or Betelgeuse, it's Venus the white-bellied, it's
Diana unfastening her tunic near a fountain of light.

Never did moons or suns run so far from the
earth, never was the night air so dense and so
heavy. I lean on my door which resists…

It opens at last, it swings and knocks against the
wall. And while the footstep moves away I decipher
on a yellow poster the word in black letters, "Plague".

THE NYMPH ALCESTIS

Two streamlets kiss, and on the midnight hour
You're born, Alcestis. Here's your cosmic dower:
Reflections, fireflies, distant lights, the seven
Torches of Ursa Major, up in heaven.

It's dark; the starting signal bids you run;
You don't suspect that night must soon disperse,
Give way, when birds are singing, and the sun
Spreads gold along the peaks with open purse.

Râle, à quoi bon les cris, la bave et le salpêtre
Un sommeil de mangeaille et de pourpre renaître
Tu, vous, les autres, nous, clames, clamez, clamons,

Trois serpents plein la gueule et l'averse d'ordure
Qui tombe sur tes yeux et dans ta chevelure.
Le jour qui t'effaça disperse les démons.

Cesse, ô Calixto, de crier qu'un ciel, ce ciel, est ton exil
Loin de l'amant olympien, celui qui ouvrit ta tunique.
(Car tu en as fait de belles sur terre aux jours de ton avril
Avant de sentir dans ta chair, non la chair, mais la flèche antique)
Un pape ou deux, à l'opposé, au dernier jour de la semaine,
Cherchent au fond des catacombes le chemin de ton domaine.

La belle engeance de tomber dans des abîmes de ténèbres
Que le vin, lui-même banni, ne peut briser à coups de trique.
Bel avantage! renoncer à l'ivresse de ton algèbre
Si on ne la retrouve, ô Calixto, dans le fond des barriques.
Ah! que le destin nous préserve toujours du pain sans levain,
Des nuits sans rêves, des ciels sans astres et des caves sans vin.

Mais ris, ô Calixto, de celui qui espère après sa mort
Retrouver le souvenir de ses amours avec sa conscience:
Autant enterrer le cheval avec sa bride, avec son mors,
Et cependant la mort ainsi ne sera que nuit et silence.
Le système du monde et la morale ont chacun leur ornière,
Crimes ou vertus, rien d'humain ne change ton itinéraire.

N'attendre rien ni châtiment, ni récompense ici ou là
Et que ce là, soit haut ou bas, à la vertu plumer les ailes
Afin de retrouver, sous son travesti d'ange à falbalas,

Why yell why rage saltpetre drooling mouth
A sleep of fodder purple stuff reborn
You, we, they, all of you, cry out and shout

Three snakes the jaws stuffed full it rains manure
Dung falling on your eyes your hair your fur.
Demons disperse when daylight scrubs you out.

Cease from crying, o Calixto, that the sky, this sky's your exile
Far from the Olympian lover, who prised your clothes apart.
(You didn't do too badly on earth in the days of your April
Before you felt in your flesh, not flesh, but the ancient dart)
No, one or two popes, on the contrary, on the week's concluding day,
Search the catacombs for your dwelling, hoping to find the way.

It's no good our falling in some shadowy abyss
If wine, that's banned and banished, cannot break the dismal mood.
It's no good renouncing your algebra's drunkenness
If we drain the casks, Calixto, and the joy is not renewed.
May providence ever preserve us from bread that has no leaven,
From dreamless nights, from wineless cellars, from a starless heaven.

But laugh, Calixto, laugh at one who hopes that when he dies
He will find consciousness again, and memories of romance:
Are bit and bridle buried too, when we inter the horse?
No, that's how death will be, no more than night and silence.
The way of the world is just a rut; there are ruts for moralities;
Crimes or virtues, nothing human can possibly alter your course.

Expect no reward nor punishment, in this or the other place.
Trust the other, high or low, to give you wings with feathers on:
You'll find again, under its disguise as an angel in furbelows,

Avec la volupté, sa chair et son sourire de femelle
Et la liberté sans laquelle il n'y a pas de vertu qui tienne.
Mais, Calixto, tout cela n'appartient qu'à la raison humaine.

Et s'il est une cause au tourbillon d'étoiles et d'atomes
Éparpillés dans ce que nous savons d'un récent univers,
Cause peut-être morte, ensevelie au fond de tant de psaumes,
Ressemble-t-elle à notre image? a-t-elle aussi squelette et chair,
Non, sans doute mais, si elle est, elle est indifférente à nous,
À nos vertus et à nos lois. Époussetez donc vos genoux!

Captive d'un paysage en perpétuelle dégradation
C'est au chant des oiseaux, c'est au chant des moissons et des fontaines
Que se tisse autour de ton corps cette robe de permission
Qui t'habille à minuit et qui sonne et tinte comme des chaînes
Froide comme le nord, chaude comme la mort, longue comme elle,
Que nous dégrafons, Calixto, dans un rêve au tien parallèle.

Et nous-mêmes, captifs de ce même univers et de sa chute,
Même à sourire, condamnés, de tout ce que nous ignorons,
Nous sourirons à l'ange avec lequel nous entamons la lutte,
Ange fantôme, ange illusoire, ange menteur et fanfaron
Qui, sans doute, vaincra mais qui ne connaîtra pas le laurier
Tant une minute de vie a triomphé du meurtrier.

Qu'il soit donc le cadavre bête, à la main gardant le couteau
Sur quoi la rouille, avec le sang, compose un visage et son masque,
Le sphinx à tête d'âne et muet, abandonné sur un coteau,
Carcasse d'un épouvantail qui s'incline dans la bourrasque.
N'y touchez pas, les vers eux seuls lui donnent vie et feu et cendre;
Il ne s'anime que si nous tentons, contre eux, de le défendre.

The flesh of desire and pleasure, and that smiling female face,
And the liberty without which no virtue blows and grows.
But all of that belongs, Calixto, merely to human reason.

And if there is a cause in the whirlwind of stars and atoms
Scattered about in what we know of a recent universe,
A cause that may have perished, buried deep in all those anthems,
Does it resemble our image? Is it of bone with a fleshy crust?
Most likely not, but if there is, it's indifferent to us,
To our virtues and our laws. So you can rid your knees of dust!

You captive of a countryside in perpetual degradation,
It's to the song of birds, the song of harvests and of streams
That there weaves itself around your limbs this garment of permission,
This robe you wear at midnight and it rings and chimes like chains,
Cold as the north and hot as death, and long as death extends:
We unfasten it, Calixto, in a dream that shadows your dreams.

We too are captives of this universe tumbling down,
Condemned to smile at something if we're ignorant about it,
We'll smile at the angel as we grapple him, locked in strife,
A phantom illusory angel, a liar and a braggart,
Who'll surely win, but who will never know the laurel crown,
So triumphant over the murderer was just one minute of life.

Then let him be the stupid corpse, clutching the dagger still,
With its rust composing a face for him, and a mask with blood on it:
Dumb sphinx with the head of a donkey, abandoned on the hill,
The carcase of a scarecrow, doubled up in a raging fit.
Don't touch him, the worms on their own will give him life and fire
and cinders;
He'll only revive if we try to fight them off, as his defenders.

Surtout taisez-vous! Lui parler serait bêtise et temps perdu
Mais, dans l'empreinte pleine d'eau de son pied dans la terre
molle,
Par ton image, Calixto, comme un œil le ciel est fendu.
L'oiseau vient boire à la fois l'ombre et la lumière en sa corolle,
Le dernier relent des charniers le vent l'emporte et le disperse,
Le sol palpite comme un ventre et pressent la prochaine averse.

TU VIENS AU LABYRINTHE où les ombres s'égarent
Graver sur les parois la frise d'un passé
Où la vie et le rêve et l'oubli, espacés
Par les nuits, revivront en symboles bizarres.

Je viens au labyrinthe où, plus gros qu'une amarre,
Se noua le vieux fil avant de se casser.
Ses deux bouts sur le sol roulent sans se lasser
Tout se tait, mais je sens naître au loin la fanfare.

Tu viens au labyrinthe et, d'un pas sans défaut,
Du seuil au seuil tu vas, tu passes sans assaut,
Ton être se dissout dans sa propre légende.

Je viens au labyrinthe oublier mes cinq sens.
J'ai choisi le courant sans en choisir le sens.
La fanfare s'éteint avant que je l'entende.

SUR LE BORD DE L'ABÎME où tu vas disparaître,
Contemple encore la rose, écoute la chanson
Qu'autrefois tu chantais au seuil de ta maison
Vis encore un instant consenti à ton être.

Not a word, above all! To speak to him would be silly, a waste of breath.
But the soft earth bears his footprint, full of water, in which the sky
Is split apart by your image, Calixto, like an eye.
The bird comes to drink from its flower-cup the light and shade
together,
The wind carries off and disperses the last stale smell of death,
The ground stirs like a belly, sensing the onset of showery weather.

YOU REACH THE LABYRINTH where shadows err,
To mark its walls with murals of the past.
Life, dream, oblivion, by darkness spaced,
Shall live again in secret signs bizarre.

I reach the labyrinth. Thick as a cable
The old thread formed a knot, and then it tore.
Its ends go rolling on, indomitable.
All's quiet. I feel the fanfare surge, from far.

You reach the labyrinth. Your step's composed,
You pass through all the doorways unopposed.
In its own myth, your entity disperses.

I reach the labyrinth, to shed my senses.
I chose the flow, but never chose its courses.
Before I hear the fanfare, it has ended.

POISED BY THE CHASM where you'll disappear,
Contemplate once again the rose, and hear
That song you used to sing at your own door:
Live with yourself a moment, as before.

Et puis tu rejoindras dans l'oubli tes ancêtres,
Ô passante! Et passée avec tant de saisons
Tu te perdras dans la planète et ses moissons.
Ne va pas espérer pourtant un jour, renaître.

Une étoile filante, au fond des temps, rejoint
Maintes lueurs, maints crépuscules et maints points
Du jour au bord d'un fleuve où tu te désappris.

La matière est, en toi, consciente d'elle-même,
Au loin l'écho se tait qui répétait «je t'aime»
Et le pur mouvement n'émeut plus nul esprit.

Abandonnons à toi, rivière,
De nous, l'infidèle reflet
Que tu laves, que tu lacères,
À qui tu restes étrangère
Et que tu laisses aux galets.
À s'endormir à la légère,
Nous rejoindrons ce faux portrait
Qui nous ressemble trait pour trait.

Baignant nos pieds, voici la Saône
Voici des ponts, voici du vent,
Voici Lyon et voici le Rhône,
Voici la lune sur son trône
Qui, dans son palais du Levant,
Éteint les torches aux pylônes
Pour mieux attirer Don Juan
À l'aisselle du confluent.

Then to oblivion you'll pass away.
Rejoin your ancestors: pass with the seasons,
Lost in the planet and its maturations.
Don't hope to be reborn, some future day.

A shooting-star, in depths of time, rejoins
A mass of glowing auras, twilights, dawns,
Beside a stream, where you learned not to be.

The stuff of you is conscious, self-aware;
The echo of 'I love you' dies away;
Pure motion stirs no spirit, any more.

River, we leave you and forswear
Our false reflection: we abjure
Our image that you wash and tear:
A stranger and a foreigner,
You leave it on your pebbly shore.
When sleeping in the open air,
We'll meet again that false portrayal
Resembling us in such detail.

We're paddling in the river Saône
Bridges and breezes are at hand
And here is Lyon and here's the Rhône
Here's the moon sitting on her throne –
She dwells in state in the Levant
And turns the pylon-lanterns down
The better to attract Don Juan
To the two rivers' meeting-point.

Car cette nuit est nuit de noces.
De par le monde on boit du vin,
On entend des bruits de carrosses
Et des aboiements de molosses
Au fond des bois et des ravins.
L'or qui tintait pour le négoce
Met le reflet des chandeliers
Au cou des femmes, en colliers.

Un couple, sous le ciel, s'épouse.
Bien loin, dans un lieu très secret,
Des violons, sur les pelouses,
Font pleurer des femmes jalouses
Et chacun boit, mais nul ne sait
Pour qui les heures de nuit cousent
Un trousseau de fièvre et d'amour
Et le linceul du petit jour.

ON DIT qu'en grand mystère, à minuit, près d'une source
Un jeune homme de pleines vertus
Va dévêtir une jeune fille dont la grâce et la pudeur
égalent l'ardeur de volupté;
On dit qu'un couple, au matin, sera réveillé
Par l'odeur de la forêt et le chant des oiseaux;
On dit qu'ils vivront longuement une inaltérable jeunesse.

On dit qu'ils seront le couple parfait,
Que la femme enfantera, dans la joie, des enfants à leur image,
On dit que leur bonheur ne cédera pas à l'ennui, ni leur
désir à la lassitude,
On dit qu'on aurait voulu naître d'un tel père et d'une
telle mère
Et vivre les années qui suivront cette noce,

This night is matrimonial.
Across the world they drink their wine
And hear the coachmen's wheels that roll
And the gigantic hounds that howl
In depths of forest and ravine.
The gold that chimed to make a deal
Shines from the chandeliers, reflects
In necklaces on ladies' necks.

A couple weds in open air.
On a remote and secret lawn
The violinists' melody
Makes jealous women start to cry.
All drink, but no-one knows for whom
The stitching hours of night prepare
A fevered, amorous wedding-gown
And the death-shroud of coming dawn.

IT IS SAID that in great mystery, at midnight, near a spring
A young man of full virtue
Will undress a young girl whose grace and modesty match the ardour of her desire;
That a couple, in the morning, will be woken
By the scent of the forest and the song of birds;
That they will live out a long and inalterable youth.

It is said they will be the perfect couple,
That the woman will bear, in joy, children in their image,
That their happiness will not yield to boredom, nor their desire to weariness,
That anyone would have wished to be born to such a father and such a mother
And to live the years that will follow this marriage.

On dit, mais on n'est pas certain, qu'ils ont, à l'instant,
échangé leur premier baiser.

On dit, et de cela on est sûr, qu'ils sont les enfants de
la terre
Que leurs vertus, leurs pensées et leurs désirs ignorent
tout ce qui n'est pas la terre,
Qu'ils goûteront sans danger à tous les fruits.
Et, toi, Calixto, étoile de la terre, à peine visible dans la
lumière,
Tu continues à servir de repère sur notre route certaine
vers un but lointain.
Mais le regard que nous portons sur toi s'envole et rompt
le fil qui devrait t'attacher à nous et nous à toi.

Mais tu te trisses, tu décarres
Et dans la boîte à réfléchir
La der des noyes, malabare,
Remet du noir et plus que mare
Nous corne qu'il faut dégauchir.
Minute! à la dernière gare
Le dur attendra mézigo:
Signé «Canrobert» ou «Gigot».

À revivre tous les naufrages
Pour en être sauvé toujours
Par la vague même et l'orage,
Tel atteignit un paysage
Au-delà des nuits et des jours.
C'était le domaine des sages,
Il en donna la clé aux fous
Pour chercher un lieu sans verrous.

It is said (but it is not certain) that they have just this moment
exchanged their first kiss.

It is said (and with certainty) that they are children of earth
That their virtues, thoughts and desires know only what is
earth,
That they will taste all fruits without danger.
And you, Calixto, star of earth, hardly visible in the light,
You continue to be a guiding-mark on our certain road to an
uncertain goal.
But our gaze, which we fix on you, flies loose and breaks
the thread that should join you to us and us to you.

YOU SCARPER THOUGH, you cut and run
And in the penitential clink
The last, the vast night-night's begun,
Puts up a black more black than ink
While loudly tipping us the wink
To dump the swag, chuck in the fun.
That's bully, but hang on a mo,
Last train, last station, rapido,
'The Canny Robert'. 'There I go!'

Re-live the shipwrecks! Sure to save,
Time after time, the stormy wave,
Which brought our hero to a place
Beyond the reach of nights and days:
Land of the wise. He gave the key
To fools, to find, quite possibly,
Somewhere no bolts and bars would be.

À s'endormir à la légère,
Ô lumière, ô Calixto,
Il prit la route buissonnière
Vers un réveil qui le libère
Autant des ports que des bateaux.
À s'endormir à la légère,
En retrouvant la pesanteur
Il retrouva son créateur,

À s'endormir à la légère:
La terre et, seulement, la terre...

CE CŒUR QUI HAÏSSAIT LA GUERRE

LE LEGS

Et voici, Père Hugo, ton nom sur les murailles!
Tu peux te retourner au fond du Panthéon
Pour savoir qui a fait cela. Qui l'a fait? On!
On c'est Hitler, on c'est Goebbels... C'est la racaille,

Un Laval, un Pétain, un Bonnard, un Brinon,
Ceux qui savent trahir et ceux qui font ripaille,
Ceux qui sont destinés aux justes représailles
Et cela ne fait pas un grand nombre de noms.

Ces gens de peu d'esprit et de faible culture
Ont besoin d'alibis dans leur sale aventure.
Ils ont dit: «Le bonhomme est mort. Il est dompté.»

When sleeping in the open air,
O star Calixto, mother-bear,
He took the hedgerow path towards
A waking dawn that frees him where
There are no boats, nor even ports,
When sleeping in the open air,
Aware again of weight, aware
Of what created, put him there,

When sleeping in the open air,
La terre, and nothing else, *la terre*...

THIS HEART WHICH HATED WAR

THE LEGACY

Hugo! So here's your name on every wall!
Deep in the Pantheon, turn in your grave,
And ask: who's done this? Hitler! Goebbels! They've
Done it, the guttersnipes: Pétain, Laval,

Bonnard, Brinon: accomplished traitors all,
High on the hog. They've done it, and they must
Face retribution, merciless and just;
And there are not that many names at all.

These mindless and uncultured men have made
A smokescreen for their filthy escapade:
'The fellow's dead and gone,' apparently.

Oui, le bonhomme est mort. Mais par-devant notaire
Il a bien précisé quel legs il voulait faire:
Le notaire a nom: France, et le legs: Liberté.

CE CŒUR QUI HAÏSSAIT LA GUERRE

Ce cœur qui haïssait la guerre voilà qu'il bat pour le combat et la bataille!
Ce cœur qui ne battait qu'au rythme des marées, à celui des saisons, à celui des heures du jour et de la nuit,
Voilà qu'il se gonfle et qu'il envoie dans les veines un sang brûlant de salpêtre et de haine
Et qu'il mène un tel bruit dans la cervelle que les oreilles en sifflent
Et qu'il n'est pas possible que ce bruit ne se répande pas dans la ville et la campagne
Comme le son d'une cloche appelant à l'émeute et au combat.
Écoutez, je l'entends qui me revient renvoyé par les échos.
Mais non, c'est le bruit d'autres cœurs, de millions d'autres cœurs battant comme le mien à travers la France.
Ils battent au même rythme pour la même besogne tous ces cœurs,
Leur bruit est celui de la mer à l'assaut des falaises
Et tout ce sang porte dans des millions de cervelles un même mot d'ordre:
Révolte contre Hitler et mort à ses partisans!
Pourtant ce cœur haïssait la guerre et battait au rythme des saisons,
Mais un seul mot: Liberté a suffi à réveiller les vieilles colères
Et des millions de Français se préparent dans l'ombre à la besogne que l'aube proche leur imposera.

The fellow's dead. Yet his bequest is clear:
His legacy is signed and proven here,
Witnessed by France; we call it Liberty.

THIS HEART WHICH HATED WAR

This heart which hated war, see now, it beats for combat and battle!
This heart that once beat only to the rhythm of the tides, seasons, hours of day and night,
See now, it swells up and sends into the veins a blood burning with saltpetre and hate
And brings to the brain a noise to make the ears whistle
And this noise cannot but spread through city and country,
Like the sound of a tocsin that summons to uprising and combat.
Listen, I hear it come back to me, sent by the echoes.
No, it is the sound of other hearts, millions of other hearts beating like mine across France.
All these hearts are beating to the same rhythm from the same need,
Their sound is that of the sea pounding the cliffs
And all this blood carries into millions of brains the same watchword:
Revolt against Hitler and death to his followers!
This heart hated war, its beat was to the rhythm of the seasons,
But a single word: Liberty was enough to awaken the old fires of anger
And millions of Frenchmen are preparing in the shadows for the demands the coming dawn will impose.

Car ces cœurs qui haïssaient la guerre battaient pour la liberté au rythme même des saisons et des marées, du jour et de la nuit.

SI, COMME AUX VENTS DÉSIGNÉS PAR LA ROSE

Si, comme aux vents désignés par la rose
Il est un sens à l'espace et au temps,
S'ils en ont un ils en ont mille et plus
Et tout autant s'ils n'en possèdent pas.

Or qui de nous n'imagine ou pressent,
Ombres vaguant hors des géométries,
Des univers échappant à nos sens?

Au carrefour de routes en obliques
Nous écoutons s'éteindre un son de cor,
Toujours renaissant, toujours identique.

Cette vision du ciel et de la rose
Elle s'absorbe et se dissout dans l'air
Comme les sons dont frémit notre chair
Ou les lueurs sous nos paupières closes.

Nous nous heurtons à d'autres univers
Sans les sentir, les voir ou les entendre
Au creux été, aux cimes de l'hiver,
D'autres saisons sur nous tombent en cendre.

Tandis qu'aux vents désignés par la rose
Claque la porte et claquent les drapeaux,

For these hearts that hated war were beating for liberty to
the very rhythm of the seasons, the tides, day and night.

THE WINDS AROUND THE COMPASS-ROSE

The winds around the compass-rose
Imply a sense in time and space;
One sense entails a thousand plus,
Even no sense can mean no less.

We all imagine or we sense
Shades roaming free of geometries,
Worlds that escape our vigilance.

We hear a dying bugle-horn
At meetings of the slanting ways,
Always the same, always reborn.

This vision of the sky, the rose,
Dissolves and merges in the breeze
Like sounds that shake us at the knees,
Or glaring light when eyelids close.

To other worlds we wander off
That no-one senses, sees or hears.
At winter peaks, at summer trough,
Seasons fall ashen round our ears.

While the winds on the compass-rose
Swell out the sails, flap flags and doors,

Gonfle la voile et sans visible cause
Une présence absurde à nous s'impose
Matérielle, indifférente et sans repos.

LE VEILLEUR DU PONT-AU-CHANGE

Je suis le veilleur de la rue de Flandre,
Je veille tandis que dort Paris.
Vers le nord un incendie lointain rougeoie dans la nuit.
J'entends passer des avions au-dessus de la ville.

Je suis le veilleur du Point-du-Jour.
La Seine se love dans l'ombre, derrière le viaduc d'Auteuil,
Sous vingt-trois ponts à travers Paris.
Vers l'ouest j'entends des explosions.

Je suis le veilleur de la Porte Dorée.
Autour du donjon le bois de Vincennes épaissit ses ténèbres.
J'ai entendu des cris dans la direction de Créteil
Et des trains roulent vers l'est avec un sillage de chants de révolte.

Je suis le veilleur de la Poterne des Peupliers.
Le vent du sud m'apporte une fumée âcre,
Des rumeurs incertaines et des râles
Qui se dissolvent, quelque part, dans Plaisance ou Vaugirard.
Au sud, au nord, à l'est, à l'ouest,
Ce ne sont que fracas de guerre convergeant vers Paris.

Je suis le veilleur du Pont-au-Change
Veillant au cœur de Paris, dans la rumeur grandissante
Où je reconnais les cauchemars paniques de l'ennemi,

An absurd presence will impose
On us, for which we see no cause:
Uncaring, blunt, without repose.

THE WATCHMAN AT THE PONT-AU-CHANGE

I am the watchman at the Rue de Flandre.
I keep watch while Paris sleeps.
Far to the north a fire glows red in the night.
I hear planes passing over the city.

I am the watchman at the Point-du-Jour.
The Seine coils in the shade, behind the Auteuil viaduct,
Under twenty-three bridges across Paris.
To the west I hear explosions.

I am the watchman at the Porte Dorée.
Around the keep, the wood of Vincennes thickens its shadows.
I have heard shouts in the direction of Créteil
And trains are rolling east, trailing their wake of songs of rebellion.

I am the watchman at the Poterne des Peupliers.
The south wind brings me an acrid smoke,
Uncertain rumours and death-rattles
That dissolve, somewhere, in Plaisance or Vaugirard.
South, north, east, west,
There is only the tumult of war converging on Paris.

I am the watchman at the Pont-au-Change
On watch in the heart of Paris, in the swell of rumour
Where I make out the panic nightmares of the enemy,

Les cris de victoire de nos amis et ceux des Français,
Les cris de souffrance de nos frères torturés par les Allemands d'Hitler.

Je suis le veilleur du Pont-au-Change
Ne veillant pas seulement cette nuit sur Paris,
Cette nuit de tempête sur Paris seulement dans sa fièvre et sa fatigue,
Mais sur le monde entier qui nous environne et nous presse.
Dans l'air froid tous les fracas de la guerre
Cheminent jusqu'à ce lieu où, depuis si longtemps, vivent les hommes.

Des cris, des chants, des râles, des fracas il en vient de partout,
Victoire, douleur et mort, ciel couleur de vin blanc et de thé,
Des quatre coins de l'horizon à travers les obstacles du globe,
Avec des parfums de vanille, de terre mouillée et de sang,
D'eau salée, de poudre et de bûchers,
De baisers d'une géante inconnue enfonçant à chaque pas dans la terre grasse de chair humaine.

Je suis le veilleur du Pont-au-Change
Et je vous salue, au seuil du jour promis
Vous tous camarades de la rue de Flandre à la Poterne des Peupliers,
Du Point-du-Jour à la Porte Dorée.

Je vous salue vous qui dormez
Après le dur travail clandestin,
Imprimeurs, porteurs de bombes, déboulonneurs de rails, incendiaires,
Distributeurs de tracts, contrebandiers, porteurs de messages,
Je vous salue vous tous qui résistez, enfants de vingt ans au sourire de source

The cries of victory of our friends and of the French,
The cries of agony of our brothers tortured by the Germans of
Hitler.

I am the watchman at the Pont-au-Change
On watch tonight not only over Paris,
This stormy night, not only over Paris in her fever and
weariness,
But over the whole world that surrounds us and presses us.
In the cold air all the tumults of war
Head for this place where for so long there have been people
living.

Shouts, songs, rumours, rattles, tumult come from every side,
Victory, suffering and death, sky the colour of white wine and tea,
From the four corners of the horizon past the obstacles of the
world,
With the perfumes of vanilla, of moist earth and blood,
Of salt water, of powder and conflagrations,
Of the kisses of an unknown giantess who at every step thrusts
human flesh into the stout earth.

I am the watchman at the Pont-au-Change
And I salute you, on the threshold of the promised day,
All you comrades from the Rue de Flandre to the Poterne des
Peupliers,
From the Point-du-Jour to the Porte Dorée.

I salute you who sleep
After the hard secret labour,
Printers, bomb-carriers, dismantlers of rails, arsonists,
Distributors of tracts, smugglers, message-bearers
I salute all you resisters, youngsters of twenty with sweet-water
grins,

Vieillards plus chenus que les ponts, hommes robustes, images des saisons,
Je vous salue au seuil du nouveau matin.

Je vous salue sur les bords de la Tamise,
Camarades de toutes nations présents au rendez-vous,
Dans la vieille capitale anglaise,
Dans le vieux Londres et la vieille Bretagne,
Américains de toutes races et de tous drapeaux,
Au-delà des espaces atlantiques,
Du Canada au Mexique, du Brésil à Cuba,
Camarades de Rio, de Tehuantepec, de New York et San Francisco.

J'ai donné rendez-vous à toute la terre sur le Pont-au-Change.
Veillant et luttant comme vous. Tout à l'heure,
Prévenu par son pas lourd sur le pavé sonore,
Moi aussi j'ai abattu mon ennemi.

Il est mort dans le ruisseau, l'allemand d'Hitler anonyme et haï,
La face souillée de boue la mémoire déjà pourrissante,
Tandis que déjà, j'écoutais vos voix des quatre saisons,
Amis, amis et frères des nations amies.

J'écoutais vos voix dans le parfum des orangers africains,
Dans les lourds relents de l'océan Pacifique,
Blanches escadres de mains tendues dans l'obscurité,
Hommes d'Alger, Honolulu, Tchoung-King,
Hommes de Fès, de Dakar et d'Ajaccio.

Enivrantes et terribles clameurs, rythmes des poumons et des cœurs,
Du front de Russie flambant dans la neige,
Du lac Ilmen à Kief, du Dniepr au Pripet,
Vous parvenez à moi, nés de millions de poitrines.

Old men venerable as the bridges, strong men, pictures of the
seasons,
I salute you on the threshold of the new morning.

I salute you on the banks of the Thames,
Comrades of all nations present and assembled,
In England's ancient capital,
Old London, old Britain,
Americans of every race and flag,
Beyond the vast Atlantic,
From Canada to Mexico, from Brazil to Cuba,
Comrades from Rio, from Tehuantepec, from New York and
San Francisco.

I've made an appointment for the whole earth at the Pont-au-Change,
Watching and fighting like you. Just now,
Forewarned by his heavy step on the echoing cobbles,
I too struck down my enemy.

He died in the gutter, Hitler's anonymous and hated German,
His face soiled with mud, his memory already rotting,
While I was already listening to your voices of the four seasons,
Friends, friends and brothers from friendly nations.

I was listening to your voices in the scent of African orange-trees,
In the heavy staleness of the Pacific Ocean,
Squadrons of hands unsheathed and extended in the dark,
Men of Algiers, Honolulu, Chungking,
Men of Fez, of Dakar, of Ajaccio.

Intoxicating and terrible clamours, rhythms of lungs and hearts,
From the Russian front blazing in the snow,
From Lake Ilmen to Kiev, from the Dnieper to the Pripet,
Born of the breasts of millions you win through to me.

Je vous écoute et vous entends. Norvégiens, Danois, Hollandais,
Belges, Tchèques, Polonais, Grecs, Luxembourgeois, Albanais
et Yougo-Slaves, camarades de lutte.
J'entends vos voix et je vous appelle,
Je vous appelle dans ma langue connue de tous
Une langue qui n'a qu'un mot:
Liberté!

Et je vous dis que je veille et que j'ai abattu un homme
d'Hitler.
Il est mort dans la rue déserte
Au cœur de la ville impassible j'ai vengé mes frères assassinés
Au Fort de Romainville et au Mont Valérien,
Dans les échos fugitifs et renaissants du monde, de la ville et
des saisons.

Et d'autres que moi veillent comme moi et tuent,
Comme moi ils guettent les pas sonores dans les rues désertes,
Comme moi ils écoutent les rumeurs et les fracas de la terre.
À la Porte Dorée, au Point-du-Jour,
Rue de Flandre et Poterne des Peupliers,
À travers toute la France, dans les villes et les champs,
Mes camarades guettent les pas dans la nuit
Et bercent leur solitude aux rumeurs et fracas de la terre.

Car la terre est un camp illuminé de milliers de feux.
À la veille de la bataille on bivouaque par toute la terre
Et peut-être aussi, camarades, écoutez-vous les voix,
Les voix qui viennent d'ici quand la nuit tombe,
Qui déchirent des lèvres avides de baisers
Et qui volent longuement à travers les étendues
Comme des oiseaux migrateurs qu'aveugle la lumière des phares
Et qui se brisent contre les fenêtres du feu.

I listen, I hear you. Norwegians, Danes, Dutchmen,
Belgians, Czechs, Poles, Greeks, Luxemburgers, Albanians
and Yugoslavs, comrades in arms.
I hear your voices and I call you,
I call you in my language known to all,
A language that has just one word,
Liberty!

And I tell you I am on watch and have killed a man of Hitler's.
He is dead in the empty street
At the heart of the unmoved city I have avenged my murdered brothers
In Fort de Romainville and in Mont-Valérien,
In the fleeting reborn echoes of the world, the city, and the
seasons.

And others besides me are watching and killing,
Marking, as I do, the resonant steps in the empty streets,
Hearing, as I do, the earth's rumours and tumults.
At the Porte Dorée, at the Point-du-Jour,
At the Rue de Flandre, at the Poterne des Peupliers,
All across France, in cities and fields,
My comrades mark the footsteps in the night
And lull their loneliness to the earth's rumours and tumults.

For the earth is a camp lit by thousands of fires.
On the eve of battle there are bivouacs across the globe
And perhaps, comrades, you hear the voices,
Voices coming from here at nightfall,
Ripping open lips that are thirsty for kisses
And flying across great distances
Like migrant birds blinded by lighthouse-beams
Who smash into the windows of the blaze.

Que ma voix vous parvienne donc
Chaude et joyeuse et résolue,
Sans crainte et sans remords
Que ma voix vous parvienne avec celle de mes camarades,
Voix de l'embuscade et de l'avant-garde française.

Écoutez-nous à votre tour, marins, pilotes, soldats,
Nous vous donnons le bonjour,
Nous ne vous parlons pas de nos souffrances mais de notre espoir,
Au seuil du prochain matin nous vous donnons le bonjour,
À vous qui êtes proches et, aussi, à vous
Qui recevrez notre vœu du matin
Au moment où le crépuscule en bottes de paille entrera dans
vos maisons.
Et bonjour quand même et bonjour pour demain!
Bonjour de bon cœur et de tout notre sang!
Bonjour, bonjour, le soleil va se lever sur Paris,
Même si les nuages le cachent il sera là,
Bonjour, bonjour, de tout cœur bonjour!

VAINCRE LE JOUR, VAINCRE LA NUIT

Vaincre le jour, vaincre la nuit,
Vaincre le temps qui colle à moi,
Tout ce silence, tout ce bruit,
Ma faim, mon destin, mon horrible froid.

May my voice reach you then
Warm and joyous and resolute,
Without fear and remorse
May my voice reach you with those of my comrades,
Voices of the ambush, the vanguard of France.

Hear us in your turn, sailors, airmen, soldiers,
We bid you good morning.
We tell you not of our sufferings but of our hope,
On the threshold of coming dawn we bid you good morning,
You who are near, and also you
Who will receive our morning greeting
When daybreak in straw shoes creeps into your homes.
And good morning anyway, and good morning for tomorrow!
Good morning, full-hearted and full-blooded!
Good morning, good morning, the sun is coming up over Paris,
Even if the clouds hide it, it will be there,
Good morning, good morning, a hearty good morning!

Signed 'Valentin Guillois', the above poem appeared in May 1944, in L'Honneur des Poètes II. *It draws on Walt Whitman's poem 'Salut au Monde'. It was recited and acclaimed in Paris in October 1944, in the presence of Général de Gaulle.*

TO CONQUER DAY, TO CONQUER NIGHT

To conquer day, to conquer night,
To conquer time's insistent hold,
This world of tumult and of quiet,
My thirst, my fate, my depth of cold.

Vaincre ce cœur, le mettre à nu,
Écraser ce corps plein de fables
Pour le plonger dans l'inconnu,
Dans l'insensible, dans l'impénétrable.

Briser enfin, jeter au noir
Des égouts ces vieilles idoles,
Convertir la haine en espoir,
En de saintes les mauvaises paroles.

Mais mon temps n'est-il pas perdu?
Tu m'a pris tout le sang, Paris.
À ton cou je suis ce pendu,
Ce libertaire qui pleure et qui rit.

CHANSON DE ROUTE

C'est avec du crottin de Pégase
Qu'Eusèbe a fumé son jardin.
Avec du crottin de Pégase?
Oh! oh!
Pour du crottin, c'est du crottin
Eusèbe appartient au gratin.

C'est avec du crottin de Licorne
Qu'Eusèbe a fumé son jardin
avec du crottin de Licorne?
Oh! oh!
Pour du crottin c'est du crottin

To rule this heart and lay it bare,
To crush this body stuffed with fable,
To plunge it in the void, somewhere
Unknowable, impenetrable.

To smash the idols of the past
And hurl them down the blackest drains,
Recover hope from hate's disdains,
Turn evil speech to good at last.

My time is spent and I am through:
Paris, you bled my arteries.
I am the hanged man, hung on you,
I, this free soul who laughs and cries.

Published posthumously, July 1947, in Les Regrets de Paris.

ROAD SONG

With horse-manure of Pegasus
Sebastian dunged his blessed plot.
With horse-manure of Pegasus?
Oh! Oh!
With horse-manure, with horse-manure
He's upper-crust and that's for sure.

With horse-manure of Unicorn
Sebastian dunged his blessed plot.
With horse-manure of Unicorn?
Oh! Oh!
With horse-manure, with horse-manure

Eusèbe n'est pas un crétin.
Avec du crottin de Minotaure
Eusèbe a fumé son jardin
ouais du crottin de minotaure!
Oh! oh!
non du crottin mais de la bouse
qu'Eusèbe a mis sur sa pelouse.

PRINTEMPS

Tu, Rrose Sélavy, hors de ces bornes erres
Dans un printemps en proie aux sueurs de l'amour,
Aux parfums de la rose éclose aux murs des tours,
à la fermentation des eaux et de la terre.

Sanglant, la rose au flanc, le danseur, corps de pierre
Paraît sur le théâtre au milieu des labours.
Un peuple de muets d'aveugles et de sourds
applaudira sa danse et sa mort printanière.

C'est dit. Mais la parole inscrite dans la suie
S'efface au gré des vents sous les doigts de la pluie
Pourtant nous l'entendons et lui obéissons.

Au lavoir où l'eau coule un nuage simule
À la fois le savon, la tempête et recule
l'instant où le soleil fleurira les buissons.

He's not some greenhorn, that's for sure.
With horse-manure of Minotaur
Sebastian dunged his blessed plot.
Yes horse-manure of Minotaur!
Oh! Oh!
Not horse-manure but cattle-splat
He fertilised his lawn with that.

Written on 4 April 1944 for his friend Eirisch in the camp at Compiègne.

SPRINGTIME

Rrose Sélavy, beyond these bounds you stray.
Meanwhile the waters and the earth ferment;
The rose on fortress-walls pours out its scent;
Love has its sweats and springtime is their prey.

The rose has torn the stone-limbed dancer's side.
While others plough and sow, he treads the boards.
The public, blind and deaf and dumb, applauds
This rite of spring, when he has danced and died.

The word that's writ in soot is wiped away
At the wind's whim by fingers of the rain.
Nevertheless we hear it and obey.

Down at the wash-place where these waters run,
A cloud portrays both soap and hurricane,
Retreating when the thickets bloom in sun.

The real 'last poem', 6 April 1944.

ROBERT LE DIABLE
de Louis Aragon

Tu portais dans ta voix comme un chant de Nerval
Quand tu parlais du sang jeune homme singulier
Scandant la cruauté de tes vers réguliers
Le rire des bouchers t'escortait dans les Halles
Tu avais en ces jours ces accents de gageure
Que j'entends retentir à travers les années
Poète de vingt ans d'avance assassiné
Et que vengeaient déjà le blasphème et l'injure

Je pense à toi Desnos qui partis de Compiègne
Comme un soir en dormant tu nous en fis récit
Accomplir jusqu'au bout ta propre prophétie
Là-bas où le destin de notre siècle saigne

Debout sous un porche avec un cornet de frites
Te voilà par mauvais temps près de Saint-Merry
Dévisageant le monde avec effronterie
De ton regard pareil à celui d'Amphitrite
Énorme et palpitant d'une pâle buée
Et le sol à ton pied comme au sein nu l'écume
Se couvre de mégots de crachats de légumes
Dans les pas de la pluie et des prostituées

Je pense à toi Desnos qui partis de Compiègne
Comme un soir en dormant tu nous en fis récit
Accomplir jusqu'au bout ta propre prophétie
Là-bas où le destin de notre siècle saigne

ROBERT THE DEVIL

by Louis Aragon

I think of you Robert

Your voice was charged with something of Nerval
You spoke of blood most singular young man
Your cruel formal verse you made it scan
Laughter of butchers flanked you in Les Halles
You seemed already to be laying odds
Across the years I hear the resonance
Poetic tyro slaughtered in advance
Avenged back then by sneers at men and gods

You left Compiègne I think of you Robert
Just as asleep one evening you had said
So you fulfilled that prophecy you made
Fate of our century lies bleeding there

Stood in a doorway with a twist of fries
St Merry overhung by thunderclouds
Impertinently staring down the crowds
You gazed like royal-blood Nereides
Enormous throbbing with a pallid haze
Ground at your foot like foam at breast of nude
Thick with fag-ends and cabbage chewed and spewed
Footfall of rain and all-too-ready lays

You left Compiègne I think of you Robert
Just as asleep one evening you had said
So you fulfilled that prophecy you made
Fate of our century lies bleeding there

Et c'est encore toi sans fin qui te promènes
Berger des longs désirs et des songes brisés
Sous les arbres obscurs dans les Champs-Élysées
Jusqu'à l'épuisement de la nuit ton domaine
Ô la Gare de l'Est et le premier croissant
Le café noir qu'on prend près du percolateur
Les journaux frais les boulevards pleins de senteur
Les bouches du métro qui captent les passants

Je pense à toi Desnos qui partis de Compiègne
Comme un soir en dormant tu nous en fis récit
Accomplir jusqu'au bout ta propre prophétie
Là-bas où le destin de notre siècle saigne

La ville un peu partout garde de ton passage
Une ombre de couleur à ses frontons salis
Et quand le jour se lève au Sacré-Cœur pâli
Quand sur le Panthéon comme un équarissage
Le crépuscule met ses lambeaux écorchés
Quand le vent hurle aux loups dessous le Pont-au-Change
Quand le soleil au Bois roule avec les oranges
Quand la lune s'assied de clocher en clocher

Je pense à toi Desnos qui partis de Compiègne
Comme un soir en dormant tu nous en fis récit
Accomplir jusqu'au bout ta propre prophétie
Là-bas où le destin de notre siècle saigne

It's you it still is you still strolling on
Shepherd of long desires dead reveries
The Champs-Élysées dim below the trees
Until your own domain the night is gone
O Gare de l'Est first croissant of the day
Black coffee percolated freshly poured
Crisp morning papers pungent boulevard
The metro-mouths where figures drained away

You left Compiègne I think of you Robert
Just as asleep one evening you had said
So you fulfilled that prophecy you made
Fate of our century lies bleeding there

Your passing haunts the city's grimy brows
With coloured shade The Sacré-Cœur is wan
As knacker daybreak flays the Pantheon
With shreds and tatters Later in the Bois
The sun rolls oranges itself an orange
The moon transfers her seat from tower to tower
Striking the belfries as they strike the hour
And the wind howls beneath the Pont-au-Change

You left Compiègne I think of you Robert
Just as asleep one evening you had said
So you fulfilled that prophecy you made
Fate of our century lies bleeding there

BIOGRAPHICAL NOTE

Timothy Adès is a translator-poet working mostly with rhyme and metre, from French, Spanish, German and, rarely, Greek. His books from French to date are *How to be a Grandfather* by Victor Hugo, *33 Sonnets of the Resistance* and *The Madness of Amadis* by Jean Cassou, and *Storysongs / Chantefables* by Robert Desnos; he has awards for translating these poets and for the Mexican, Alfonso Reyes. His book from Spanish is *Florentino and the Devil* by Alberto Arvelo Torrealba. Most of these books are in bilingual facing text. In *Loving by Will*, Shakespeare's Sonnets appear alongside new versions written without using the letter e. Other favourites are Ricarda Huch, Bertolt Brecht, and Ángelos Sikelianós. He is married to a professor of both Surrealist and Latin American art history.

Arc Publications would like to thank everyone
who contributed to the crowdfunding campaign
to support the production of this book.
Without their generosity it could not
have been completed.

We would particularly like to thank
the following individuals:

Harry Ades
Rose Ades
R. J. Allen
David Andrew
Stephen & Jackie Benson
Leon Burnett
Nicola
Nicholas Faulkner
Peter France
Olivia Hanks
Andrew & Audrey Heald
Miranda Kendall
Dave Laing
Chris Lord
Stephanie and Ron Moncrieff
Alvin Pang
Ian Patterson
Jonathan Sieders
Dan Skillicorn
Martin Sorrell
Benjamin Wachs
Jeffrey Wainwright
Tony Ward